Exemplary Practices *for* Secondary Math Teachers

Alfred S. Posamentier

Daniel Jaye

Stephen Krulik

 Association for Supervision and Curriculum Development • Alexandria, Virginia USA

Association for Supervision and Curriculum Development
1703 N. Beauregard St. • Alexandria, VA 22311-1714 USA
Phone: 800-933-2723 or 703-578-9600 • Fax: 703-575-5400
Web site: www.ascd.org • E-mail: member@ascd.org
Author guidelines: www.ascd.org/write

Gene R. Carter, *Executive Director;* Nancy Modrak, *Director of Publishing;* Julie Houtz, *Director of Book Editing & Production;* Katie Martin, *Project Manager;* Georgia Park, Senior Graphic Designer; Vivian Coss, *Production Specialist.* For Bytheway Publishing Services: Jean Blackburn, *Project Manager;* Kate Brown, *Copy Editor;* Leslie Phillips, *Designer;* Exeter Premedia Services Private Ltd., *Compositors*

Printed in the United States of America. Cover art copyright © 2007 by ASCD. ASCD publications present a variety of viewpoints. The views expressed or implied in this book should not be interpreted as official positions of the Association.

PAPERBACK ISBN: 978-1-4166-0524-9   ASCD product #106005   s3/07

Also available as an e-book through ebrary, netLibrary, and many online booksellers (see Books in Print for the ISBNs).

Quantity discounts for the paperback edition only: 10–49 copies, 10%; 50+ copies, 15%; for 1,000 or more copies, call 800-933-2723, ext. 5634, or 703-575-5634. For desk copies: member@ascd.org.

Library of Congress Cataloging-in-Publication Data
Posamentier, Alfred S.
   Exemplary practices for secondary math teachers / Alfred S. Posamentier, Daniel Jaye, and Stephen Krulik.
      p. cm.
   Includes bibliographical references and index.
   ISBN 978-1-4166-0524-9 (pbk. : alk. paper) 1. Mathematics—Study and teaching (Secondary) 2. Effective teaching. I. Jaye, Daniel. II. Krulik, Stephen. III. Title.

   QA11.2.P6385 2007
   510.71'2—dc22

                          2006038319

To Barbara *for her suport, patience, and inspiration.*

To my children and grandchildren: David, Lisa, Danny, Max, and Sam, *whose future is unbounded.*

And in memory of my beloved parents,
Alice and Ernest, *who never lost faith in me.*

—ALFRED S. POSAMENTIER

To my wife, Tae-Jin, *who has made every sacrifice to ensure my happiness and success.*

To my children, Jennifer and Rebecca,
who are an eternal source of pride and joy,

And in memory of my parents, Stanley and Beatrice,
who were always there for me.

—DANIEL JAYE

To my wife, Gladys, *my best friend, critic, and love of my life, who gives me the shot-in-the arm to keep going.*

—STEPHEN KRULIK

CONTENTS

INTRODUCTION

In recent years, numerous new teachers have taken their positions through alternate certification routes. This has been most prevalent in what is referred to as hard-to-staff areas; chief among these is mathematics. Many of these transitioning professionals rely on various forms of school-established support to enrich their development while performing their teaching role.

To supplement the usual support on matters of curriculum and methodology typically provided by assistant principals, some schools have hired experienced teachers trained to be math coaches. These individuals are usually master teachers with many years of experience, and they spend much of their time mentoring new teachers. The math coach's role involves observing the teacher, making constructive comments, and offering to teach model lessons. Follow-up discussions afford the opportunity to delve into aspects of teaching beyond the observed lesson. All this is critical, because it's during the first few years of a teacher's experience that he develops the practices—the habits, methods, procedures, and techniques—that will persist in one way or another throughout the teacher's career.

Unfortunately, not every new teacher (i.e., a teacher in the first 3–4 years of teaching) will have the advantage of having a math coach. Such a teacher will have to rely on being his own coach: a self-coached teacher.

It is common that we best see ourselves through the eyes of others. Opinions about our dress, humor, intelligence, and yes, our teaching skills, are usually established by the comments of others. If you do not have a math coach, then you will have to do some serious self-inspection. Videotaping is a clever way to get a new perspective on your practice. Watching your teaching performance in this way can be enlightening—a way to pick up on any distracting habits and see if you conduct the class efficiently. You will see yourself as your students see you.

This takes care of part of self-coaching. What about the professional development that should be spurred on by a good math coach? This book is designed to assist you in this area. In the chapters ahead, we touch on many aspects of the teaching profession, both in and out of the classroom. Our objective is not necessarily to give you the answers to all the outstanding issues; rather, it is to share with you what our years of experience tell us are the practices and habits of exemplary secondary math teachers and ignite your thinking about the many salient issues there are to be considered and explored. By prompting you to think about what the best math teachers know and do, we hope to open new pathways for you. And we recommend that you concomitantly develop a professional library so you can have easy reference to books on teaching, books that discuss the underlying concepts of school mathematics, books that provide you with the history of mathematics and mathematics education so you can enrich instruction with anecdotes, books on higher mathematics so you can continue to grow professionally, books on topics in mathematics beyond the curriculum so you can appropriately enrich your instruction, and books on such overarching topics as problem solving, which often merits special consideration as it is ubiquitous in a math teacher's work.

In sum, we hope that reading this book will pique your interest in delving more deeply into the practices we discuss, and that it will generate discussions with your colleagues so that they too can offer input to help you become the truly exemplary math teacher your students deserve.

1

STARTING OUT AS A MATH
TEACHER TODAY

This book is intended to "replace," or at least complement, a coach assigned to a new math teacher. In this first chapter we address the first issues that a new teacher might be puzzled about and bring to the fore some issues that might prevent a lot of learning by mistakes. Your first concern might be to consider what support personnel are available in your school. Is there an assistant principal directly assigned to support your teaching? What might you expect from your immediate supervisor? Is he a curriculum specialist or just an administrator to whom you cannot turn regarding pedagogical issues, such as how best to teach certain topics? Soon, the concerns turn to how you might behave when you meet with your new class. What issues should you be conscious of?

We have a natural tendency to recall our school days as the model to follow when setting the tone in our class. This chapter will help you determine how today's classroom might be different from the one you were in as a student. You will need to read up on educational reports and consider today's issues. For example, is there a philosophical split on how to teach mathematics? If so, what are the various positions and their respective justifications? What role should technology play in your lessons? Although teachers are encouraged to incorporate technology in their lessons, a basic rule of thumb for the use of any software or technology is that it should enhance what you are teaching and be a preferred alternative to presenting the lesson without it. Two examples of software that can enhance the teaching of geometry are Geometer's Sketchpad and Cabri Geometry. Both dynamic software packages enable students to discover geometric relationships and examine them as they change in real time. The handheld (graphing) calculator should also be thoughtfully employed to extend student thinking beyond notebooks and chalkboard. Throughout the book, we provide few recommendations for software for fear that it will become obsolete and replaced by better products. Teachers are encouraged to keep professional knowledge current and to learn new technologies as they evolve. These are just some of the ways this introductory chapter will help you acclimate to better understand your position as a teacher of mathematics.

To Whom Can a New Teacher Turn for Advice?

As a new teacher (or for that matter, a second-year teacher), you must begin by lining up all the aspects of your professional responsibilities before the school year begins. In addition to preparation for the subject you will be teaching, you will need to know about your particular school environment. First, focus on the physical plant where you will be teaching. You can walk around the building with an experienced colleague or simply do your own inspection. Familiarize yourself with the school and the many support services in both social and academic areas available to the students. Guidance counselors or other administrators should be available to discuss this with you.

Technical Support

Of ever-increasing importance is the technical support that you may need to help with the many forms of technology you can use to enhance your instruction. Consider issues like these: Are students expected to supply their own laptops, graphing calculators, and the like, or will the school supply them? How will your classroom be outfitted to support your technological needs, such as provision of a SMART Board or a computer projector? These questions are best posed to either a colleague or a supervisor. If your school has a library, then learn about its holdings and about the services offered to both you and the students. The school librarian is the logical person to approach to learn about the library.

Mentoring

Throughout your first few years as a teacher, you would be well advised to select an experienced teacher to serve as your professional buddy. You may be assigned a mentor, but in the absence of that you would be wise to select someone who you respect and who can guide you through your initial years with the tricks of the trade rarely found in a book. (Of course, there are many books that can be helpful to meet certain needs and address your various areas of concern. See the References and Resources for many books we recommend.)

As often as you can, try to observe your buddy/mentor teaching classes similar to yours. Look for and list what you believe are the strong points of the lesson as well as its weaknesses. Do not try to copy everything you observe other teachers doing in the class. Remember, a teacher's personality is definitely embedded in teaching performance, and if your personality differs from that of your mentor, you may find the successful lesson you observed flops when you try it in the same way. Teaching is part art and part science. The science part is that there are proven "rules" one can follow that will usually produce a fine performance, yet these may not be exclusive or sacrosanct. The art part is the way each teacher brings ideas to the classroom—embedding her personality into the performance in a special way. The teacher is a professional and, as such, must use judgment about the best way to bring personal skills and talents to the classroom. Ask your mentor to observe you whenever possible. This should be particularly useful because she will not be rating your teaching performance, so it ought to be nonthreatening.

What to Expect from Your Immediate Supervisor

To receive your specific teaching assignment, you should meet with your immediate supervisor; often, this is the assistant principal, but you can also get this information from a lead teacher or department chair. If you are fortunate to have a supervisor who is a mathematics specialist, then you know immediately who your source will be for all curriculum and methodology matters. In smaller schools, it is not always possible to have an assistant principal for each subject area, as is more often the case in a larger school. There, one might even find a math coach— a senior teacher to whom you can turn for issues of instruction and content. This person will provide you with the local curriculum guides and with the state standards: your two most important guideposts regarding what to teach and how much emphasis you should place on the required topics. In the wake of the federal law No Child Left Behind (NCLB), states have been forced to improve their students' performance in mathematics; as a result, much greater emphasis is placed on mathematics achievement. The school district's expectations for each math teacher will have passed through your immediate supervisor.

Your supervisor will also familiarize you with the customs of the school and with the various procedures you are expected to follow both in and outside your classroom. You might be assigned to extra classroom duties, and you might want to know what extracurricular opportunities there are for your students. Perhaps you will find that an extracurricular activity you hold dear is not available in the school. This would give you an opportunity to present it to the supervisor as something you might be willing to take on: setting up a math team or a math club, sponsoring a student math journal, or providing a math fair for students or a math assembly program in which your students could exhibit the power and beauty of mathematics to the rest of the students in the school. It might be wise to present any of these ideas to your supervisor after you have become better established in the school. Otherwise, the supervisor may discourage your suggestions so there is no interference with the beginning of your teaching assignment.

Without placing an undue burden on your supervisor, you might invite her to observe you when you teach and offer some advice to improve your performance. This has a number of advantages; the obvious one is that you will be getting some expert advice to improve your teaching. When you are starting out as a teacher, you will be much more receptive to others' advice on good teaching practices. Many who have been teaching for a long time seem to be convinced that they have adopted the best methods to suit their personality and are often not open to new ideas, especially ones contrary to their style of teaching. By asking the supervisor to visit your classes, you will be giving the signal that you are eager to learn from her new approaches to teaching. This not only is flattering but also will give a clear signal that you are a true professional, open to new ideas and eager to incorporate them into your lessons. Try to obtain from your supervisor—typically a seasoned educator—the best practices you can. This is the best time in your career to obtain alternate ways to conduct your lessons.

What Happens When You Close the Classroom Door?

Once you close the door to your classroom, you are in charge. To perform appropriately, you should be familiar with your school district's policies and with the rules and regulations that the school expects you to enforce. These might include the circumstances under which a student may leave your classroom during an instructional period or the type of instruction you are expected to give.

There may be policy on the quantity, length, and timing of homework assignments. There may be dress codes that teachers are expected to enforce (e.g., not wearing hats in class). In addition to these policies, rules, and regulations, you will need to establish carefully thought out procedures to conduct your class. It is of paramount importance to define your procedures very clearly at the beginning of the school year because modifying them during the semester usually exhibits teacher unsureness and can generate subsequent student discipline problems. So, it is best that you get your act in place from the very start. It is better—and easier—to begin with a strict set of rules and procedures and then relax them, if appropriate, than to try to "get tough" later in the year. The tone you set in the beginning usually lasts throughout.

Let us emphasize one point clearly: The best way to maintain good discipline is to conduct effective and highly motivational lessons. Yet, there are certain procedures you may want to put in place from the first day to make the rest of your lessons clear and orderly. Before your first class, decide if you want to seat the students in your class or let them select their seating. Having them select their seating can lead to problems down the road if they choose to sit next to their friends for all the wrong reasons, or if the "wrong students" choose to sit in the back of the room hoping to avoid involvement in the lessons. On the other hand, you might want to seat students in alphabetical order (or some other random arrangement) to show that you are in charge. Again, this will depend on your personality and whether you plan to have your class sit in the traditional fashion or work in small groups. You supervisor or mentor can help you make this decision.

The way you begin each lesson sends students a clear signal about the way you will conduct your class. Although there are definite advantages to beginning each lesson differently (suspense about what to expect—done effectively—can be motivating), there should be a fixed expectation regarding what students should do when they enter the classroom. Otherwise, students will usually do what they can to stall the class so that they (in their belief) will cover less work and be responsible for less information.

Before each lesson, make sure that any technology you will be using is functional; once the door is closed, things must move smoothly or you run the risk of ruining a perfectly well thought out lesson. Also, make sure that the physical environment is conducive to learning. As a self-coach, you will want to build an arsenal of books that can help guide you through effective teaching methods. There are many such books on the market (see Krulik, Rudnick, & Milou, 2003; Posamentier, Smith, & Stepelman, 2006).

How Is Teaching Mathematics Now Different from When You Went to School?

One major influence causing a change in mathematics instruction rests with technological advances. Perhaps the most dramatic change is seen in the way logarithms are presented in the high school. In the past—albeit the distant past—logarithms were taught with the notion that they could be used as a way for students to do complicated arithmetic calculations more easily. Today, we introduce logarithms as functions to be studied for their mathematical properties. A simple calculator can do far more efficiently what the slide rule and logarithms did in the past. The graphing calculator allows students to graph functions accurately and efficiently, providing more time to study other important aspects of functions, such as how functions behave with certain parts changed. Geometry can now be investigated much more economically with dynamic software such as Geometer's Sketchpad. One could essentially say that this software can replace the traditional Euclidean tools—an unmarked straightedge and a pair of compasses. Perhaps more important, software like Geometer's Sketchpad can allow the student to observe geometric phenomena better than any other past aid. Students can justify geometric theorems and see what it means to prove that something is true in all cases. Students can discover geometric relationships and make conjectures—only then to do a proof. This brings much more meaning to the exercise of proof, which often in the past turned into a rote procedure, leaving students without a true understanding of what they actually accomplished with the proof.

Even the classroom organization now shows some changes. Many teachers now use the workshop style of organization, in which students sit at tables and work together in a cooperative mode instead of sitting in nicely arranged rows. Depending on the lesson topic, some classes will need to be conducted in a combination of styles, old and new. Your supervisor is the person to consult about the teaching style preferred in your school; however, remember that you are a professional, and you must determine the way you will be most effective. Discuss this with your supervisor, if you find the prescribed method (if there is one) is too restrictive to your style of teaching.

Another change in many of today's high schools is the de-emphasis of the former two-column proof in geometry. The two-column format is often replaced by a more flowing paragraph style, and the role of proof in the course is somewhat diminished. Perhaps more than any other subject in the mathematics curriculum, geometry has been discussed in a quest to determine the best way it should be taught. Because it is the only time a high school student is asked to work as a mathematician—developing a logical axiomatic system with axioms, postulates, and proofs—it has been kept intact that way. A feeling that this course might be too difficult for many students has led to recent modifications. There is a continuing debate about what should be emphasized: transformational geometry, vector geometry, non-Euclidean geometry, three-dimensional geometry, and so on. So, this is an area of continuous change that might manifest itself differently around the United States.

In some states, topics such as symbolic logic (truth tables) have come and gone from the curriculum. You should review the textbook and the curriculum materials of the school or school district in which you are going to teach for changes that may be particular to your immediate concerns. Finally, there is a major, and increased, emphasis on reasoning, thinking, and problem solving (see Chapter 8). A major thrust of the curriculum in mathematics is not only to teach the algorithms and skills of mathematics—which we will agree are very important—but also to teach for understanding, with an emphasis on reasoning. The current goal in most states is "Mathematics for all!" This thrust includes an emphasis on process skills as well as algorithmic skills at every grade level.

The Impact of Various Position Papers and Documents

With strong influence from the federal government, states are ramping up their mathematics standards. Some states have found that existing standards were not written in a way that proved helpful to teachers. Often, teachers only discovered what was expected of them regarding curriculum from the various standardized tests, both statewide and local. As a new teacher, you should request a copy of the latest mathematics standards documents and study them because these are the materials that most clearly define what you are responsible for teaching to your students.

National Council of Teachers of Mathematics

Much of today's teaching of mathematics is based on the *Principles and Standards for School Mathematics* published by the National Council of Teachers of Mathematics (NCTM) in 2000. This followed their *Curriculum and Evaluation Standards for School Mathematics* (1989). What emerged from the later document was a new emphasis on problem solving, communication, reasoning, and connections in the teaching of mathematics. These were known as the Process Standards because they dealt with thought processes rather than content as such. For the first time, the mathematics teacher was required to devote time to helping children develop their reasoning skills, sharpen their problem-solving abilities, see how mathematics connects to other branches of mathematics and other subjects, and communicate their thought processes to others using the language of mathematics in written and oral form. The new thinking is that when students are able to verbalize their ideas, they will better understand what is taking place. This ability to read, write, listen, and speak about mathematics, using the language of mathematics, will enable your students to function better in the scientific society in which they will spend the rest of their lives.

Third International Mathematics and Science Study

The Third International Mathematics and Science Study (TIMSS) found that students in the United States do not do as well as their counterparts throughout the world. Indeed, the United States ranked in the lower third of the countries taking part in the study. One reason for this low ranking has been shown to be the kind of homework assignments that we give our students. In many cases, they emphasize skill execution rather than reasoning. For example, a student was given the following pair of equations to be solved simultaneously:

$$4x + 6y = 42$$
$$6x + 9y = 85$$

Multiplying the first equation by 9 and the second equation by 6, we obtain

$$36x + 54y = 378$$
$$36x + 54y = 510$$

Subtracting, we obtain

$$0 = -132$$

This is a strange result. Students will ask what they did wrong. In many cases, the students were asked to write an explanation of what took place. The U.S. students were often unable to understand what had happened. We can regard a linear equation in two variables x and y as the equation with solution pairs that represent the points on a graph. Thus, (0,7) and (3,5) are two members of the solution set of the first equation. A straight line drawn through these points will represent all the points, which are in the solution set of $4x + 6y = 42$. If the students find the slope of the line represented by each equation, then they will discover that the two lines have the same slope and are therefore parallel. Because the solution of a pair of equations solved simultaneously is the coordinates of their point of intersection, and because these lines are parallel, they will have no point of intersection. Thus, there is no solution set for the original equations when considered simultaneously.

Backward Design

TIMSS, together with several major universities, has helped to develop something referred to as *backward design*. This procedure develops curriculum in a back-to-front direction using a series of eight steps. The first four steps are usually done at an administrative level, most often outside the school itself. Curriculum committee involvement is mostly in these first four steps. For more information see *Understanding by Design* (Wiggins & McTighe, 1998).

1. *Analyze the standards.* Decide how the standards map onto your curriculum. In other words, what is it we want our students to learn? This will have been further determined by the standards your state promulgates. Under the NCLB law, these standards are to be taken seriously because the tests given by the state will be based on them. Some states have also developed curriculum guides set apart from the standards in that they suggest ways to teach topics to meet the standards.
2. *Develop an assessment task.* Based on what we wish our students to learn, an assessment task is developed. This could be a test question, a project, or some type of assessment device to determine achievement.
3. *Develop a scoring rubric.* A scoring rubric is developed to ensure that all students are scored in the same manner. This device enables all teachers who are scoring papers to score them in approximately the same manner. As a new teacher, you must be more sensitive to the alternate forms that students

may present as they solve atypical problems. Just because a student does not present a solution that is one of the rubric models does not mean it is incorrect. Some of the most talented youngsters—because of their superior insight—provide solutions that many teachers just did not anticipate. Give them lots of praise for such innovative responses, but by no means penalize them for not matching the prescribed anticipated answers.

4. *Design the curriculum.* Based on the assessment device and its rubric, the curriculum to be taught is written. There may be many other support materials available as a resource.

5. *Plan the instructional strategies.* Now, the classroom teacher enters into the teaching process. Lesson plans are developed with an eye on the curriculum and assessment devices. As you plan your lessons, remember that your personality must be reflected in your teaching. You will perform best if you feel comfortable doing "your thing"—of course, within the bounds of appropriate instruction.

6. *Deliver the instruction.* The teacher now uses the lesson plans to teach the subject matter. You always ought to be aware of your performance—a form of metacognition.

7. *Administer the assessment.* The assessment device developed in Step 2 is administered to the students.

8. *Evaluate and redefine Steps 1–7.* Based on the results of the assessment, the preceding seven steps are refined.

You will find that, as the curriculum is reconstructed in this manner, what you are asked to teach will change. For example, NCLB is continuously being reviewed and modified to meet the vastly diverse needs across the United States. Its assessment requirements are driving states' curriculum and instruction like never before. It is incumbent on you to remain aware of the ways in which your state's education practices and regulations change over time.

2

THE TEACHING ASSIGNMENT

You have your class assignments for the coming school term. You know which subjects you will be teaching. But what do you teach? Algebra, geometry, trigonometry? These generic terms do not tell you what you will be teaching from day to day. You will have to do some planning, but you need some sort of guidelines.

In addition to the standards and curriculum materials published by state agencies, many schools and school districts publish what is often called a scope-and-sequence guide. This at least provides some broad guidelines of what your students should know when they arrive in your room that first day. It will also tell you in general terms what you should be teaching during the year. Ask your chairperson or principal for a copy of the curriculum or course of study guide for each course you will teaching, then check the administrative requirements. Will you be expected to reach a particular place in the algebra curriculum by a specific date? You need this information so that you may pace yourself properly. Will there be a departmental final examination or broader examination at the end of the school year? This can affect your course preparation or pacing. You might try to get copies of previously administered exams to use as a guide.

Examine the curriculum guide carefully. Does it give a day-by-day plan or just a collection of units or topics? Remember, this is a curriculum *guide*, and you can modify it to fit with your expertise. Some guides give suggestions in detail. For example, the guide might suggest that you teach algebraic factoring in a specific order in an Algebra 1 course:

1. Find the common factor in the expression $3xy - 5x$. The factor common to both terms is x. The factored expression is then $x(3y - 5)$. Then they might

have you consider factoring the expression:

$$5(x + y) - x(x + y),$$

where the common factor is $(x + y)$, so the factoring gives

$$(x + y)\,(5 - x).$$

Remember, this is really the distributive property of multiplication over addition/subtraction in reverse.

2. Factoring the difference of two perfect squares, using, for example, $x^2 - 16$. Because both terms are perfect squares, we get $(x + 4)(x - 4)$.

3. To combine the two previous factoring techniques, the students examine the expression for factoring procedures in the order they have been taught, that is, first for the common factor, then for the difference of two squares. For example, to factor the expression $3x^2 - 27$, first check for a common factor (here it is 3) to get $3(x^2 - 9)$. Then, because both terms in the parentheses are perfect squares, we get

$$3(x + 3)(x - 3)$$

Trinomial factoring can also be simplified by first finding the common factor and then doing the usual trinomial factoring. Consider the trinomial $2x^2 + 24x + 54$. Factor the expression for the common factor 2: $2(x^2 + 12x + 27)$. Then, factor the trinomial to get $2(x + 9)(x + 3)$.

In some cases, you may discover that there is no curriculum guide; consider asking a more experienced teacher if you can borrow a lesson plan book from a previous year. This can provide a tremendous amount of material to direct your teaching. Although the content of this teacher's plan book may not fit your teaching style, it at least provides a guide regarding the amount of material that can be presented during a given time span. It also provides a lesson-by-lesson sequence you can examine as you plan your lesson. A word of caution is necessary: Don't directly adopt someone else's lesson plans (tempting as this may be). That will not work. Regard this borrowed plan book simply as a guide to help plan your lessons. You'll see more about lesson planning in Chapter 5.

Above all, don't hesitate to ask for help. Try to find a teacher who can act as a mentor for you for each course you are teaching for the first time. Most experienced teachers will be glad to share their knowledge and experience with you—it is flattering to be asked—as an acknowledgment of mastery!

Is Your Textbook the Curriculum?

Not all curriculum guides go into detail. In fact, it is possible that your school may not even have a curriculum guide. Don't worry. You always have your old friend the textbook to rely on. The textbook is an excellent guide to tell you which topics to teach and in what order. If all else fails, examine the Teacher's Edition of your textbook. It should give you ideas for teaching and many other features to help you. Most textbook publishers provide potentially useful supplementary materials to accompany their textbooks. A word of caution: Do not use these materials just because they are available. Always use your personal judgment so that the instruction is yours and not one provided by prescription. (For more on this, see Chapter 4.)

Your textbook also gives many exercises you can use with your students. Although not a curriculum guide per se, your textbook is definitely a curriculum guide of last resort. Also look at the standards of your local district. The state often generates these because they are ultimately responsible for enforcing the standards in all fields and at all grade levels. Under the No Child Left Behind law, states now require teachers to adhere to the state standards, yet local districts might have some modifications for you to follow. Do not confuse the standards with a curriculum guide. The latter is designed to help you teach the material by providing a suggested order of topics, indicating the depth of your responsibility for covering the material, and providing suggestions for teaching: possible motivational activities, developmental suggestions, and assessment options.

Differentiation Within the Curriculum

Your curriculum may have special sections for teaching gifted or special education students. Yet, you are responsible for providing instruction for all student types: English language learners, "average" students, struggling students, gifted students, as well as special education students. Rest assured your classes will include students from many of these groups. (Note: The Appendix includes more technical information about special education law and the inclusive mathematics classroom.)

The English Language Learner

Teaching mathematics effectively is a daunting task for even the most experienced teacher. However, teaching English language learners is particularly challenging because the teacher must teach both mathematics and English at the same time. The task is more difficult if teachers and students cannot communicate in a common language.

There are several strategies you might employ to create a classroom that is warm, nonthreatening, and rewarding for English language learners. Consider using small groups to allow students who share the same first language to communicate with each other in a relaxed environment. This gives them a chance to ask questions of each other and clarify concepts in both languages while you "manage" the groups. To address the varying levels of understanding a group of English language learners may bring to the classroom, employ a variety of instructional strategies in your classroom not only to keep the classes lively but also to reach more students. Manipulatives enable the English language learner to discover relationships and learn concepts while circumventing the language barrier. You can then ask the student to express the relationship using informal language that does not stress grammatical structure but rather focuses on the mathematical concepts.

Teachers should be sensitive to the frustrations of English language learners and present activities that are both interesting and relevant to the students' lives. English language learners can relate to situations that they are experiencing and are more likely to respond when relevant material is presented. Activities involving sports, music, movies, and games are likely to capture their interest. English language learners can benefit greatly from visual aids, so try to reinforce concepts and skills using charts, graphs, diagrams, and pictures.

Another important factor in the effective instruction of English language learners is the simultaneous acquisition of a mathematics vocabulary and the English language. You should spend some time each day building the English language learners' mathematics vocabulary and making certain that they are well versed in the vocabulary words essential to the day's lesson. You may have students keep a separate vocabulary journal so they can review vocabulary. English language learners may feel more comfortable writing in a journal than speaking up in class. This is natural, and you may wish to first check the journal entries and then call on students to share entries aloud with the class. Knowing that their responses are correct will instill confidence in them and allow them to contribute in a nonthreatening environment.

Teachers must constantly monitor their teaching habits when working with English language learners. Remember to speak slowly and pause often to allow students to thoroughly comprehend what they are saying. Paraphrase your thoughts using different vocabulary and always write key words on the blackboard. Keep spoken sentences short and build in wait time to allow students to process the information before proceeding with the lesson. By following these guidelines, you are more likely to provide your English language learners rich mathematical experiences.

The Average Student

Working with the average student presents teachers a great opportunity to gauge their own teaching effectiveness. Many teachers of average learners are complacent and forget to challenge these students. Outstanding teaching, however, can transform the average student into an above-average student by engaging the student in interesting and relevant activities that will better reinforce conceptual understanding. In addition, the new mathematics standards require that students have a deeper understanding of mathematics and the ability to apply it to various problem-solving activities. Mathematics instruction is no longer restricted to presenting simple procedural tasks; rather, it has broadened into formulating a process to solve provocative problems using careful analysis and the synthesis of many skills.

Although average students may not be expert mathematicians, each average student is an expert at something. The effective teacher finds a way to include opportunities for the average student to show off personal strengths. By incorporating writing, art, and even sports statistics into your activities, you give each student a chance to shine. The average student's motivation in the mathematics classroom increases with this opportunity to feel confident.

Consider asking average students to pair up with struggling students to provide support in some activities. Being asked to explain a concept to a struggling student can be an effective means of motivating an average student to acquire a fuller grasp of the associated concepts; this often results in a valuable learning exercise for both students. In short, the average student, like all students, should be exposed to a mathematics classroom that is lively, engaging, and rich in content.

The Struggling Student

Teaching is not an exact science. Although teachers plan to reach all students with a single clear explanation, it would be naïve to think that just because you've explained something all students necessarily get it. The realization that some of your students are struggling does not imply that you are failing as a teacher. The real failure comes from refusing to accept the challenge of reaching those struggling students.

Struggling students may need to be retaught, and there are two ways of doing that: Either use the same approach or use a new approach. Simply reteaching using the same approach may not be too inventive, but it can be effective for some students. Mathematics can be considered like a language, and in language learning, repetition can bring benefits. Just rehearing an explanation may help concepts "sink in." However, if you can make the same points in a modified fashion, then there is a good chance that you will avoid student boredom and possibly strike a chord that resonates with the student. Such action can even be the break in the learning frustration that may have begun to set in.

If your re-explanation doesn't work, then it is time to search for a new angle. Try to incorporate visuals, manipulatives, or real-world examples to which struggling students can relate. Your goal might be to enable the struggling student to help himself. If the textbook is beyond that student's reading level, then provide a book that is more appropriate.

If the student is still struggling, consider teaming the student with an average or accelerated student for peer tutoring. The tutoring process benefits the struggling student as well as the student tutor by reinforcing both students' understanding. Working with the parents to devise strategies is another way to effectively address the needs of the struggling student. You might ask parents to monitor their child's study and homework time. This may reveal that simple measures such as increasing study time might improve performance in mathematics. Such parental involvement also sends an important message to the student: There is genuine interest in improved performance. This prominent parent involvement has proved successful in increasing student effort. Without increased effort, improved student achievement might prove evasive.

As you identify struggling students, you can try to prevent future difficulties by anticipating which prerequisite skills each student may lack. An astute teacher will also consider many factors that could impinge on student achievement. Some of the considerations are as follows:

1. Are there any undetected learning disabilities that may need to be addressed?
2. Is there a language problem (e.g., for an English language learner)?
3. Is there adequate support in the home, where many feel that true learning really takes place while doing homework?

4. Are there any psychological issues that need to be addressed?
5. Does the student have the proper prerequisites for the course?
6. Are optimum methods of instruction in use for this student?

The Gifted Student

Teaching the gifted student can be as difficult as teaching the weaker student. The challenge is different, but it is a challenge nevertheless.

You will be able to identify gifted students by their creative talent, curiosity, and ability to achieve at a high level. The gifted student will often come up with an innovative or unusual method for solving problems, reflecting a rare insight into mathematics. You can use these unexpected responses to exhibit to the rest of the class alternative ways to look at the mathematics under discussion. Often, the gifted youngsters take pride in sharing their ideas with the rest of the class.

In some schools, gifted students are moved ahead or accelerated. They may begin their algebra work in 7th grade or earlier and complete geometry by the end of 8th grade. This enables them to continue taking mathematics courses and complete a year of college-level mathematics, such as calculus, while still in high school. In some cases, students may accelerate beyond the capabilities of the high school and be forced to take courses at a nearby college or to take a "vacation" from math. The latter would have deleterious effects on the development of a talented student. A high school may offer advanced (i.e., college-level) courses that do not involve calculus (e.g., probability, number theory, advanced Euclidean geometry, etc.). These are all options to consider.

Within your class, however, you will want to challenge gifted students. You do not want them to be bored by moving along with the class at the regular pace. One way to challenge gifted students is to have them delve more deeply into certain topics. For example, the class may be studying the Pythagorean theorem. You might challenge your gifted students to extend the theorem to non-right triangles. (For an obtuse-angled triangle, $a^2 + b^2 < c^2$; for an acute-angled triangle, $a^2 + b^2 > c^2$.) Or, you might ask them to generate Pythagorean triples using the following parametric equations:

$$a = u^2 - v^2$$
$$b = 2uv$$
$$c = u^2 + v^2$$

Then, have them examine some of the triples that result from these equations:

3, 4, 5
7, 24, 25
5, 12, 13
8, 15, 17
9, 40, 41

Will all primitive Pythagorean triples[1] have exactly one leg of even measure? Will the product of the three members of a primitive Pythagorean triple always be a multiple of 60? And so on.

In a geometry class, for example, introduce gifted students to the elements of simple topology. The four-color map problem, the Möbius strip, and the bridges of Königsberg are all topics that will interest gifted students. (See the References and Resources for sources of material on topology.)

There are many questions that can be assigned to the gifted students to inter-est and intrigue them. Here are some you might consider:

When is $\frac{1}{x} > x$?

If $a^2 = b^2$, then will $a = b$?

For what value(s) of x will $x^2 + 6x + 6$ be a negative number?

If x lies between 0 and 1, then can x be less than x^2? Explain your answer.

When does $x = \frac{1}{x} + 1$?

The Special Education Student

The special education student comes into your class under guidelines of an entirely different set of rules. In addition to the rules set by your school or school district, these students are governed by the Individuals with Disabilities Education Act (IDEA). (See the Appendix for more information regarding IDEA and your classroom.) If you have a classified special education student in your class, then that student will probably come with an Individual Education Program, or IEP. This has been prepared by the student's previous teacher together with a child study team and the child's parents.

You must follow what appears in this plan; it is a legal document. If a problem arises, you may need to consult with the child study team and discuss modifying the IEP. However, you should always plan to modify your instruction to accommodate the needs of the learning disabled (LD) child. A typical procedure is to have a teacher aid or special education teacher work with the individual student while you are working with the rest of the class. Be certain, however, that the teacher aid has a good understanding of the mathematics taught.

There are other techniques you can use to help these children achieve in your class. For example, you should obtain permission to give the LD child a grade of Pass or Fail rather than a letter or numerical grade. This is often specified in the IEP. You may have to modify what you teach. For instance, when you teach factoring in an algebra class, use simple numbers. Instead of asking the LD child to factor an expression such as $2x^2 - x - 6$, which factors into $(2x + 3)(x - 2)$, you could ask the child to factor $x^2 + 5x + 6$, which factors into $(x + 3)(x + 2)$.

Remember, students with disabilities are not necessarily slow. They *can* learn mathematics. Consider reducing the number of problems expected of the child for a class or home assignment. Ask a bright child to work with the LD child and assist with the work. (This might be an excellent way to challenge the gifted child, who might otherwise be bored.) You might consider the following problem:

Ian has $1.35 in nickels and dimes. He has 15 coins altogether. How many nickels and how many dimes does Ian have?

The majority of students in your algebra class would immediately resort to a system of two equations with two variables (where x = the number of dimes, y = the number of nickels):

$$x + y = 15$$
$$10x + 5y = 135$$

The student working with the special education child might instead encourage a guess at the answer. After all, intelligent guessing and testing is a valid problem-solving strategy and should be encouraged for everyone. Then, the two students could consider how to move on to the pair of equations solved simultaneously as a more efficient method of solution.

Many special education students may not have a good command of the basic arithmetic facts. For example, they may not always recall the multiplication facts. It's usually wise to make a calculator available for the special student. (All students might well have a calculator available all the time.) At the same time, break the various tasks into smaller pieces. Instead of an entire proof of a theorem in

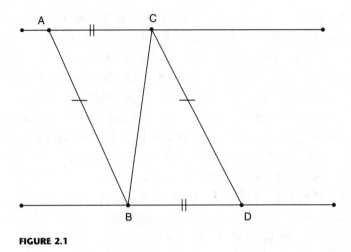

FIGURE 2.1

geometry, you might have the special education child just do the first part, such as simply proving triangles *ABC* and *DCB* congruent (see Figure 2.1). Then, in a second assignment, have the child prove that the line segments *AC* and *BD* are parallel by establishing that $\angle ACB \cong \angle DBC$.

It is good to have models of geometric figures available. Many LD students need to physically touch geometric shapes to understand them. For example, you might help them grasp the concept of congruence by asking them to place one triangle on the other and make the parts coincide. The student may even have problems associating the symbol for congruence ($\cong$) with the word *congruence* or the concept of congruence. The word and symbol may have to be placed side by side for several days. Some special education students may forget material within a day or two. For these children, make reteaching and extended drill and practice a regular part of their lessons. Some special education students have trouble organizing numbers on their papers. For example, they might easily misalign numbers in a simple subtraction problem or when adding a column of figures. To help them, always provide graph paper.

How Do You Get Ideas to Teach Something Beyond the Textbook?

There are numerous books that can provide you with ideas appropriate for your class and yet not included in your textbook. These enrichment units, along with student materials, can be found in several books about teaching algebra and geometry (see Posamentier, 2000a, 2000b, 2000c).

Teaching Secondary Mathematics: Techniques and Enrichment Units (Posamentier, Smith, & Stepelman, 2006) provides enrichment units for all secondary grades, as well as methods of teaching mathematics in the secondary school.

As a new teacher, begin to collect books for a resource library, which will serve you well as you select topics that can be used to enhance your lessons and will enrich your students. A little secret is to find topics and small units you find exciting and you will continue to rejuvenate your professional outlook and become a more enthusiastic teacher. Students appreciate when you take time to show them math "things" not necessarily part of the standard curriculum. You shouldn't think of these short digressions as "wasting time" that could otherwise be used to move ahead in your syllabus; rather, the time spent on these activities will serve you well because they will motivate your students, making them more receptive learners. In that spirit, a list of some of the books that you might obtain as you build your professional library is provided in the References and Resources.

3

YOUR ROOM AS A MATH LAB

When students enter your classroom, they should feel the excitement of mathematical discovery. Your room should be unmistakably dedicated to mathematics and show many mathematical themes, including polyhedral models, posters of famous mathematicians, and colorful bulletin boards. Students should regularly check the bulletin board as a source of information. This bulletin board can include a problem of the week, results of recent mathematics competitions, and a calendar of events for all mathematics activities, including math competitions, math fairs, math assembly programs, math club meetings, and other math-related activities. You might also include some information about math-related careers. Exceptional student work can be displayed on the bulletin board.

The mathematics classroom should be equipped with technological and nontechnological teaching aids, including computer stations, laptop computers, SMART Boards,[1] overhead projectors, math manipulatives, graphing calculators, and a mathematics library. Your classroom should have a warm and inviting atmosphere that will encourage students to look forward to learning mathematics.

Arranging Your Room to Support Student Learning

When students enter a room, the arrangement of desks and other furniture sends a strong message to them about the learning that is to take place. If you want students to work collaboratively, then arrange the room in a manner that supports student interaction and cooperation. Consider the tasks that students will be asked to complete and make sure that your room arrangement will allow them to do it comfortably.

Technology in the Mathematics Classroom

Today's students rely on technology for most of their out-of-school communication and entertainment, and we encourage teachers to consider using technology in their lessons. Even the simplest uses of technology can add a new dimension to a lesson, but like everything else in the classroom, these uses require careful planning. Technology ranges from basic to very sophisticated. Each type can play an important role when used appropriately.

Perhaps the overriding rule in using technology is not to abuse its use. That is, if you can do something in a simple fashion without technological aid, then by all means do so. On the other hand, if a concept can be better explained with technological assistance, then that would be the wise way to go. For example, some geometrical relationships can be best demonstrated with dynamic software, such as Geometer's Sketchpad.

The Overhead Projector: Basic Use

After pencil, paper, chalk, and the blackboard, the overhead projector is the most basic form of technology for the classroom. Although long overlooked in favor of more modern forms of technology, the overhead projector can provide stimulating enhancements to a lesson. You can employ the overhead projector in a few ways as a powerful teaching aid and transform the classroom into a dynamic laboratory for learning mathematics. Two types of transparencies can be used with an overhead projector. The first is the write-on transparency, which you can mark on with either a permanent or an erasable marker. Second, a laser/inkjet transparency can be printed directly from your laser or inkjet printer or you can make a copy from a document copier. Transparencies can be used in many ways to enhance instruction.

Having students prepare solutions on transparencies and displaying them to the class is an effective way of comparing and contrasting solution methods. Students feel empowered when they display their work on the overhead projector. In some ways, they feel like they are the star performers of the moment, captivating all of the attention as their work is displayed in bright lights. Students can also display transparencies of their solutions to selected homework problems for a brief review during class.

The greatest benefit in using the overhead projector is to economize on time and to add a new, visual dimension to the lesson. In most cases, you should not plan to use an overhead projector for an entire lesson. The projected image is limited to a small space and can be monotonous. Above all, be sensitive to the amount of time you show a transparency. Often, the transparency is put up in a flash and then abruptly removed, leaving too little time for students to "digest" the material, much less copy it in their notebooks.

Laser-made transparencies can provide an unlimited expansion to your visual library. Transparencies can display Web pages, computer documents, or images. Teachers can spice up their lessons with newspaper or magazine pictures found online or scanned to their computer. Articles about sports and statistics provide good opportunities to motivate lessons. For example, if you are trying to motivate a lesson on the relationship between decimals and percents, then you can project an image containing the statistics of baseball players and determine exactly how a batting average is calculated. The next transparency could be from a newspaper's financial section for calculation of price/earnings ratios and dividend yields from the earnings per share and the stock price.

During a lesson, the artful use of the overhead projector can make a static lesson dynamic. You can place two transparencies on top of one another to demonstrate the congruence of overlapping triangles as shown in Figure 3.1. Use of two transparencies allows the teacher to "separate" the triangles so that students can visualize the congruent parts. In this manner, students can better deduce that the common segment $\overline{EF}$ must be added to the congruent segments $\overline{AE}$ and $\overline{BF}$ to complete the proof.

Transformations such as reflections and rotations are easily demonstrated using transparencies. Figure 3.2 shows a reflection in the line $\overline{EF}$. Rotations can also be easily presented with transparencies (Figures 3.3, 3.4).

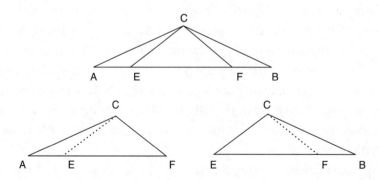

FIGURE 3.1. Given: Isoceles $\triangle ABC$, where $\overline{CA} \cong \overline{CB}$, $\overline{AE} \cong \overline{BF}$. Prove: $\triangle ACF \cong \triangle BCE$.

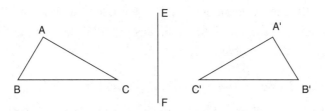

FIGURE 3.2. A reflection of $\triangle ABC$ in the line *EF*.

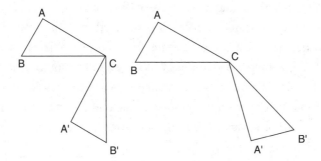

FIGURE 3.3. *Left:* Rotation of $\triangle ABC$ 90° about Point *C*. *Right:* Rotation of $\triangle ABC$ 135° about Point *C*.

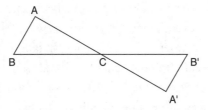

FIGURE 3.4. Rotation of $\triangle ABC$ 180° about Point *C*.

There are many educator tools available that are designed for the overhead projector, including dice, coins, spinners, see-through calculators, geo-boards, polygons, compasses, and protractors. These enable you to conduct experiments, find measurements, and record the results for the class's analysis while the students observe it. Data generated in class have more meaning to students than a chart that lists data from someone else's experiments. Of course, if you have access to a computer attached to an interactive whiteboard, a SMART Board, or other similar device, the same activities can be done using random generators, virtual spinners, and dynamic software. As mentioned in Chapter 5, the Illuminations Project of the National Council of Teachers of Mathematics (NCTM) contains a "tools" section that has many Java-based demonstrations for classroom use.

More Advanced Use of the Overhead Projector

The preceding section discussed how to use the overhead projector in its most basic form, but it should be noted that the overhead projector can be used along with other technologies to create dynamic class presentations. Most notable is the use of a graphing calculator and a view screen. With a view screen, everything that appears on the graphing calculator can be projected onto the wall. Students will see, in real time, the behavior of certain functions or objects as they change dynamically. The graphing calculator has become an important force in mathematics education, and its use is written into the mathematics standards documents of many states. In addition, facility with the graphing calculator is required for the college entrance exams and for advanced placement classes in mathematics, statistics, and the physical sciences.

The Appropriate Use of the Graphing Calculator in the Mathematics Classroom

"Based on research studies including meta-analysis, correlational analysis, and experimental and quasi-experimental methods, research has found that use of graphing calculators in a variety of instructional situations leads to improved student achievement in specific middle school and high school mathematical skills" (Interactive Educational Systems Design, 2003). So, although it is generally agreed that graphing calculators can provide meaningful enhancement to student learning, this does not imply that it is appropriate for all instructional situations. Before determining when you will use the graphing calculator, it is important to ascertain if there is a classroom set of calculators for your use. Many teachers do not have access to such a set. The view screen enables teachers to present effective calculator-based lessons.

If equipment is scarce, then the teacher can use the graphing calculator and view screen to project various graphs (or geometric figures). If there is a class set of graphing calculators, then students can work at their seats or in small groups. In either case, students should be asked to view the graphs and draw conclusions and generalizations from them. Let's consider a middle school example in which the teacher uses the view screen graphing calculator to introduce students to the slope-intercept form of a line.

1. Give students a few equations in standard form.
2. Ask students to re-express the equation in $y = mx + b$ form.
3. Enter the equations on the view screen calculator. Ask students to make a sketch of what they see from the projected image. To make the graph as accurate as possible, press ZOOM, then 6, then ZOOM, then 5. This will produce a window that has equal spacing between tick marks on the x and y axes.
4. Use the calculate function of the calculator to find the slope of each line and its y intercept.

Challenge students to draw conclusions about the effect of m and b on the resulting graphs.

In Figure 3.5, the graphing calculator is used to allow the students to see a variety of examples before drawing conclusions. Students enjoy the challenge in

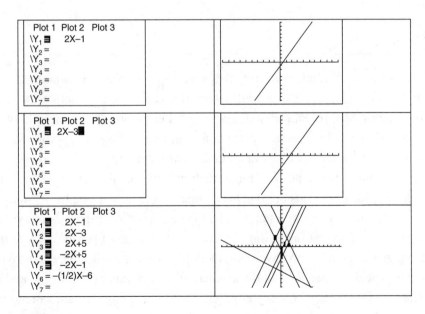

FIGURE 3.5

discovering a relationship. Educational research supports the notion that students retain knowledge attained through experimentation and discovery.

Consider an example at the high school level. When presenting a lesson on solving quadratic equations, you may ask the class to inspect the graphs of the following equations:

$$(1)\ y = x^2 + 6x + 9$$
$$(2)\ y = x^2 - 2x - 3$$
$$(3)\ y = x^2 + 3x + 5$$

Students studying algebra can be asked to generalize how the graph of the function can be a predictor for the number of its roots. More advanced students can be asked to make more sophisticated generalizations about the graph of the function and its relationship to the value of the discriminant. By completing the following table, students will be guided to discover the relationship between the number of roots and the value of the discriminant.

EQUATION	a	b	c	$b^2 - 4ac$	NO. OF ROOTS (x-INTERCEPTS)
(1) $y = x^2 + 6x + 9$					
(2) $y = x^2 - 2x - 3$					
(3) $y = x^2 + 3x + 5$					

Teachers must remember that the graphing calculator is simply a tool; although it might be a part of a well-designed lesson, it should not be the entire lesson. When planning your lesson, give careful consideration to the role of the calculator. Using it to replace repetitive and mundane tasks is appropriate and frees valuable time for discovery and inquiry-based learning.

The graphing calculator is an extremely useful tool for exploring functions and their graphs. Let's consider quadratic functions and their graphs. In studying quadratic functions, it is important to develop the equation of the axis of symmetry. This can be done by inspecting the graphs of a series of parabolas. You may want to pique student interest by telling them that there are little clues in the equations that provide a means to find the equation of the axis of symmetry and the coordinates of the vertex. Thus, you might want to challenge the students to find the relationship between the coefficients of the quadratic equation and the equation of the axis of symmetry by presenting the graphs in Figure 3.6.

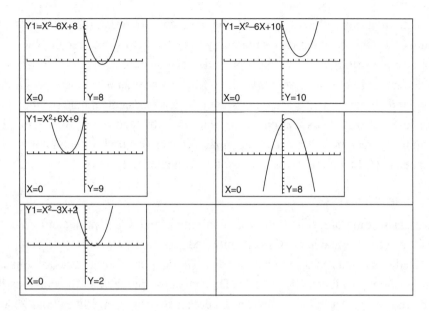

FIGURE 3.6. Coefficients of the quadratic equation and the equation of the axis of symmetry.

At this point in the lesson, some students may wish to hypothesize the relationship between the coefficients of the quadratic and the equation of the axis of symmetry. Of course, under your careful questioning (see Chapter 6), you will orchestrate the discovery if students don't find it on their own.

To lead the discovery of the equation of the axis of symmetry from the given equation, the teacher must ask students to write the equations for the five axes of symmetry. Having students create a table of values is helpful as you ask them to discover relationships. By examining the following table of values, students can more easily be guided to the discovery that the equation of the axis of symmetry is $x = \dfrac{-b}{2a}$.

EQUATION OF QUADRATIC	EQUATION OF THE AXIS OF SYMMETRY	a	b	c
$y = x^2 - 6x + 8$	$x = 3$	1	-6	8
$y = x^2 - 6x + 10$	$x = 3$	1	-6	10
$y = x^2 + 6x + 9$	$x = -3$	1	6	9
$y = x^2 - 3x + 2$	$x = 3/2$	1	-3	2
$y = -x^2 + 2x + 8$	$x = 1$	-1	2	8

Although this activity can clearly be done without a graphing calculator, the tedium of graphing the parabolas manually may distract from a student's ability to recognize the pattern or draw the appropriate conclusions.

Systems are now available that allow teachers to monitor student progress by linking individual student's calculators with the teacher's calculator. Technological advances enable students and classes to interact with each other from home. It is important to recognize that it is essential for you to employ technology as an enhancement, not a replacement for a solid mathematics lesson.

The LCD Projector

Many classrooms are equipped with computers and LCD projectors. With an LCD projector, the teacher can show animated images, movie clips, and computer-generated models to capture student interest. The support material that accompanies many textbooks includes CDs and DVDs containing pictures and animations that can be shown to a class. These multimedia demonstrations can enliven your lessons.

Are Scientific Calculators Obsolete?

The scientific calculator is a valuable tool because of its simplicity and availability. Although students should possess strong mathematical skills, it might be wise to use scientific calculators for long and laborious calculations to free valuable class time for more meaningful activities. Many states have assessments that require the use of calculators (of one type or another). Examinations that include trigonometry require the use of a scientific or graphing calculator because trigonometric tables are no longer in vogue. Some veteran teachers continue to use traditional trigonometric charts along with scientific calculators so that students can better see the behavior of the trigonometric functions.

Using Dynamic Software to Make Your Lesson Come Alive

The computer has become an important tool in mathematics instruction. It can be used in various of ways to deliver exciting presentations to students and facilitate learning through inquiry, discovery, and connections to the real world. As software continues to develop, the technology choices available to educators will continue to increase dramatically.

Dynamic software enables students to view mathematics in motion. It enables teachers to challenge students with a variety of "what if" scenarios that can be investigated in a matter of minutes. Many different dynamic software packages are appropriate for mathematics, and each has features that can be used to enrich a lesson.

Using Geometer's Sketchpad or Cabri Geometry, draw a quadrilateral and join the consecutive midpoints of its sides (Figure 3.7). Ask students if quadrilateral EFGH appears to have any special properties. Some students will suggest that EFGH is a parallelogram. Use the slope tool of the software to test this hypothesis (Figure 3.8).

The student's conjecture is verified for this example, but will it always be true? Dynamic software now becomes an invaluable tool. By dragging Points B and C to different locations, we can examine quadrilateral EFGH in a new scenario (Figure 3.9). Dynamic software enables the class to view, in real time, the effect of moving one or more of the vertices. In this example, quadrilateral EFGH remains a parallelogram in every case. This supports the conjecture that the line segments joining the consecutive midpoints of the sides of a quadrilateral form a parallelogram. The students can also experiment and then make conjectures regarding the circumstances for which this interior parallelogram will be a rectangle (Figure 3.10), a square, or a rhombus. This makes geometry really "come alive."

Students must be reminded that, until proven, this remains a conjecture and not a theorem. This is a great time to prove, using deductive geometry, that this conjecture is indeed a theorem. The proof is relatively short. Use auxiliary line segment $\overline{AC}$ and apply the triangle midsegment theorem that states that the line joining the midpoints of two sides of a triangle is parallel to the third side and half its length, so that we can establish that $\overline{EF}$ and $\overline{HG}$ are both parallel to and half the length of $\overline{AC}$.

Dynamic software can be used in three ways to enhance a lesson: teacher demonstration, students working as a class in a computer lab, and take-home activity or

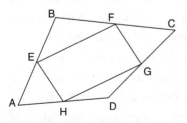

FIGURE 3.7

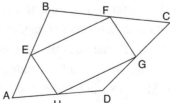

Slope $\overline{FE}$ = 0.47
Slope $\overline{HG}$ = 0.47
Slope $\overline{EH}$ = −1.50
Slope $\overline{GF}$ = −1.50

FIGURE 3.8

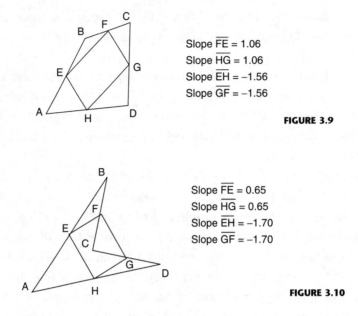

Slope $\overline{FE}$ = 1.06
Slope $\overline{HG}$ = 1.06
Slope $\overline{EH}$ = −1.56
Slope $\overline{GF}$ = −1.56

FIGURE 3.9

Slope $\overline{FE}$ = 0.65
Slope $\overline{HG}$ = 0.65
Slope $\overline{EH}$ = −1.70
Slope $\overline{GF}$ = −1.70

FIGURE 3.10

guided discovery lesson. Teachers are advised to mix and match among them based on their particular school's infrastructure, equipment, and computer lab availability.

- *As a presentation tool.* In this model, a portion of the lesson is projected onto a screen or SMART Board from a computer using an LCD projector. The teacher has the ability to project images that can be manipulated and examined to investigate and discover relationships. These can be elementary or complex relationships. The Geometer's Sketchpad is a powerful yet relatively simple dynamic software program that can be used for many purposes beyond the exploration of geometry. Cabri Geometry is another dynamic software program that allows student investigation. Cabri Jr. can be installed on some graphing calculators for handheld explorations in geometry.

- *In a computer lab.* Dynamic software can also be used effectively in a computer lab. Guided activities allow students to discover certain properties or relationships. Students can be paired to follow the guided activity to discover relationships in algebra, geometry, trigonometry, precalculus, and calculus. The Geometer's Sketchpad and Cabri Geometry have a series of guided activities that lead the students through investigative lessons from which they can form conjectures after discovering relationships. Teachers now have the option of having students prove these conjectures.

- *At home.* Another effective use of the dynamic software is to have students use it at home (with a guided activity sheet) and share their discoveries with the class. Many companies provide student versions of their software for this purpose, particularly if your school has a site license for their product. Ask your supervisor to request student copies for their home computers for this purpose.

In any of the three scenarios, dynamic software can enrich instruction and capture the interest of students.

Creating a Mathematics Library in the Classroom

Most of this chapter has been devoted to technology that can be integrated into instruction in the mathematics classroom. Although technology provides teachers with many opportunities to enliven a lesson, a basic mathematics library can promote student interest by providing enrichment activities to supplement the day's lesson. Vignettes from the history of mathematics show mathematics in a context that many students find fascinating. For example, before presenting a proof of the Pythagorean theorem, you may wish to ask students to investigate some of the notable people who have devised proofs of this theorem. Students are intrigued to learn that such prominent historical figures as Euclid, Leonardo da Vinci, Napoleon Bonaparte, and President James A. Garfield have fashioned proofs of the Pythagorean theorem.[2] There are always new proofs being developed—some even done without words. Using the history of mathematics to inspire students makes mathematics more meaningful to students and allows students to investigate and report back to the class.

The mathematics library is undergoing change, as technology becomes the rule rather than the exception. Print journals are being replaced by their digital (electronic) counterparts, as the Internet provides access to libraries across the street and around the world. Teachers should encourage students to view the collections in a print library as a tiny fraction of the resources available to them. The Internet is now considered an integral part of any library and not a separate and distinct entity. The Internet provides a great way for students to investigate a given topic; it is a good medium for discovering interesting topics that relate to mathematics. One excellent resource can be found at www.mathforum.com. By using Google or some other search engine, students should get instant responses to any issue they wish to pursue. It is important for students to select the appropriate keywords so that the document search can be as effective as possible.

Allowing students the time and opportunity to browse leisurely through a book or journal with a wide variety of enrichment topics will undoubtedly pay huge dividends. Teachers must give direction when students are given library time. Students should be given a library lesson to make their time most productive. A mathematics library should contain a selection of books and periodicals at or slightly above the students' current level. Many students enjoy the challenge of comprehending and mastering some topics slightly beyond the scope of the syllabus and the average ability level of the class.

A classroom library can begin with just a few titles and a few magazines. If you join the NCTM, you will receive a subscription to one of their publications, either *Mathematics Teaching in the Middle School* or *The Mathematics Teacher* (high school). These monthly journals have many interesting explorations for teachers and students. The Mathematical Association of America's *College Math Journal* has interesting articles that may be appropriate for upper-level high school honors students. The Canadian Mathematical Society also publishes monthly journals that contain articles about mathematics and math education for middle school and high school teachers. The magazine *Chance,* published by Springer-Verlag, contains stimulating articles that are based on statistics. These real-life studies provide outstanding motivation for mathematics lessons. *Scientific American* is another magazine that would be appropriate for your math library. By subscribing to these magazines and periodicals, your library will continually grow; in a few years, you will have a substantial collection.

Finding appropriate books for your library is not a difficult task. There are many books on recreational mathematics that are suitable (see References and Resources). You want to expose students to a variety of topics at this time, and they can then use the Internet to delve into these topics in more depth. Because the mathematics standards require students to express themselves mathematically, the math library presents a wonderful opportunity for students at all ability levels to investigate and write about mathematics. Teachers are advised to reserve some time so that students can share their findings with each other.

Math libraries should be used to promote independent student research and investigations. Most curricula and syllabi are too restrictive to allow for student research outside the scope of the syllabus. In addition, new teachers have to concern themselves with following the prescribed syllabus or risk falling behind. A mathematical library in each classroom gives students the opportunity to investigate many interesting topics in mathematics. Assigning projects for extra credit on the history of mathematics similarly promotes the goal of students learning to appreciate mathematics as the foundation of science and discovery. Using your classroom as a mathematics laboratory encourages students to think beyond the textbook and make connections between the mathematics taught in the classroom and the world around them. There is an extensive list of books at the end of this book.

4

USING YOUR TEXTBOOK
EFFECTIVELY

Probably the least understood and the most erroneously used aid to teaching is your mathematics textbook. It is an important component of your teaching in a middle or high school because often the textbook essentially serves as the curriculum guide for the course you are teaching. Many teachers tend to rely on the textbook to determine what to teach, how to teach it, and the best order in which to teach the various topics. How can you make the best use of this valuable aid?

Your textbook is a guide. Think of it as a blueprint or a road map that can help you decide what to teach and provide at least one way to teach it. In fact, we recommend that you acquire several textbooks from various publishers and compare the different approaches to developing the same topics. Some of these approaches may be new to you and should enhance your understanding of the topics. This deeper insight into the common topics of the course you are teaching will enable you to provide a much "richer" lesson than otherwise.

Keep in mind that the traditional textbook is designed for the mainstream teacher, one who believes that following the textbook and its approaches is the best way to succeed. Yet, it is extremely difficult for a printed text to present problem-solving activities or reasoning tasks in a style that matches the teacher's personality so that the individual teacher can just use the material as presented and discuss it with the class. It is difficult to put a discussion in a textbook. This would make the teaching too rigid and would not compensate for individual teaching styles. There have been textbooks written that reflect an author's particular teaching style rather than embracing a sort of neutral path; these books have rarely been successful.

A good textbook must allow you to exercise freedom to exhibit professional judgment in presenting lessons in a fashion consistent with your teaching style.

To insist that a teacher follow a specific method for teaching the more thought-provoking topics could produce an ineffectual performance. Use the textbook as your guide, not your "lesson plan."

The Teacher's Edition

Most textbooks have a Teacher's Edition available, which usually reproduces the student page of the textbook and surrounds it with ideas and hints for teaching. For example, in one typical series designed for the middle school grades, the Teacher's Edition consists of an oversize volume with three main sections:

- Scope and Sequence
- Starting Off Right
- Becoming a Better Test Taker

Under the Scope and Sequence heading, there is a large chart that lists the topics taught in each grade level in the series. You can read across the Scope and Sequence to see what your students should know when they reach your class and what they will have learned after they leave you. This helps put the topics you will teach into their proper perspective. Everything you teach is merely a link in a long chain of mathematical topics. You should be aware of what came before and what comes afterward. In addition, the Scope and Sequence permits you to see how closely your textbook actually follows the curriculum from which you will be teaching.

The section Starting Off Right is the main part of the Teacher's Edition. The book shows the students' page and surrounds it with a series of topics such as: "Lesson Organizer," "Introduction," "Teaching," "Summarizing," and "Checking." In addition, there are "Alerts" or "Warnings" set off in boxes and scattered throughout the text to alert you of some errors that are commonly made by students.

The Becoming a Better Test Taker section provides support for student assessment. The Teacher's Edition generally provides solutions to all the exercises in the textbook. Let's see how the Teacher's Edition can help you plan a typical lesson.

Teacher's Edition Features

Lesson Organizer

Some textbook publishers provide a lesson organizer that offers an overview of what the lesson under consideration might look like. It is usually a one- or two-word phrase offering things discussed in the following categories: introduction, teaching, summarizing, checking, and alert. A quick glance at this section provides an overview of what your lesson might look like.

Introduction

The introductory section may provide a motivation for the lesson. It might also offer a problem designed to catch the students' interest. For example, in one 8th grade textbook, the lesson is listed as "Exploring Independent Events." The lesson begins with the description of an event:

> The captains of the two opposing football teams toss a coin to decide which team will kick off and which will receive. Mike is the captain of the Storms. Should he call heads or tails? Why?

The Teacher's Edition suggests that the teacher begin the lesson by discussing this with the class and listen to the students' reasons for selecting heads or tails. It advises you to accept all answers that are supported by a reason and to discuss them with the class.

Teaching

A Teacher's Edition may suggest that a lesson be taught by placing the students into groups. The textbook for such an arrangement might provide students with directions for performing an experiment in coin tossing. The Teacher's Edition then would suggest how to divide the class into groups of four and provides a task for each member of the group. One student will actually toss the coin, one will announce heads or tails, one will record the data in a table, and the fourth will report the results to the class. The teacher could then introduce the concept of probability of heads or tails in fraction form:

$$P(\text{Heads}) = \frac{\text{Favorable outcome}}{\text{Possible outcomes}}$$

Summarizing

Here, the Teacher's Edition tells the teacher to discuss what has taken place in the lesson. Begin with the original problem, discuss whether it matters if Mike calls heads or tails, and why.

Checking

The Teacher's Edition suggests to the teacher that the students should develop an experiment to decide which number is most likely to occur when a pair of dice is tossed. They should carry out the experiment and decide which number occurs most often and then substitute their decision.

Alert

Although this lesson did not have an alert in it, let's look at one typical alert from the Teacher's Edition. Here is the problem suggested:

> A commuter looks at the tickets in his tunnel-toll ticket booklet. He sees that Number 11 is the top ticket, and number 20 is the last ticket. How many tickets does he have left?

Under the alert box, the Teacher's Edition states that students may fail to count the number 11 ticket in their total; actually there are 10 tickets, not 9. You should read the Teacher's Edition carefully to find the possible mathematics pitfalls of the lesson.

The Teacher's Edition also delves into how to provide algorithmic practice in each lesson. This practice may not always be a page of practice problems similar to those done in class. For example, having taught a lesson on exponents, the following question is suggested:

> Are the values of 3^4 and 4^3 the same? Why or why not?

Notice that this problem provides the student with practice in using exponents, but at the same time puts the practice into a situation that is not mere drill. This emphasis on problem solving and reasoning pervades the entire book, so that the Teacher's Edition is an invaluable tool for finding appropriate problems.

Becoming a Better Test Taker

This section delivers exactly what its name promises. In this day of frequent testing and assessment (see Chapter 9), it is more important than ever that your students improve their test-taking abilities. Most current textbook series either add a section to their Teacher's Edition or produce a separate assessment booklet to go along with the series. The Teacher's Edition should account for all types of questions—multiple choice, short answers, open-ended problems, and long answers. Students should be provided with an excellent example of a response to the problem as a model, a suggestion for thinking it through, and some basic tips for avoiding common errors. In addition, the students should be given practice in writing out their thought processes as they solve problems. Some text series now even have a section for the student to read about how to avoid careless mistakes when taking a test.

With the current emphasis on problem solving, the Teacher's Edition is an excellent source of problems to use with your students. Some Teacher's Editions will provide a series of problems listed by problem-solving strategy, so that students can practice each strategy separately, if you wish. The Teacher's Edition might also include a "problem of the day" for each lesson or a "problem of the week." These regular challenges should be within reach of many of your students so that most can achieve some success. This is a fine motivating device.

You should read the beginning sections of your Teacher's Edition carefully to find out how up to date the text series is. Is the writing based on the latest research? The mathematics classroom is changing rapidly; it is important to keep up with what we are finding out about how children learn mathematics.

You should look through the Teacher's Edition for other teacher support materials. For example, does the daily lesson include something for everyone? Is there material designed for slower learners? For rapid learners who finish early? For gifted and talented learners?

The Teacher's Edition should also provide you with pages of extra practice after each section. This will help you when looking for test and review questions for your students. These questions might also be useful later in the school year for reviewing something taught earlier.

How You Should Use Your Textbook

Remember that your textbook is just a printed page. It has limitations and may not always offer the best way to teach a topic. As a result, consider the following ideas.

Let the speed with which you "cover" a topic be dictated by how well and how quickly the students learn it. Most lessons in a textbook encompass two pages. The first page usually introduces the topic and explains the algorithm or skill.

The second page usually contains illustrative examples and problems for practice, both in class and at home. Don't be driven by a desire to finish the two-page lesson in one day. The textbook is merely a guide, and you are the best judge of how much time a particular class requires to properly learn the material. It's more important that your students understand the mathematics you are teaching. Even if you do cover the two-page lesson, that doesn't necessarily mean your students understood it.

The textbook can provide an excellent source of problems for review or homework assignment. Don't try to assign every problem in the textbook. Select those activities, problems, and exercises that best suit your goals, both instructional and content. You can easily skip problems and even pages that you think are not appropriate for your students. Remember that clever students are wise to the teacher who, sometimes out of a lack of caring, assigns merely the odd- (or even) numbered exercises for homework. This gives the students the impression that little time and effort was put into examining the problems and selecting appropriate ones for the homework. So, why should they spend a lot of time doing it? Take the time to carefully read each exercise, work several of them out, and select those that provide direct practice in the various skills you would like your students to have learned in that lesson. Try to eliminate exercises with difficult computation, thus focusing on the real intent of the practice on the topic taught. Don't get caught up in unnecessary complications.

Here's a hint: Save some of the practice exercises for later in the semester. You will want the students to spiral back and review topics periodically. To do this, you should save some problems from each topic to assign throughout the year.

The textbook should be used for more than a set of problems to be assigned as homework. It is hoped the material will be written at a reading level that is appropriate to the students who will use the book. In a mathematics class, a "reading assignment" can be frowned on by students. They need to understand that the best way to solidify their learning is to review it at their own pace, which means reading the expository material in the textbook at home and in a quiet setting. Besides their class notes (which sometimes are not the easiest to follow), the textbook is an excellent resource for student test preparation. They can reread the sections on which they will be tested and try some of the exercise examples (which you might assign as a practice test).

Building a Personal Library of Textbooks and Other Math Books

You should try to build a personal library of textbooks from several different publishers. As mentioned, each textbook often has a different approach to teaching a particular topic. Thus, if you examine how something is taught in more than one textbook, then you might find a more interesting way to teach the topic to your classes. Furthermore, if a fair portion of your students don't "get it" the first time you teach something, then it may have to be retaught. Using a different approach from another textbook is one way to keep the students' interest and possibly reach them more effectively.

The first thing you should do is see which textbooks are already available in your school. Often, different teachers use different texts. Ask your supervisor. You might be able to obtain a copy of each text used in your school—that's a good start.

Another approach you might consider is attending meetings of the local, state, or national professional organizations held in your local area. These meetings are usually accompanied by exhibits from many various publishers. If you ask the publishers' representatives at their exhibits, they might be willing either to give you a copy of their latest text for your grade level or to send one to you at your school. After all, they cannot sell their books to a school system in which the teachers don't know the books exist. The last few hours of the meeting is the best time to request a textbook—the exhibitors don't really want to carry the textbooks home and would much rather give them to interested teachers who might consider adopting them.

Also consider writing a letter (on your school's stationery) asking the publisher to send you an examination copy of the textbooks you want to see. In most cases, publishers are happy to do so. Believe it or not, this is an inexpensive way for publishers to advertise their books. They believe that the more copies that get into the hands of teachers, the more sales they will be able to realize.

All the while you are collecting textbooks—some as resources, some to use in class—you should also be building a personal library of mathematics books that can be used as a source of problem-solving activities, class enrichment, historical anecdotes to enhance a lesson, background material for different topics, and underlying support for the material to be taught throughout the school year. These books, usually not too expensive, can be found in bookstores, through advertisements or reviews in professional journals, and at publishers' exhibits at professional conferences. You might even find some gems in a used book store. Old books sometimes provide interesting alternatives and background information that you can use to enhance your lesson. Remember, the Internet offers an almost boundless way to search for common books as well as out-of-print ones.

Selecting a New Text

You may be asked to serve on a committee to select a textbook to use in your school. In some schools, a panel of teachers and the supervisor select the texts from an approved list of books. In others, you may find that there are virtually no restrictions on which book to select. In either case, however, there are some key points to consider.

First, do the topics in the textbook under consideration match the topics in your curriculum guide? It's no problem if there are extra topics (you can always skip those or enrich your instruction), but the text won't be of much value if it is missing a fair number of topics you require. In such a case, it is advisable not to consider that book further, even if it appears to be attractive. Try matching the Scope and Sequence in the Teacher's Edition with your curriculum to see how closely they match. This may be the most efficient way to judge the book's appropriateness.

Second, read through and check the mathematical accuracy presented. Are there any conceptual errors? Are the definitions and algorithms expressed in good, clear mathematical language and easily understood? For example, one text might define absolute value as "A number without a sign." This is hardly a worthwhile definition to give students. Similarly, it might be considered inappropriate to define an infinite set as "a set that can be brought into one-to-one mapping onto a proper subset of itself." The age appropriateness must also factor into your decision about the usefulness of a textbook.

Third, does the book include both algorithmic practice and problem-solving/ reasoning lessons? For the longest time, most textbooks included only skill-building topics; this is no longer true. Today, most textbooks include problem solving and reasoning as topics to be taught, and these topics appear as lessons throughout the text. If the textbook shows only separate lessons for problem solving and reasoning, however, a red flag should go up. These skills are not reserved for mathematics;

they occur in every facet of daily living. They not only should be taught as separate lessons, but also should be appropriately integrated throughout the textbook.

Fourth, is the book at a reading level appropriate for your students? According to the National Council of Teachers of Mathematics' standards (1989, 2000), the ability to read mathematics is important. The text must be written at the grade level for which it was intended. You shouldn't be put in a position of feeling that you will have to rewrite each lesson to make certain that the students understand it.

Fifth, is the textbook based on up-to-date research on how children learn mathematics? Or will you have to redo each lesson to make certain your students can understand the topic? The introduction to the Teacher's Edition will usually discuss this important topic and give you the proper guidance in this regard.

Sixth, what are the teacher support materials that come with the textbook? There will usually be a Teacher's Edition for you to use, but there may also be sample lesson plans, test items for each section or chapter, unit tests, a CD-ROM with supportive material (including test items, geometric diagrams, some interactive support, etc.), and laboratory experiments with the appropriate equipment. Current research supports the notion that students learn better with a hands-on approach, even in middle school and in high school. Do the materials come with the text series? Or are they an additional expense? Is their use carefully explained in the Teacher's Edition? Does the publisher offer free workshops for the teachers on some of the ways to make best use of their text? Most publishers will provide a consultant to come into your school and work with teachers if the publisher's text series is adopted. Check on this; it can be an important part of your decision making.

Finally, what does the book cost? This may affect your decision. Be careful about the copyright date. When a book is more than two years beyond the copyright date, it is generally already three years old because publishers usually issue a book with a copyright date of the following year. As a book approaches the fifth year, the publisher will already be preparing a new edition, making the current one obsolete and ordering replacement copies difficult and sometimes impossible.

If you are asked to serve on a textbook selection committee, then examine all the textbooks carefully. Don't let yourself be swayed by the use of color and fancy printing. In some cases, these may only add to the cost without adding to usability. It has been said that too much glitz on a page can distract from the purpose of the book: presenting mathematics in a pedagogically sound manner.

5

DESIGNING AN EFFECTIVE
LESSON PLAN

Although theories abound about the best way to teach mathematics to children, it is universally accepted that a well-designed lesson plan is the main ingredient of a successful lesson. Examining the professional practice of effective teachers reveals two commonalities: great organizational skills and the thoughtful design of the lesson plan. A lesson plan serves at least two main functions. The obvious purpose is to provide the teacher with a guide or notes for conducting a lesson. The less obvious but no less important purpose is to give the teacher an opportunity to mentally rehearse the lesson while writing the plan. Just as an actor would hardly ascend a stage without rehearsal, so, too, should a teacher not teach a lesson without a rehearsal: the writing of the lesson plan.

Enthusiastic young teachers, in an effort to maintain a lively and spontaneous classroom, may wish to avoid a "scripted" and "confining" lesson, but a well-designed lesson plan is neither. The lesson plan should serve as a guide that provides the classroom teacher great flexibility in presenting the day's lesson. Lesson plans must be designed to reflect continuity of purpose from one day to the next. In general, the teacher should begin planning a lesson by identifying the student learning outcomes: exactly what the student is expected to learn, and what the teacher will use as evidence of a successful learning outcome.

What Are the Components of a Lesson Plan?

There are nine major components that might be included in the design of an effective lesson plan:

1. Prior skills inventory (preassessment).
2. The aim of the lesson, or its purpose.

   3. A start-up activity.
   4. A motivational activity.
   5. The body of the lesson (discovery, developmental, application of new concepts, pivotal questions, etc.).
   6. The planning of differentiated instructional paths for the gifted, average, and weaker students.
   7. The generalizations and conclusions (to be modified, if necessary, based on the progress of the lesson).
   8. The homework assignment.
   9. If time permits . . . (a brief interesting activity, if there is time left after you have completed your lesson).

These basic elements are designed to be both universal and flexible and lend themselves to a variety of instructional approaches.

Prior Skills Inventory

Most lessons have a set of prerequisite skills that will be used in the lesson. For instance, students must know how to find the least-common multiple of two numbers before learning how to add fractions with unlike denominators. Before you begin to plan the lesson, you should take a "skills inventory" of your students, a sort of preassessment to determine their readiness for the lesson. Relevant skills obtained from previous years should be reviewed so that your lesson proceeds smoothly. Otherwise, you may be forced to break the continuity of the lesson to provide review for only a few students. One way to ensure that students are prepared for the day's lesson is to include review problems in the preceding days' homework assignments. Effective teachers anticipate potential student weaknesses and address them well in advance of the lesson. Of course, this clearly implies that you should begin a rough plan a few weeks ahead of time. You can refine your lesson a few days before presenting it to ensure that it suits the actual class needs and abilities.

The Aim of the Lesson

The aim of the lesson should be clear to you and to all members of the class. It can either be written on the board before students enter the room or be elicited from members of the class during the development of the lesson. In either case, it clarifies for the students exactly what is to be learned in class. It gives them a purpose for being in class that day. In some districts, the aim will be requested to be phrased in the form of a question. This is a style issue.

The Start-up Activity

Most mathematics lessons begin with a start-up exercise. The purpose of the lesson-starting activity is to engage students in something that will contribute to the lesson. This activity can include review of past work and previously learned concepts, foreshadow topics to be learned, or motivate students in some novel way. You might lead students through a series of previously learned exercises and conclude with a related problem that cannot be completed without mastering the day's lesson.

The second use for the start-up activity can be to review some specific skills that may be essential to the day's lesson. In our sample Lesson 2 (page 70), an important prerequisite skill is solving an equation such as $(x - 3)^2 = 5$ and understanding that the solution is $(x - 3) = \pm\sqrt{5}$ or $x = 3 \pm \sqrt{5}$. By using this example in the start-up exercise, the teacher derives the benefit of anticipating a potential "rough spot" in the lesson that might cause a break in the continuity of instruction. Anticipating student skill deficiencies and providing appropriate support and review in the start-up exercises can be part of the design of an effective lesson.

What should you do while the class works on the motivational (start-up) exercise? Here are several options:

1. Put up the next day's homework assignment (which can be modified later, depending on the progress of the lesson).
2. Take attendance; deal with yesterday's absentees to formulate plans to make up the work.
3. Circulate among the students, offering some assistance when necessary.
4. Check student homework at their seats. (This is merely a cursory spot-check and should not be considered as anything comprehensive.)

The Motivational Activity

The motivational activity addresses the question, Why do we have to learn this? One motivational technique is to highlight the utility of learning a topic. Teachers are encouraged to use current events, present a problem involving recreational mathematics, or make connections to students' interests to motivate a lesson (for a series of techniques, see Posamentier, Smith, & Stepelman, 2006). Anecdotes from the history of mathematics can also motivate a lesson. Students are surprised to learn that mathematics has been important from ancient civilizations through modern times. (See Chapter 7 for more ideas on starting a lesson.) Another method is to present a challenging puzzle that relates to the day's lesson. After they struggle with it for a while, tell them that the puzzle will be very easy to solve with the mathematical techniques they will learn that day.

The Body of the Lesson

The development of the lesson. Now that you have students motivated to learn, you have to lead the class through a series of discoveries and the development of the lesson. Using a technique called backward design (Wiggins & McTighe, 1998), consider which concepts and skills you hope to have the students attain by the end of the instructional period. You now must create a series of activities that will artfully lead them to your intended goal. This is sometimes referred to as *guided discovery*. Students must be active participants in the lesson and provide explanations, conjectures, and thoughtful questions. The development and design of a good lesson include anticipating opportunities to embrace students in the instructional process. Sending students to the board while other students work at their seats promotes a lively classroom where a weaker student can seek help from the teacher, work with their ordered pair,[1] or sneak a peek at the board to overcome a small hurdle in negotiating the task at hand. The foregoing can easily be adapted to a workshop-type class organization model.

Application(s) of newly acquired concepts. Allow time in each lesson for students to apply what they have just learned. These application problems (exercises) present an opportunity to solidify the concepts, methods, and rationale developed in the body of the lesson and to extend the concepts through a series of increasingly complex problems. This is the time for the teacher to present differentiated instruction to advanced students and to provide support for weaker students. It is also an ideal time to have students exhibit their work on the chalkboard, overhead projector, or projection device and to provide supporting explanations. If these problems and exercises are left on the board, then they can be used to summarize the day's lesson.

Planning pivotal questions. Students are likely to remain actively engaged if challenged with questions that effectively lead them through the discovery and development of the lesson. Students become stakeholders in the success of the lesson when they contribute to it. Effective questioning clarifies and validates learning for the student, and it informs the teacher of student progress. Pivotal questions should be written out beforehand and be a part of every well-designed lesson plan. The structure of the question is important, and most methods books deal with this in great detail (see Posamentier et al., 2006). See Chapter 7 for specific "dos and don'ts" of questioning.

Planning Paths of Differentiated Instruction

Because many mathematics classes have students with varying skill levels, design lessons to engage learners of all abilities. This means you must come to class prepared to present advanced students with some challenging problems and somewhat weaker students with a series of simpler exercises that gradually lead to the point at which the average student is functioning. Weaving these plans into the instructional design is tricky but can be done by finding a time when most of the class is working on a similar (parallel) problem of an easier nature. For instance, if the entire class is solving (by factoring) the quadratic equation $x^2 - 2x - 15 = 0$, advanced students can be asked to solve (by factoring) $6x^2 = 2 - x$. Having students place solutions to the problems on the board for a side-by-side comparison shows the similarity in their solution, although the second problem requires more algebraic (symbolic) manipulation and factoring skills than the first problem. This is what your chalkboard might look like:

$$x^2 - 2x - 15 = 0$$
$$(x - 5)(x + 3) = 0$$
$$x - 5 = 0 \text{ or } x + 3 = 0$$
$$x = 5 \text{ or } x = -3$$

$$6x^2 = 2 - x$$
$$6x^2 + x - 2 = 0$$
$$(3x + 2)(2x - 1) = 0$$
$$3x + 2 = 0 \text{ or } 2x - 1 = 0$$
$$x = -\frac{2}{3} \text{ or } x = \frac{1}{2}$$

The average student should be able to complete the first problem; the more advanced student could tackle the second problem. Without drawing attention to the differences, this differentiated instructional model supports the goals of the lesson in a seamless fashion but allows students to work at their appropriate levels of sophistication. Students can also work cooperatively in ordered pairs when presented with problems of varying difficulty. For homework, problems at all levels can be assigned because students can refer to their notes for clarification (see Chapter 2 for levels of student abilities).

Generalizations and Conclusions

Every lesson should end with a summary and conclusion to clarify the concepts and skills presented. Either summarize the lesson or ask student volunteers to do it. Encourage students to communicate about mathematics. When students articulate what they understand, either verbally or in written form, the main points of the lesson are reinforced. Listening to student summaries serves as an informal assessment of both student comprehension and the effectiveness of your instruction.

Homework Assignment

Have your planned homework assignment, but always be prepared to modify it, based on the students' performance in the lesson.

If Time Permits: Some Ideas

Because teaching and learning are individual aspects, it is important to recognize that, for a variety of reasons, some lessons may finish early. You may find that a lesson has gone more smoothly than the same lesson did in previous classes. Thoughtful planning can include an extra application problem or the presentation of a tantalizing tidbit (Posamentier, 2003) to whet students' appetites in other areas of mathematics. Some teachers routinely assign a "problem of the week" that can be reviewed if time permits. These do not have to relate to the theme of the lesson and thus can be saved for an appropriate time. These problems typically reward students who think creatively and fashion elegant solutions. Here is an example of a quick problem that you can give to your students if time permits:

> Find the value of $1-2+3-4+5-6+7-8\ldots-1000$. Explain how you arrived at your answer.

Planning Group Work in the Mathematics Classroom

Much research has been devoted to the efficacy of using group work in the mathematics classroom. In addition to the ordered-pair construct, there are many other ways to design effective lessons that employ group work. Organizing the routines and delineating student responsibilities during group work is essential for its success. Students should know exactly what is expected of them during group work. Basic principles that make group work successful are as follows:

1. Groups should consist of three or four students.
2. Students should have a clear understanding of how to form groups.
3. Students are to complete the entire assignment, in the same order, at the same time. How can students help one another, if they are not working on the same problem?
4. Each student in the group must assume all the roles in the group, including that of the facilitator, the recorder, the contributor, and the presenter. Thus, everyone should be writing, calculating, and contributing.
5. Anyone from the group may be called on to present their findings to the class.
6. Students must understand that they are responsible for each other. All members of the group should benefit from the learning activity. There can be no leisure learners in group work.
7. Students should understand that any member's notes can be collected and graded. This grade will be assigned to all of the members of the group.

Teacher-Centered Versus Student-Centered Instructional Models

As you plan your lesson, decide the extent to which the lesson will be student centered. Teacher-dominated lessons (sometimes referred to as *chalk and talk*) are usually not too effective because they do not adequately engage students. However, students should not be expected to learn everything without your structure and guidance. An effective lesson includes opportunities for student discovery and for teacher-guided learning. Some topics lend themselves to one instructional model over another; consider this as you design your lessons. We discuss the developmental and workshop models.

The Developmental Lesson Model

The developmental lesson model relies primarily on the teacher as the main source of information, if not by lecturing, then as the guide who elicits the information from students. Until recently, this was the predominant lesson format, and it still remains popular, particularly with veteran teachers. In this model, the teacher orchestrates the lesson from the chalkboard through a series of questions and discussions. The teacher typically controls the flow of the lesson and the pace of student learning. When done properly, this format can be effective and engaging for students. Students feel comfortable when they are led, step by step, through a difficult concept. Some teachers misinterpret their role in the presentation of the developmental lesson and simply lecture the students, providing them with little or no opportunity to discover or make meaningful contributions to the lesson.

The Workshop Model

The student-centered workshop model, also known as discovery learning, has had great success in science and humanity classes. It can also be adapted for use in a math class with thoughtful planning. In this model, the teacher presents a mini-lesson (of about 10–15 minutes) with four major components:

- Connection to some previously learned concept.
- An explicit statement of what is going to be taught and modeling it.
- Active engagement that allows students to try it out during the lesson.
- Provision of a link to independent or group work.

As the students work independently or in groups, the teacher circulates among them, providing guidance and encouragement. This is followed by a "share," with the teacher asking individuals or groups to report on their results. The teacher then restates these results to reinforce the aim of the lesson. Obviously, if you plan to use the workshop model, you have to plan accordingly.

Calculating the value of π is a classic discovery lesson. Teachers can distribute circular objects to group members and ask them to measure and record the circumference and diameter of each, using string. Using a calculator, each group computes the ratio of the circumference to the diameter for each object. Encourage groups to identify the patterns they notice and use them to predict the circumference of the sun given its diameter (870,000 miles).

Students get great satisfaction from discovering mathematical patterns. They learn to look at math as problem solving instead of something that they must be "told" how to do. On the other hand, this model has several pitfalls. Planning a lesson using the workshop model often requires a significant amount of time. As is the case with most group work, you may find it difficult to assess individual members of a group.

The workshop model may not be appropriate for all lessons. For example, developing a formula for the sum of an arithmetic series or finding a relationship between the number of sides of a polygon and the sum of its interior angles are examples of lessons that can be effective in a workshop model class. A middle school lesson on order of operations would be difficult to present using the workshop model and is more suitable as a developmental lesson. A high school lesson on the derivation of the quadratic formula would probably be most effective if presented using the developmental lesson format.

Solving Systems of Equations Using the Developmental Lesson Model and the Workshop Model

Sample Lesson 1: Using the Developmental Model

Aim. The lesson aim is to solve systems of equations by eliminating a variable.

Start-up activities. Ask students to complete the following tasks:

Solve for x, given the value of y: $3x + 2y = 10$, when $y = 2$.
The sum of two numbers is 10, and their difference is 4. Find the two numbers.

Motivation. Although the first start-up problem reinforces previously learned skills, the second exercise is a more obvious look at a system of equations. Many students will use trial and error and arrive at the correct answer, 7 and 3. The teacher will now present the class with a problem that cannot easily be solved by trial and error and will work with the students to develop a universal method that can solve all systems of linear equations.

Solve for x and y and check:

$$2x + 5y = 5$$
$$3x - 5y = 3$$

Comment: It is highly unlikely that students will be able to solve the third exercise by trial and error. The expert teacher will solicit ideas from the students and direct them to look at an easier problem of the same type as the third start-up exercise. This question is to remain on the chalkboard so that students are reminded that solving it is today's goal.

Developing the lesson. The two major concepts that should be introduced are writing verbal expressions algebraically and combining two linear equations to form a third one.

Write the following on the board and ask students to verify its accuracy:

$$
\begin{array}{r}
5 \text{ nickels } + 2 \text{ dimes } = 45 \text{ cents} \\
+ \quad 2 \text{ nickels } + 4 \text{ dimes } = 50 \text{ cents} \\
\hline
7 \text{ nickels } + 6 \text{ dimes } = 95 \text{ cents}
\end{array}
$$

Engage students in a discussion about the accuracy of these statements and lead them to conclude that if two true equations of this type are added, then the resulting equation is also true. Have students practice with the following examples:

$$
\begin{array}{r}
x + 2y = 9 \\
+ \quad 5x + 4y = 3 \\
\hline
\end{array}
$$

$$
\begin{array}{r}
3x + 5y = -10 \\
+ \quad 6x - y = 13 \\
\hline
\end{array}
$$

After students have combined these equations, you will place the following problem on the board:

$$
\begin{array}{r}
x + y = 10 \\
+ \quad x - y = 4 \\
\hline
\end{array}
$$

Ask students:

1. What significance do the equations in the last item have in relation to today's lesson? (They are an algebraic representation of the second start-up question.)
2. When you combined these equations, how did the answer differ from the two sets of equations above? (The y term drops out when we add the two equations.)
3. Look at the result when the equations are added: $2x = 14$ and $x = 7$.
4. Now that we have solved for x, how can we solve for y?
5. Now that you have solved for x and y, how can you check your answers? (You must substitute your answers into *both* equations.)

Write the following on the board: "After solving for one variable, you can determine the value of the other variable by substituting the known value into *either* equation. However, to check you must substitute your answers into both equations."

Activity. Students will work either individually or in small groups to solve for x and y and check:

1. $2x + y = 9$
   $3x - y = 1$

   Answer (2, 5)

2. $3x + 2y = 9$
   $4x - 2y = 26$

   Answer (5, –3)

3. $-2x + 6y = 2$
   $2x - 3y = 7$

   Answer (8, 3)

4. The sum of two numbers is 15, and their difference is 5. Find the two numbers.

   Answer: 10 and 5

Comment: During this activity, circulate among the groups of students and send students to the board to share their solutions with the class.

Summary. After having students explain their solutions to these problems, ask students to summarize the lesson in their math journals or notebooks.

If time permits. Solve for x and y and check:

$$3x + y = 22$$
$$x + y = 12$$

Answer (5, 7)

Comment: Tomorrow's lesson will focus on solving more complex systems of linear equations in which one or more of the equations needs to be multiplied by a constant.

Homework. Figure 5.1 is the homework for this lesson; see the section on designing a homework assignment.

Sample Lesson 2: Using the Workshop Model

Aim. The aim of the lesson is the introduction to solving systems of linear equations.

Start-up activity. Students are seated at desks arranged in groups of three or four.

Tuesday, October 18	Homework 28	Due: October 19
Solving Systems of Equations by Eliminating a Variable		

Read Section 4.5, pages 227–235	Read Example 3, page 231, and Example 4, page 232

Write a paragraph that summarizes the concepts and techniques presented in today's lesson.

Pages 235–236	Pages 225–226	Page 211	Page 199	Page 188
{1, 2, 4, 7} A {12, 13} B {14, 21} C	{22, 27} D	{18, 34} E	{23, 44} F	{37} G

Next test: Thursday Section 4.1 through Section 5.2
After-school tutoring: Tuesday and Wednesday, 3:00–4:00, Room 404

Problem of the week: http://mathforum.org/algpow/. Submissions must be handed in by Friday, October 20, in class for extra credit.

FIGURE 5.1. Homework assignment, developmental model.

Activity 1. Each group is asked to investigate and answer the following:

1. Find five pairs of numbers with a sum of 20.
2. Are these the only five pairs?
3. Find five pairs of numbers with a difference of 8.
4. Are these the only five pairs?
5. Find one pair of numbers with a sum of 20 and a difference of 8.
6. Is this the only pair? Explain how you arrived at your answer.

Comment: The teacher's role during this discovery activity is that of a facilitator. The teacher should circulate among the groups and identify those groups that have made significant progress. Students may arrive at their answers in various ways, including making charts, guessing and checking, or taking an algebraic approach. The teacher should give opportunities for all of the different approaches to be shared. After this sharing, the teacher should guide the class to use variables to express the relationship of the pair of numbers with a sum of 20 in Activity 1. It is advisable for the teacher to inform the class that the algebraic method will always work, but that other methods some groups may have used, like guess and check or making charts, depend on luck or good intuition.

Ask students to do the following:

1. Write an algebraic expression to represent the pair of numbers whose sum is 20.
2. Write an algebraic expression to represent the pair of numbers whose difference is 8.

The teacher takes a few minutes to make certain that the class understands that, in this instance, when these two algebraic expressions are combined in a certain fashion, one variable will drop out; they are then left with a simple equation in one variable to solve. The class then returns to their small groups to begin Activity 2.

Activity 2.

1. Find 10 pairs of numbers with a sum of 50.
2. Find 10 pairs of numbers with a difference of 18.
3. Find 1 pair of numbers with a sum of 50 and a difference of 18.
4. Express the relationship between the numbers in Questions 1 and 2 algebraically. Use the algebraic method from Activity 1 to find the pair of numbers with a sum of 50 and a difference of 18.
5. Use an algebraic method to solve the following: The sum of two numbers is 174, and their difference is 92. Find the two numbers. (Answer: 133 and 41)

Comment: Notice that the scope of this lesson is much smaller than that of the developmental lesson. However, in this lesson, students are challenged to make conjectures and discover relationships for these and similar problems.

Share time. Each group will share the method they used to solve the problems in Activities 1 and 2.

Homework. Write a paragraph about how to use an algebraic method to solve Question 4 in Activity 2.

Solve using an algebraic method:

1. Find two numbers with a sum of 83 and a difference of 27.
2. Find two numbers with a sum of 2,346 and a difference of 1,024.
3. Find two numbers with a sum of 7,489 and a difference of 2,159.

Comment: This homework assignment can also include problems from previous lessons and should not be limited to only those concepts covered in this one lesson.

Activity 3 (if time permits). Make up three problems similar to those in Activities 1 and 2. Use the algebraic method developed to find the numbers. Exchange your three problems with another group and compare your answers.

Designing the Homework Assignment

Designing a series of meaningful homework assignments requires thoughtful planning and outstanding organizational skills. Homework reinforces the aim of the day's lesson and supports the goals of future lessons. Homework assignments should be designed to practice, reinforce, and extend the concepts presented in class, as well as review or revisit previously learned material. Homework provides the teacher valuable information about student progress and ideas for future lessons. When homework assignments include problems that are well beyond students' capabilities, the students can be frustrated, lose confidence, and may give up.

Homework must be assigned thoughtfully and be limited to enable completion in a reasonable amount of time. The homework assignment is your communication to the student about what you view as important, what you value conceptually, and which specific tasks you expect students to be able to master. It is advisable to include a reading assignment about the day's lesson before asking students to begin the written portion of the assignment. Although the majority of your homework problems should be within the reach of your students, you may include some problems that present an extra challenge. If you choose to assign problems that you know will be a bit difficult for many students, then you may wish to inform them of the difficulty ahead of time. This is not to excuse them from attempting the problem but rather to communicate the difficulty level so that they do not become frustrated if they fail to complete it.

Consider this homework assignment and determine if it supports your educational objectives:

Homework: Pages 352–353, do odd-numbered exercises 1–31.

This homework assignment sends a negative message. It appears as if the teacher did not take time to choose appropriate problems but rather assigned a series of problems as "busy work." There is also no reading assignment or any review exercises from previous lessons. An item that foreshadows what is to come in future lessons also is missing.

Teachers may wish to design *spiraled* homework assignments. As the name indicates, these assignments spiral back to previously learned materials. With spiraled assignments, students can spend time reinforcing the current material while taking a small amount of time every night refreshing their memories of prior lessons.

Figure 5.2 is a sample assignment that reflects best practices in homework design. You can choose some or all of these features as you design your homework assignments to reflect your teaching style and tastes.

Tuesday, December 6	Homework 42			Due: December 7
Solving Quadratic Equations by Completing the Square				
Read Section 10.3, pages 345–351		Read Example 2, page 348, and Example 4, page 350		
Write a paragraph that summarizes the concepts and techniques presented in today's lesson.				
Pages 352–353	Pages 344–345	Page 336	Page 227	Page 198
{1, 2, 5, 6} A {8, 9, 12} B {15, 21} C	{23, 26, 28} D	{30, 35} E	{29, 41} F	{57} G
Next test: Thursday, Dec. 15, Section 9.5 through Section 10.8 After-school tutoring: Tuesday and Wednesday, 3:00–4:00, Room 404				
Problem of the Week: http://mathforum.org/algpow/. Submissions must be handed in by Monday, December 19, in class for extra credit.				

FIGURE 5.2. Homework assignment reflecting best practices.

The elements of the homework assignment that make it effective are as follows:

1. The assignment is clearly numbered, with a date, a title, and a due date.
2. It contains a specific reading assignment.

3. Specific examples from the textbook are highlighted for the students to review.

4. It includes a short writing assignment that asks the student to summarize the concepts and procedures involved in the day's lesson. Asking students to communicate mathematically addresses the "communication standard" that has become a staple of national and statewide mathematical process standards.

5. The homework assignment spirals. Even if students do not fully comprehend or are absent for this day's lesson, they can still do a significant portion of the homework. Notice that the class is reminded of an examination in 1 week, which begins the reviewing process.

6. Notice how problems are grouped and labeled with a capital letter, A through G, to the right of each grouping. This is the teacher's method of assigning problem sets to individual students *the day before they are due* so that students come to class prepared to place their problems on designated areas of the board according to their grouping letter. This eliminates much of the commotion at the beginning of the lesson as students have clearly defined roles and responsibilities with respect to the homework. An added advantage of this method is that the homework is likely to be placed on the board correctly because students are assigned the problems in advance. In addition, students can easily refer to a specific problem because it is placed in a designated area. Homework can also be prepared on transparencies for display on an overhead projector or on a laptop computer. Of course, as new technologies evolve, there will be more options available to students and teachers.

7. The upcoming test is announced more than one week ahead of time. The material that the students are responsible for is clearly defined by both the textbook sections and the homework assignments. After-school tutoring schedules are included in the homework as well.

8. This homework assignment contains a "problem of the week" that students may do for extra credit. More importantly, it initiates an online relationship with a respected mathematics organization that can serve as an outstanding resource in the future.

How Do You Know Which Problems to Choose for the Homework Assignment?

Select several problems from the textbook that are aligned with this lesson. Now, actually work them out in advance to determine their complexity and the amount of time required for the student completion. Often, a problem that appears elementary has hidden complexities that make it unsuitable for homework. In such instances, you may wish to include these problems in future spiraled assignments because students will have had more time to master the concepts. Problems relating to the day's lesson should be elementary to moderately challenging; problems from previous lessons can be more difficult.

Routines for Checking Homework

Teachers must develop routines for checking homework. Students should understand that homework is an essential component of learning, and that you value their time and efforts in completing the assignment. Students prepare homework with increasing care when they receive positive feedback for their efforts. There are many ways to check homework; it is important to adopt one or more of these techniques to validate student achievement.

The model that is most efficient for checking homework is to circulate among the students during the start-up exercises and spot-check certain problems in the assignment. You are checking homework for two reasons: to reward students who completed the assignment and to determine the effectiveness of the previous lesson by gauging students' success in completing the homework. Choose at least three problems to check, two from the previous day's lesson (one elementary and one more challenging) and one that is a review problem from some earlier lessons. The first two provide a good idea whether the students grasped yesterday's lesson. The third clearly identifies those students who require remediation or those who did not seriously attempt to do the homework. Remind students that because the homework assignment contains a significant amount of review, they are *always* expected to be successful with a portion of the assignment. This eliminates the excuse "I didn't understand the lesson, so I couldn't do the homework." Note when a student comes unprepared for class. A student who continually comes to class unprepared may be experiencing problems that require a referral to a guidance counselor. You should ask students who are unprepared to see you after class for a private chat about the importance of doing homework and to ascertain the reason for not having done the homework.

Another model that you can use is to collect the homework and spot-check it for accuracy. This might be advisable for an inexperienced teacher, but this takes a lot of time, and the record-keeping task can be onerous. Some teachers find it appropriate to randomly select a row of students and ask them to hand in their homework for inspection. Of course, you can mix and match these methods and collect homework on some days but check homework at their seats on others.

Every now and then, you can collect a homework assignment and grade it as a quiz. Regardless of which method you choose, you must make students realize that homework is important, and it must be done regularly to be successful at learning mathematics.

Review of the Previous Day's Homework

It is important that the homework be placed on the board for inspection and review. You do not have to ask each student to explain the problem that he placed on the board. You should have a clear idea of which problems you consider essential for the day's lesson. However, students should have the opportunity to check their solutions against those placed on the board. It is a good practice to come to class with a notebook that contains the solutions to the homework problems, which makes it easy for you to compare the solutions on the board with your solutions. Most important, when you actually do the homework assignment, you can choose an appropriate subset for explanation in class to ensure that students see the solution to a variety of problems without redundancy.

Planning for Students Who Are Absent

It is highly recommended that each student have the phone numbers and e-mail addresses of three other students in the class. You may wish to put aside a few minutes of class time during the first week of school for students to choose their partners. Encourage students to call their absentee partners to keep them abreast of class activities. Should an absent student find the homework assignment daunting, they can always do the part that is a review of previously learned material. When students return to class after an absence, you may want to lend them your homework solution book. Many teachers use technology to communicate with their students. Homework assignments can be posted on your Web site, and your school may have educational chat rooms for student communication. As new technologies evolve, there will be more opportunities for members of a class to communicate with the teacher and each other.

The Importance of Planning Your Board Work

What you and your students write on the board is typically recorded in students' notebooks. The modern classroom may now be equipped with SMART Boards, interactive whiteboards, or LCD projectors to augment the overhead projector and chalkboard. It is advisable to be extremely organized when you plan your board work or the use of a technological alternative. You should know exactly where the aim, the start-up, and homework will be written. This is typically done at the beginning of the period and can be placed on a single panel of the board. Some teachers, in an effort to save time, have these items prepared on an overhead projector transparency. Although it may save time at the beginning of the lesson, this practice has many drawbacks, the most serious of which is that it may not remain projected. Thus, students arriving late to class cannot record the motivational start-up exercise or copy the homework assignment. One effective technique is to have the aim, the start-up activity, and the homework prepared in advance on a small portable whiteboard. This is particularly valuable when teachers are not teaching the same class back to back or are scurrying from one room to another for instruction. The time saved at the beginning of the period is significant and allows teachers to attend to other classroom routines, such as greeting students, taking attendance, checking homework, and providing support to students as they work on the start-up exercise.

Dealing with the Alternative Solutions

Be ready to deal with unexpected strokes of genius or creative solutions. Although some of these may be invalid, they often provide valuable insights into how students think. You need to judge the validity of the statement and its value to the lesson. Do not feel pressured to draw an immediate conclusion. It is acceptable to tell the class, "I will think about that and get back to you tomorrow." You can also ask the class to ponder the conjecture. For example, take a careful look at the problem to solve for x and check: $2x^2 - x = 15$. This problem was presented in a class, and two students gave convincing arguments supporting their solutions, yet their answers did not match:

Unexpected solution:

$$2x^2 - x = 15$$
$$x(2x - 1) = 3 \cdot 5$$

$$\therefore x = 3 \text{ and } (2x - 1) = 5$$
$$2x = 6$$
$$x = 3$$

Correct solution:

$$2x^2 - x = 15$$
$$2x^2 - x - 15 = 0$$
$$(2x + 5)(x - 3) = 0$$
$$x - 3 = 0 \text{ or } 2x + 5 = 0$$
$$x = 3 \text{ or } x = -\frac{5}{2}$$

Although clever, the first solution was "lucky." A good teacher will use the first solution as an opportunity to clear up mathematical misconceptions. Because of the spontaneity of these "novel" solutions, it is not always easy to convert them into meaningful instructional moments.

Incorporating Technology into Your Lessons

Teachers are encouraged to integrate technology into the mathematics classroom. To be successful, you must carefully plan the use of technology with your other classroom activities. The National Council of Teachers of Mathematics (NCTM) has a series of interactive, online "tools" that can be used by students and teachers to explore mathematical concepts (NCTM, n.d., Illuminations Project). The NCTM also provides a variety of lesson plans that are technology based. Let us consider presenting a lesson on the properties of the medians of a triangle. This lesson can be presented with compass and straightedge, with software installed on a graphing calculator, or with dynamic software, such as Geometer's Sketchpad, that can be displayed with a SMART Board or projected with an LCD projector. In each scenario, an exciting lesson can be presented.

Scenario 1: Low Tech (Compasses, Straightedge, Cardboard, Scissors)

Students should either be familiar with the geometric construction to determine the perpendicular bisector of a given line segment or be taught it at the beginning of this lesson.

1. Give students a piece of cardboard (8.5 × 11 inches) and ask them to draw a large triangle on it.
2. Lead students through the construction of the perpendicular bisector of each of the sides of the triangle to find each midpoint.
3. Students should draw the three medians to the sides of the triangle. At this point, students should make some observations about the medians of the triangle. Students will "discover" that they meet at a common point (the centroid). Most students will be surprised that their classmates' triangle displays the same property.
4. For each of the three medians, students should measure the distance from the vertex to the centroid and the distance from the centroid to the midpoint. Ask students to make conjectures about these lengths. They will be surprised to find that, for each of the three medians, these distances maintain a 2:1 ratio.
5. Instruct students to use their scissors to cut out their triangle from the rectangular cardboard. Ask them to experiment and attempt to balance the triangle on the tip of a pen or pencil. Students will discover that the centroid is the balance point or center of gravity of the triangle.

Scenario 2: High Tech (Dynamic Software with a SMART Board or LCD Projector)

Presenting the same lesson using a high-tech approach can also be exciting. Using a dynamic geometry software program, perform the same constructions as in Scenario 1 (Figure 5.3). Students will see a series of diagrams that will allow them to discover the concurrency of the medians. The dynamic software will also reveal the ratio of the segments of the medians.

As the software computes the lengths of the segments, students should be asked to make conjectures and draw conclusions. Note that the demonstration of the centroid as the balance point can only be accomplished using the low-tech approach with cardboard and scissors. Dynamic software allows further exploration of some additional properties in this diagram involving areas. There are more properties that can be revealed using dynamic software. Consider the areas of the six interior triangles (Figures 5.4 and 5.5). Students will discover that they all have the same area. Dynamic software enables the teacher to alter the diagram to support the conjecture that this relationship holds in all cases.

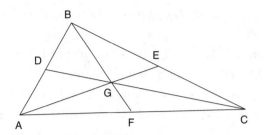

m $\overline{CG}$ = 4.70 cm　　　m $\overline{GA}$ = 3.38 cm　　　m $\overline{GB}$ = 2.45 cm

m $\overline{GD}$ = 2.35 cm　　　m $\overline{EG}$ = 1.69 cm　　　m $\overline{FG}$ = 1.23 cm

$\dfrac{\text{m } \overline{CG}}{\text{m } \overline{GD}}$ = 2.00　　　$\dfrac{\text{m } \overline{GA}}{\text{m } \overline{EG}}$ = 2.00　　　$\dfrac{\text{m } \overline{GB}}{\text{m } \overline{FG}}$ = 2.00

FIGURE 5.3

Area △ GFA = 1.99 cm²

Area △ ADG = 1.99 cm²

Area △ GEB = 1.99 cm²

Area △ GEC = 1.99 cm²

Area △ FGC = 1.99 cm²

Area △ GFA = 1.99 cm²

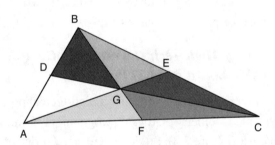

FIGURE 5.4

Area △ GFA = 2.36 cm²

Area △ ADG = 2.36 cm²

Area △ GEB = 2.36 cm²

Area △ GEC = 2.36 cm²

Area △ FGC = 2.36 cm²

Area △ GFA = 2.36 cm²

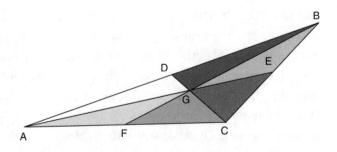

FIGURE 5.5

Planning a Series of Lessons (Unit Planning)

Just as careful planning must accompany any given lesson, a series of lessons must also be planned thoughtfully. Units of study consist of a series of lesson plans that build on one another and complete a discrete topic. In planning a series of lessons, you must determine the number of lessons necessary to cover the material. If you have never taught this material, then solicit the advice of your colleagues. They can provide valuable insights about motivation, timing, and instructional techniques that should be considered as you begin your planning. Consider how technology can be used to enhance the lesson. Many teachers use a backward design process (Wiggins & McTighe, 1998) that employs three stages in unit planning. Stage 1 identifies the desired results. Stage 2 determines acceptable evidence of mastery. Stage 3 is actual lesson planning. You should consider what previously acquired skills will be needed for each lesson. These concepts and skills can be included in preceding homework assignments so that if review is necessary, it will not break the flow and continuity of the lesson.

In the following example, we consider the outline for planning three days of instruction in algebra leading up to the derivation and use of the quadratic formula:

Lesson 1: To solve quadratic equations by factoring.
Lesson 2: To solve quadratic equations by completing the square.
Lesson 3: To solve quadratic equations using the quadratic formula.

Lesson 1

Aim. The aim of Lesson 1 is to solve quadratic equations by factoring.
Start-up. Factor each of the following expressions:

1. $x^2 + 6x + 8$.
2. $x^2 - 10x + 25$.
3. $2x^2 + x - 1$.

Skills inventory for Lesson 1.

- Multiplying binomial expressions.
- Recognizing perfect trinomial squares.
- The zero-product rule for multiplication.

The lesson should now be developed as the class is challenged to solve a series of problems that are related to the start-up exercise. Solve for x:

1. $x^2 + 6x + 8 = 0$.
2. $x^2 - 10x = -25$.
3. $2x^2 = 1 - 2x$.

Comment—Using Technology: Ask students to graph each of the quadratic expressions in Lesson 1 after they have placed them in standard form. Use a view screen and ask students to draw correlations between the graphs and the solutions to the quadratics.

Lesson 2

Aim. The aim of Lesson 2 is to solve quadratic equations by completing the square.

Start-up. Solve for x and check:

1. Mulitply $(x-3)^2$.
2. Factor $x^2 + 10x + 25$.
3. Solve for all values of x: $x - 2 = \sqrt{3}$.

Then later have the class do:

4. Solve for all values of x: $x^2 - x - 6 = 0$.
5. Solve for all values of x: $4x^2 - 9 = 0$.
6. Solve for all values of x: $(x-3)^2 = 4$.
7. Solve for all values of x: $(x-3)^2 = 5$.
8. Solve for all values of x: $x^2 - 6x + 4 = 0$.

Skills inventory for Lesson 2.

- Factoring trinomials.
- Solving quadratic equations by factoring.
- Recognizing patterns in perfect trinomial squares.
- Forming perfect trinomial squares.
- Solving $x^2 = a$ as $x = \pm\sqrt{a}$.

MOTIVATING THROUGH THE HISTORY OF MATHEMATICS

Over 4,000 years ago, the Babylonians studied algebra and geometry. They used cuneiform script that pressed numbers and letters on soft clay tablets that were baked in the hot sun. Over 500,000 tablets have been recovered. The Babylonians solved quadratics by completing the square. This is a typical problem that was translated from a tablet: "I added twice the side to the square, and the result is 1, 26, 40." This translates into the expression $x^2 + 2x = 5,200$. Students will be curious about the notation 1, 26, 40; again, you can discuss the base 60 system (sexagesimal) that was employed by ancient civilizations.

Of course, you can now engage students in a discussion about the rich history of mathematics and the methods that were employed over 4,000 years ago. Students will be surprised to learn that the completing the square method was used by ancient civilizations. Students can be asked to do extra credit reports on topics from the history of mathematics.

Students should be able to complete the first four problems of Lesson 2 in a matter of minutes. Of course, Problems 4–6 are your motivational exercises that create a rationale for extending their knowledge. At this point in the lesson, it is important to have unanimity among members of the class that a solution to Problems 6 and 7 cannot be obtained by previously learned methods. Students may assume that because they cannot factor these quadratics, they may not have any solutions. In some cases, students may have encountered imaginary roots. Encourage student discourse and praise students who take academic risks.

APPROPRIATE USE OF TECHNOLOGY

Ask the students to use their graphing calculators to solve Equations 3–8 by finding the intersection of the graphs of the right and left sides of the equations.

As you guide the discussion, students should conclude that there are solutions to the equation $x^2 - 6x + 4 = 0$. At this point, develop the lesson in detail using Problems 4 and 5 as the foundation for instruction. Because solving $(x - 3)^2 = 5$ is much easier than solving $x^2 - 6x + 4 = 0$, a majority of the lesson may be devoted to forming perfect trinomial squares. In this example, the transformation of $x^2 - 6x + 4 = 0$ into $(x - 3)^2 = 5$ is the most challenging component of the process. The final steps are simply procedural:

$$(x-3)^2 = 5$$
$$\sqrt{(x-3)^2} = \sqrt{5}$$
$$(x-3) = \pm\sqrt{5}$$
$$x = 3 \pm \sqrt{5}$$

The body of the lesson should include many exercises involving the forming of perfect trinomial squares and this should have been reinforced through pattern recognition in factoring in the preceding lesson(s) and homework assignments. Remember to include a summary at the conclusion of each lesson. The summary may be more meaningful if students are asked to provide it.

Lesson 3

Aim. The aim of Lesson 3 is to solve quadratic equations using the quadratic formula.

Start-up. Solve the following equations:

1. $(3x-1)^2 = 8$.
2. $x^2 - 4x - 3 = 0$.

Check your answers using a graphing utility.

Skills inventory for Lesson 3.

- Recognizing patterns in perfect trinomial squares.
- Forming perfect trinomial squares.
- Simplifying radical expressions.
- Solving $x^2 = a$ as $x = \pm\sqrt{a}$.

TIPS FOR TEACHERS

If it appears that the motivational exercise may take too long for each member of the class to complete, then you can split up the assignment and have designated teams of students working on specific problems. They can then report their results to the class or send a representative to place their answers on the board. The use of ordered pairs is a valuable technique that can be employed in many situations, including ones like this.

You can expect that Problem 1 will be solved quickly. Students may attempt to use factoring to solve Problem 2; however, they will discover that it is not factorable over the rational numbers. As you circulate among the students, make certain that, after a few moments, they begin to tackle the second start-up problem by completing the square. You may wish to pair students up to ensure that students are not sitting idly. You can also have some students place their solutions to start-up Problem 2 on the board. After a few more minutes, you can call the class to order and allow students to explain their work. Highlight the formation of the perfect trinomial square in Problem 2 and extend their ability to complete the square when the coefficients are fractional.

Ask the students to complete the square:

3. $x^2 - \dfrac{2}{3}x.$

4. $x^2 + \dfrac{3}{4}x.$

When you are satisfied that they can complete the square with fractional coefficients, ask them how they might solve a problem like this:

5. $4x^2 - 4x + 1 = 3.$

Many students in the class will recognize the clues from the start-up activity and suggest solving this quadratic by completing the square. Inform them that today's lesson will simplify their mathematical tasks and prove to be a useful timesaving method for solving all types of quadratic expressions, regardless of their form. Students should be guided through the solution of this problem, paying careful attention to the details of the algebraic manipulation and the formation of the perfect trinomial square. This will serve as your model for the derivation of the quadratic formula.

$$4x^2 - 4x - 2 = 0 \qquad\qquad ax^2 + bx + c = 0$$

$$4x^2 - 4x = 2 \qquad\qquad ax^2 + bx = -c$$

$$4(x^2 - x + \quad) = 2 \qquad\qquad a\left(x^2 + \frac{b}{a}x\right) = -c$$

$$(x^2 - x + \quad) = \frac{2}{4} \qquad\qquad \left(x^2 + \frac{b}{a}x\right) = -\frac{c}{a}$$

$$\left(x^2 - x + \frac{1}{4}\right) = \frac{2}{4} + \frac{1}{4} \qquad\qquad \left(x^2 + \frac{b}{a}x + \left(\frac{b}{2a}\right)^2\right) = -\frac{c}{a} + \left(\frac{b}{2a}\right)^2 = \frac{b^2 - 4ac}{4a^2}$$

$$\left(x - \frac{1}{2}\right)^2 = \frac{3}{4} \qquad\qquad \left(x + \frac{b}{2a}\right)^2 = \frac{b^2 - 4ac}{4a^2}$$

$$\sqrt{\left(x - \frac{1}{2}\right)^2} = \sqrt{\frac{3}{4}} \qquad\qquad \sqrt{\left(x + \frac{b}{2a}\right)^2} = \sqrt{\frac{b^2 - 4ac}{4a^2}}$$

$$\left(x - \frac{1}{2}\right) = \pm\frac{\sqrt{3}}{2} \qquad\qquad \left(x + \frac{b}{2a}\right) = \pm\sqrt{\frac{b^2 - 4ac}{4a^2}}$$

$$x = \frac{1}{2} \pm \frac{\sqrt{3}}{2} \qquad\qquad x = \frac{-b \pm \sqrt{b^2 - 4ac}}{2a}$$

Using the solution of Problem 5 that remains on the board, ask students to compare $4x^2 - 4x - 2 = 0$ with $ax^2 + bx + c = 0$. Ask students to identify a, b, and c. Now, ask students to proceed with a step-by-step solution of $ax^2 + bx + c = 0$ by following the model set by the solution of $4x^2 - 4x - 2 = 0$. Have students do them side by side so that they can see that they are employing the exact same steps on the literal constants as they did for the coefficients in the original problem.

This can be reinforced through the following problem. Solve for x and check using your calculator:

6. $9x^2 - 6x + 1 = 0$.

Have students turn to their neighbor and work in ordered pairs to determine which methods can be used to solve this problem and which of these is the most desirable. Have students justify their conclusions. Depending on your time constraints, you may ask one group of students to attempt this by factoring, another group by completing the square, and a third group by using the newly derived quadratic formula. Others may be left to choose whatever method they want. Students will be unaware that they already have the solution to this problem as it was the first start-up exercise that was solved by the completing the square method. This is a good time to highlight that there are many ways to solve problems, and that they can choose among them.

Practice: Use the quadratic formula to solve for the variable. Check using your graphing calculator.

7. $3y^2 - 2y - 5 = 0$.
8. $5x^2 - 3x - 1 = 0$.

Conclusion and Summary

Whereas only some quadratic equations can be solved by factoring, any quadratic equation can easily be solved using the quadratic formula. To use the quadratic formula, you must place the quadratic in standard form, $ax^2 + bx + c = 0$, and then put the appropriate values of a, b, and c in the formula:

$$x = \frac{-b \pm \sqrt{b^2 - 4ac}}{2a}.$$

Solutions should be checked with a graphing utility.

In summation, units should be planned with both hindsight and foresight to build on prior knowledge and to extend the students' conceptual understanding and procedural fluency in mathematics.

6

SOME SPECIFIC IDEAS FOR TEACHING CERTAIN LESSONS

Most math teachers rely on the textbook for the way a topic should be presented. Good textbooks develop a mathematical concept in a creative way. However, it is always exciting for the class when a topic is introduced differently from the way the textbook does it. There is also an additional excitement on the part of the teacher to be able to "show off" a clever way to envision a topic or concept. In this chapter, we present a selection of alternative ways to introduce topics from the curriculum that are different from most textbooks. Our purpose is to show you that sometimes alternative methods might be more efficient, or even more elegant, but may not fit the style of the textbook. The topics are not presented in any particular order because the order of topics taught may vary from state to state.

Angle Measurement with a Circle by Moving the Circle

This lesson is designed to prove the theorems on measuring angles related to a circle using a physical model, such as cardboard, string, and a pair of scissors, or using the Geometer's Sketchpad software program. Rather than follow the usual textbook method of treating each of the theorems as separate entities, this lesson takes care of all the theorems with one procedure. The applications that follow this lesson may be handled either together (as we present the theorems here) or individually over a few lessons following this one.

We demonstrate that all of the measurements of the various angles related to a circle can be carried out nicely by cutting out a circle from a piece of cardboard and drawing a convenient inscribed angle on it (see Figure 6.1). The measure of that angle should be the same as that formed by two pieces of string affixed to a

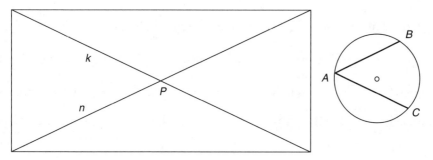

FIGURE 6.1

rectangular piece of cardboard as in Figure 6.1. The lesson prior to this one should have proved the theorem establishing that the measure of an inscribed angle of a circle is one-half the measure of the intercepted arc.

By moving the circle to various positions, we are able to find the measure of an angle formed by

- Two chords intersecting inside the circle (but not at its center).
- Two secants intersecting outside the circle.
- Two tangents intersecting outside the circle.
- A secant and a tangent intersecting outside the circle.
- A chord and a tangent intersecting on the circle.

We begin by demonstrating the relationship between the arcs of the circle and the angle formed by two chords intersecting inside the circle (but not at its center). Place the cardboard circle into a position so that $\overline{AB} \parallel n$, and $\overline{AC}$ is on k, as in Figure 6.2.

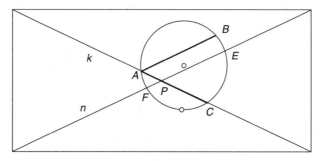

FIGURE 6.2

Notice that $m\angle A = \frac{1}{2}\overset{\frown}{BEC}$, and $m\angle A = EPC$. Therefore $m\angle P = \frac{1}{2}m\overset{\frown}{BEC} = \frac{1}{2}(m\overset{\frown}{BE} + m\overset{\frown}{EC})$. But, because parallel lines cut off congruent arcs on a given circle, $m\overset{\frown}{BE} = m\overset{\frown}{AF}$. It then follows that $m\angle P = \frac{1}{2}(m\overset{\frown}{AF} + m\overset{\frown}{EC})$, which shows the relationship of the angle formed by two chords $\angle P$ and its intercepted arcs $\overset{\frown}{AF}$ and $\overset{\frown}{EC}$.

Consider next the angle formed by two secants intersecting outside the circle. Place the cardboard circle into the position shown in Figure 6.3.

Begin by remembering that $m\angle A = \frac{1}{2}m\overset{\frown}{BC}$ and $m\angle FPC = m\angle A$. Because $m\overset{\frown}{AE} = m\overset{\frown}{BF}$, we can add and subtract it to the same quantity without changing the value of the original quantity. Thus, $m\angle P = \frac{1}{2}(m\overset{\frown}{BC} + m\overset{\frown}{BF} - m\overset{\frown}{AE}) = \frac{1}{2}(m\overset{\frown}{FBC} - m\overset{\frown}{AE}$.

In a similar way, we can demonstrate the relationship between an angle formed by two tangents intersecting outside the circle and its intercepted arcs. We move the cardboard circle into the position shown in Figure 6.4. In this case, the equality of arcs $\overset{\frown}{AE}$ and $\overset{\frown}{BE}$ as well as that of arcs $\overset{\frown}{AF}$ and $\overset{\frown}{CF}$ are key to demonstrating the desired relationship. We have

$$m\angle P = m\angle A = \frac{1}{2}m\overset{\frown}{BC} = \frac{1}{2}(m\overset{\frown}{BE} + m\overset{\frown}{BC} + m\overset{\frown}{CF} - m\overset{\frown}{AE} - m\overset{\frown}{AF})$$

$$= \frac{1}{2}(m\overset{\frown}{EBCF} - m\overset{\frown}{EAF}).$$

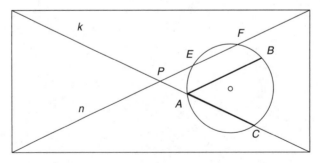

FIGURE 6.3

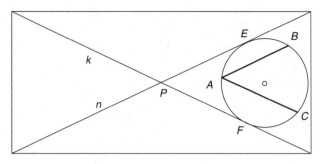

FIGURE 6.4

Again, by sliding the cardboard circle to the following position (see Figure 6.5) we can find the measure of the angle formed by a tangent and a secant intersecting outside the circle. This time, we rely on the equality of arcs $\widehat{AE}$ and $\widehat{BE}$. We get the following by adding and subtracting these equal arcs:

$$m\angle P = m\angle A = \frac{1}{2}(m\widehat{BC}) = \frac{1}{2}(m\widehat{BC} + m\widehat{BE} - m\widehat{AE})$$

$$= \frac{1}{2}(m\widehat{EBC} - m\widehat{AE}).$$

To complete the various possibilities of positions for the cardboard circle, place it so that we can find the relationship between an angle formed by a chord and a tangent intersecting at the point of tangency and its intercepted arc (see Figure 6.6). The crucial arc equality this time is $m\widehat{AP} = m\widehat{CP}$, and $m\widehat{AP} = m\widehat{BE}$. We begin as before:

$$m\angle P = m\angle A = \frac{1}{2}(m\widehat{BEC}) = \frac{1}{2}(m\widehat{BE} + m\widehat{EC} + m\widehat{PC} - m\widehat{AP})$$

$$= \frac{1}{2}(m\widehat{EC} + m\widehat{PC}) = \frac{1}{2}m\widehat{PCE}.$$

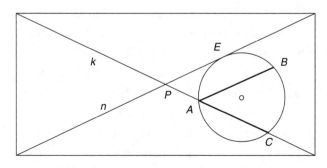

FIGURE 6.5

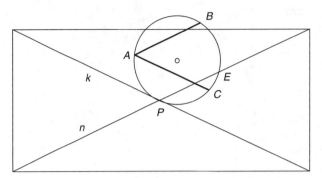

FIGURE 6.6

This activity can also be done quite nicely with a computer drawing program such as Geometer's Sketchpad.

You should remember that, although this was presented as a demonstration lesson, it could very well be adopted as a student activity in which students work in small groups to investigate—each working with a cardboard model—the measures of the various angle positions mentioned.

Sum of an Arithmetic Progression

This lesson uses one of the most famous "stories" math teachers tell students when they introduce the formula for the sum of an arithmetic progression. We use the story, but also use its conclusion to develop the formulas rather than (as most textbooks do) merely go to an alternative method for developing the formula. Let us begin by telling the famous story.

Carl Friedrich Gauss (1777–1855) was perhaps one of the most gifted mathematicians of all time. Part of his success in mathematics can be attributed to his uncanny ability to "number crunch," that is, to do arithmetic calculations with incredible speed. Many of his theorems evolved from this ability to do what most others could not. It gave him much greater insight into quantitative relationships and enabled him to make the many breakthroughs for which he is still so famous. The often-told story[1] about his days in elementary school can be used as an excellent lead-in to the topic of adding an arithmetic sequence of numbers.

As the story goes, young Gauss's teacher, Mr. Büttner, wanted to keep the class occupied, so he asked the class to add the numbers from 1 to 100. He had barely finished giving the assignment, when young Gauss put his slate down with simply one number on it, the correct answer. Of course, Mr. Büttner assumed Gauss had the wrong answer or cheated. In any case, he ignored this response and waited for the appropriate time to ask the students for their answers. No one, other than Gauss, had the right answer. What did Gauss do to get the answer mentally? Gauss explained his method as follows.

Rather than to add the numbers in the order in which they appear,

$$1+2+3+4+\cdots+97+98+99+100,$$

he felt it made more sense to add the first and the last, then add the second and the next to last, then the third and the third from the last, and so on. This led to a much simpler addition:

$$1+100=101; \quad 2+99=101; \quad 3+98=101; \quad 4+97=101$$

Simply put, there are now 50 pairs of numbers with 101 the sum of each pair, or $50 \cdot 101 = 5,050$.

Although many textbooks may mention this cute story, they fail to use the Gauss technique to derive a formula for the sum of an arithmetic progression.

We generalize Gauss's method of addition. Consider the following arithmetic progression sum:

$$S = a + [a+d] + [a+2d] + [a+3d] + \cdots + [a+(n-2)d]$$
$$+ [a+(n-1)\,d]$$

where a is the first term, d is the common difference between terms, and n is the number of terms. Following Gauss's method, adding the first and nth term gives

$$a + [a+(n-1)d] = 2a + (n-1)d$$

Adding the second and $(n-1)$th term gives

$$[a+d] + [a+(n-2)d] = 2a + (n-1)d$$

Adding the third and $(n-2)$th term gives

$$[a+2d] + [a+(n-3)d] = 2a + (n-1)d$$

If we continue in this same manner until all the pairs have been added, we obtain $\frac{n}{2}$ such pairs, giving us the formula

$$S = \frac{n}{2}[2a + (n-1)d].$$

Students may be shown another derivation of this same formula by considering the arithmetic progression written in the expected order and then in the reverse order. First, the "proper" order is

$$S = a + [a + d] + [a + 2d] + [a + 3d] + \cdots + [a + (n-2)d] + [a + (n-1)d],$$

where a is the first term, d is the common difference between terms, and n is the number of terms. Then, in the reverse order,

$$S = [a + (n-1)d] + [a + (n-2)d] + [a + (n-3)d] + \cdots + [a + 2d] + [a + d] + a.$$

We then add these two equations:

$$2S = [2a + (n-1)d] + [2a + (n-1)d] + [2a + (n-1)d] + \cdots + [2a + (n-1)d]$$

$$S = \left(\frac{n}{2}\right)[2a + (n-1)d].$$

Now that the formula has been derived, first using Gauss's experience and then in the more traditional way, students ought to practice using the formula to find the sums of given arithmetic progressions. Remember, an effective teacher will allow students to discover most of this by themselves. All they need to do is to represent Gauss's procedure algebraically. Just by showing a class two different ways to reach the same result is also enriching because it opens the students' minds to alternative solutions to a problem—both correct.

Novice teachers are sometimes perplexed by the most effective way of introducing students to the concept that the product of two negative numbers is a positive number. The remaining combinations of multiplication of signed numbers are usually intuitive enough not to cause a problem. Let us next consider the product of two negatives.

Introducing the Product of Two Negatives

It is always desirable to have students understand intuitively and abstractly why the product of two negatives is positive. Typically, a discussion of the product of two negative numbers follows a discussion of the product of a negative number and a positive number (which may be shown by the multiple addition of a negative number or by some other convenient method). This product generally poses no great difficulty for the teacher to demonstrate or the student to understand.

It is more difficult to develop an analogue for the product of two negative numbers. One can show that the product of two negatives evolves from the following pattern:

$$(-1)(+3) = -3$$
$$(-1)(+2) = -2$$
$$(-1)(+1) = -1$$
$$(-1)(0) = 0$$
$$(-1)(-1) = +1$$
$$(-1)(-2) = +2$$
$$(-1)(-3) = +3$$

How can the student get a more genuine intuitive feel for this concept? Perhaps a "real-life" illustration will clarify it.

Consider making a videotape recording of a clear plastic water tank that has a transparent drain tube we know can empty (negative) the tank at the rate of 3 gallons per minute. We tape this event for several minutes, allowing the tank's contents to decrease. If we run the tape for 2 minutes, then the tank will show a decrease of 6 gallons. After 3 minutes, 9 gallons will be emptied.

Suppose we run the tape in reverse (negative) for 1 minute. The tank will refill by 3 gallons. At twice the normal rate in reverse (negative), the tank will gain (positive) contents at the rate of 6 gallons per minute. Here, a student can see that the product of two negatives (emptying a tank and running a film in reverse) results in a positive.

If this is not sufficiently convincing, then perhaps tell students to consider good guys (positive) or bad guys (negative) who are entering (positive) or leaving (negative) a town:

1. If the good guys (+) enter (+) the town, that is good (+) for the town. $(+)(+) = +$

2. If the good guys (+) leave (−) the town, that is bad (–) for the town. $(+)(–) = –$

3. If the bad guys (−) enter (+) the town, that is bad (−) for the town. $(−)(+) = −$

4. If the bad guys (−) leave (−) the town, that is good (+) for the town. $(−)(−) = +$

This example gives students an intuitive feel for the product of two negatives. The teacher should choose that approach most likely to succeed with the particular class.

For the more curious or gifted students, a proof of this concept might be in order. They should know that $(−1) + 1 = 0$. By multiplying both sides of this equation by $−1$, we get

$$(−1)[(−1) + 1] = (−1)[0].$$

Using the distributive property, we get

$$(−1)(−1) + (−1)1 = (−1)0$$

Because we know that $(−1)1 = −1$ and $(−1)0 = 0$, we then have $(−1)(−1) + (−1) = 0$. By adding 1 to both sides of this equation, we get $(−1)(−1) = 1$, which proves the relationship.

One might also like to reach back to another topic for further convincing that the product of two negatives is a positive. Recall that $(a^x)^y = a^{xy}$, which holds true for $a = 2$, $x = y = −1$. Therefore, $(2^{-1})^{-1} = 2^{(-1)(-1)}$. By the definition of a negative exponent, we get $(2^{-1})^{-1} = \left(\dfrac{1}{2}\right)^{-1} = 2$. We can then conclude that $2^1 = 2^{(-1)(-1)}$ or $1 = (−1)(−1)$ because, if the bases are equal, so must the exponents be equal. By now your students must have a good feeling for the notion of the product of two negatives.

Rationalizing the Denominator

Most textbooks approach the topic of rationalizing the denominator of a fraction by simply delving into it without much justification regarding why we even need to do this procedure. As a growing teacher, it is powerful (not to mention motivating) to show your students how useful this procedure can be. Before the advent of the calculator, you could have convinced your students that to find the value in decimal form of $\frac{5}{\sqrt{41}}$ was complicated. To get $\frac{5}{\sqrt{41}} = .780868809\ldots$, you had to divide 5 by $\sqrt{41}$. Today, the teacher must be far more resourceful to find a reason for rationalizing the denominator of a fraction. To do this, we will search for some problem "off the beaten path" that almost cannot be done without rationalizing the demoninator.

Begin by presenting the following problem to your students. Evaluate the series sum

$$\frac{1}{1+\sqrt{2}} + \frac{1}{\sqrt{2}+\sqrt{3}} + \frac{1}{\sqrt{3}+\sqrt{4}} + \cdots + \frac{1}{\sqrt{1999}+\sqrt{2000}}.$$

Starting to solve this problem can be difficult if one is not accustomed to expressing denominators in terms of rational numbers. This procedure should be discussed and taught at this point before the problem is revisited.

When the process of rationalizing a denominator of a fraction has been mastered, the problem can be approached by considering the general term

$$\frac{1}{\sqrt{k}+\sqrt{k+1}}.$$

Rationalizing this denominator yields

$$\frac{1}{\sqrt{k}+\sqrt{k+1}} \cdot \frac{\sqrt{k}-\sqrt{k+1}}{\sqrt{k}-\sqrt{k+1}} = \sqrt{k+1}-\sqrt{k}.$$

This will allow us to rewrite the series as

$$\left(\sqrt{2}-\sqrt{1}\right) + \left(\sqrt{3}-\sqrt{2}\right) + \left(\sqrt{4}-\sqrt{3}\right) + \cdots$$
$$+ \left(\sqrt{1999}-\sqrt{1998}\right) + \left(\sqrt{2000}-\sqrt{1999}\right),$$

which equals $\sqrt{2000} - \sqrt{1} = 20\sqrt{5} - 1 \approx 43.7213596$.

By showing how the process of rationalizing the denominator of a fraction makes the fraction much more workable, students now can see a purpose for learning this procedure. It ought to become a tool in the arsenal of techniques taught in algebra.

The Pythagorean Theorem

Perhaps one of the most popular topics to teach in various ways is the Pythagorean theorem. It can be introduced in many ways, but the trick is to have students discover interesting proofs of this famous theorem. One might begin by asking the class the following question: What did Pythagoras, Euclid, and President James A. Garfield have in common? They each proved the Pythagorean theorem.

In 1876, while still a member of the House of Representatives, James A. Garfield published in the *New England Journal of Education* an original proof of the Pythagorean theorem. This theorem, believed to have been originally proved by Pythagoras in about 525 BC was also proved by Euclid in 300 BC. Proving the Pythagorean theorem has fascinated mathematicians for centuries. In 1940, Elisha S. Loomis published a book (reprinted by the National Council of Teachers of Mathematics in 1968) with 370 different proofs. There are many more known today. However, there will never be a proof using trigonometry. You should try to ask your students why trigonometry cannot be used. They should see this as circular reasoning because the entire field of trigonometry depends on the Pythagorean theorem. In the discussion that follows, we briefly consider these extraordinarily clever proofs, especially considering the level of development of mathematics at the time. How you use them in introducing the theorem can only be decided by considering the students' strengths.

You may wish to begin the introduction of the Pythagorean theorem by having students consider the problem of getting a circular tabletop with diameter of 7.5 feet through a doorway with a height of 7 feet and a width of 3 feet. Students should see that the problem is to determine the length of the diagonal of the doorway. This will lead to a need for the Pythagorean theorem. Now, continue the lesson while you keep "an ear to the ground" because this pivotal theorem has many ways it can be introduced to students. What works for one class may not with another. You must be sensitive to the motives of your students. In that spirit, we offer several proofs of the Pythagorean theorem with the hope that you will find one or more that will be appropriate for your students. Sometimes, students are intrigued and motivated by the notion that a theorem can be proved in so many different ways. To that end, you might want to show the class a number of these proofs, particularly the uncommon ones, such as the last one presented here, which proves the theorem by paper folding.

To prove the theorem, use the relationships among the sides of a right triangle in which the altitude is drawn to the hypotenuse. This can be done simply by completing a few exercises.

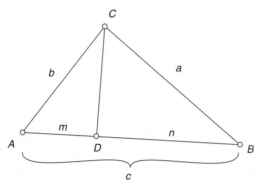

FIGURE 6.7

In Figure 6.7, $\overline{CD}$ is an altitude of right $\triangle ABC$, with right angle at C, so that $\triangle ADC \sim \triangle CDB \sim \triangle ACB$. The lengths of the segments are indicated in the figure. Referring to Figure 6.7, complete each of the following:

1. AC is a mean proportional between _____ and _____. $[c, m]$

2. Therefore, $\frac{c}{b} = \frac{b}{m}$, or $b^2 =$ _____. Why? $\left[\frac{c}{b} = \frac{b}{m}, cm \right]$

3. _____ is the mean proportional between AB and BD. $[a]$

4. Therefore, $\frac{c}{a} = \frac{a}{n}$ or $a^2 =$ _____. Why? $\left[\frac{c}{a} = \frac{a}{n}, cn \right]$

5. Adding the results of items 2 and 4, we get
    $a^2 + b^2 =$ ___ $+$ ___ $=$ ___$(m + n)$. $[cn + cm = c(m + n)]$

6. But, $m + n =$ _____. $[c]$

7. Therefore, $a^2 +$ _____ $=$ _____. $[a^2 + b^2 = c^2]$

This essentially proves the Pythagorean theorem.

Students will enjoy the novelty of proofs by Pythagoras, Euclid, and President Garfield. Begin by showing the demonstration that is believed to be the one that was used by the Pythagoreans to show this famous theorem.

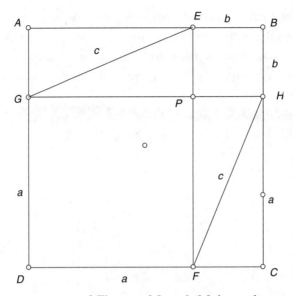

FIGURE 6.8

The two squares of Figures 6.8 and 6.9 have the same area. Figure 6.8 is composed of four congruent right triangles and two squares: $4\left(\dfrac{1}{2}ab\right)+a^2+b^2$. Figure 6.9 is composed of four congruent right triangles and one square: $4\left(\dfrac{1}{2}ab\right)+c^2$.

After establishing that the quadrilateral inside the square of Figure 6.9 is also a square (with side length c), one may conclude that $a^2+b^2=c^2$.

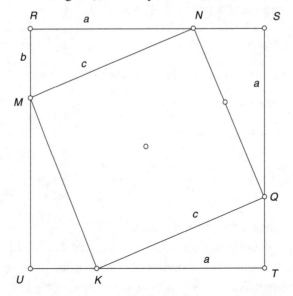

FIGURE 6.9

Euclid's proof also uses area but in a much different way. We are given right $\triangle ABC$ with $m\angle C = 90$; *BAED*, *CAKH*, and *CBFG* are squares (Figure 6.10). We are to prove that (area) $\mathcal{A}$ square *CBFG* + $\mathcal{A}$ square *CAKH* = $\mathcal{A}$ square *BAED* (that is, $a^2 + b^2 = c^2$). Draw $\overline{FA}$ and $\overline{CD}$. Then, we can show that $\triangle FBA \cong \triangle CBD$, so that $\mathcal{A} \triangle FBA = \mathcal{A} \triangle CBD$. Draw $\overline{CL} \parallel \overline{BD}$. Because $\triangle CBD$ and rectangle *BJLD* share the same base and altitude, $\mathcal{A} \triangle CBD = \dfrac{1}{2} \mathcal{A}$ rectangle *BJLD*; likewise, $\mathcal{A} \triangle FBA = \dfrac{1}{2} \mathcal{A}$ square *CBFG*. Therefore, $\mathcal{A}$ rectangle *BJLD* = $\mathcal{A}$ square *CBFG*.

We can also show that $\triangle BAK \cong \triangle EAC$. It follows that $\mathcal{A}$ rectangle *JAEL* = $\mathcal{A}$ square *CHKA*. Therefore, $\mathcal{A}$ square *CHKA* + $\mathcal{A}$ square *CBFG* = $\mathcal{A}$ rectangle *BJLD* + $\mathcal{A}$ rectangle *JAEL*. But, $\mathcal{A}$ rectangle *BJLD* + $\mathcal{A}$ rectangle *JAEL* = $\mathcal{A}$ square *BAED*. Thus, $\mathcal{A}$ square *CBFG* + $\mathcal{A}$ square *CHKA* = $\mathcal{A}$ square *BAED*, or $a^2 + b^2 = c^2$.

To begin President James A. Garfield's proof, we consider right $\triangle ABC$ (Figure 6.11) with $m\angle C = 90$; we let $AC = b$, $BC = a$, and $AB = c$. We need to show that $a^2 + b^2 = c^2$. Select D on $\overline{BC}$ so that $BD = AC$ and $\overline{CBD}$. Consider $\overline{DE} \perp \overline{CBD}$ so that $DE = BC$. We can show that quadrilateral *ACDE* is a trapezoid. Also, $\mathcal{A} \triangle ABC = \mathcal{A} \triangle BED$, and $AB = BE$.

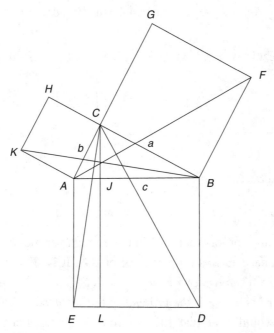

FIGURE 6.10

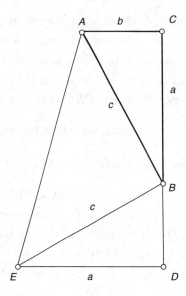

FIGURE 6.11. President James A. Garfield's proof.

$\mathcal{A}$ trapezoid $ACDE = \dfrac{1}{2}CD(AC + DE) = \dfrac{1}{2}(a+b)\cdot(a+b) = \dfrac{1}{2}(a+b)^2$

$\mathcal{A} \triangle ABE = \dfrac{1}{2}AB \cdot BE = \dfrac{1}{2}c^2$. Also $\mathcal{A} \triangle ABC = \dfrac{1}{2}AC \cdot BC = \dfrac{1}{2}ab$.

However, $\mathcal{A}$ trapezoid $ACDE = \mathcal{A} \triangle ABE + 2\mathcal{A} \triangle ABC$. Substituting, we get

$$\frac{1}{2}(a+b)^2 = \frac{1}{2}c^2 + 2\left(\frac{1}{2}ab\right)$$
$$(a+b)^2 = c^2 + 2ab$$

and it follows that $a^2 + b^2 = c^2$.

A Simple Proof

There are many more proofs that are simple enough for the average high school student. Here is one that uses properties of circles. It is simple but based on the following theorem: *When two chords intersect in the circle, the product of the segments of one chord is equal to the product of the segments of the other chord.* In Figure 6.12, this would mean that, for the two intersecting chords, $p \cdot q = r \cdot s$.

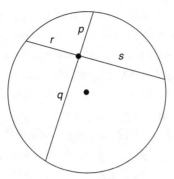

FIGURE 6.12

Let us now consider the circle of Figure 6.13 with diameter $\overline{AB}$ perpendicular to chord $\overline{CD}$. From the theorem, $(c - b)(c + b) = a^2$. Then, $c^2 - b^2 = a^2$; therefore, $a^2 + b^2 = c^2$. The Pythagorean theorem is proved again.

Proving the Pythagorean Theorem by Paper Folding

The paper-folding method of proof will surely win favor among your students. They ought to appreciate it for no other reason than that they will be able to "see" the Pythagorean theorem before them. After all the struggles students go through to prove the Pythagorean theorem, imagine that we can prove this famous theorem

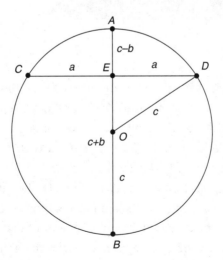

FIGURE 6.13

simply by folding a piece of paper. Your first thought might be, why didn't my teachers ever show me this when I was in school? This is a good question, but perhaps it is one of the reasons many adults need to be convinced in later life that mathematics is beautiful and holds many delights as yet unexposed. Here is an opportunity to show your students beauty they are not likely to forget.

We can extend from the statement of the Pythagorean theorem as follows: *The sum of the squares on the legs of a right triangle is equal to the square on the hypotenuse of the triangle.* By replacing the word *squares* with *areas of similar polygons,* we now have: *The sum of the areas of similar polygons on the legs of a right triangle is equal to the area of the similar polygon on the hypotenuse of the triangle.* This replacement can be shown to be correct and holds true for any similar polygons appropriately (correspondingly) placed on the right triangle's sides.

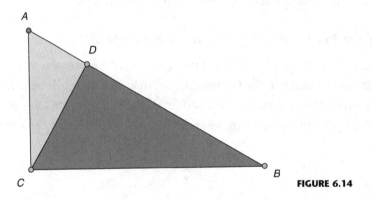

FIGURE 6.14

Consider the right triangle with altitude $\overline{CD}$ in Figure 6.14. The figure shows this with three triangular flaps folded over the $\triangle ABC$. The flaps are $\triangle ABC$, $\triangle ADC$, and $\triangle BDC$. Each student should be working along with you as you develop this demonstration. Notice that $\triangle ADC \sim \triangle CDB \sim \triangle ACB$. In Figure 6.14, $\triangle ADC$ and $\triangle CDB$ are folded over $\triangle ACB$. Clearly, $\mathcal{A} \triangle ADC + \mathcal{A} \triangle CDB = \mathcal{A} \triangle ACB$. If we unfold the triangles (including the $\triangle ACB$ itself), then the result is as shown in Figure 6.15. The relationship of the similar polygons (here, right triangles) is the extension of the Pythagorean theorem. The sum of the areas of similar *right triangles* on the legs of a right triangle is equal to the area of the similar *right triangle* on the hypotenuse of the triangle. This essentially proves the Pythagorean theorem by paper folding.

It is now up to you to select the proof or proofs that would best convince your students of the veracity of the theorem as well as the beauty of mathematics as shown by the many different proofs of this famous theorem.

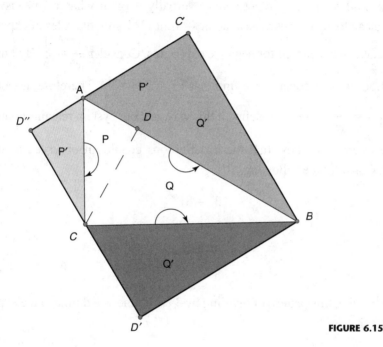

FIGURE 6.15

Introduction to Nonpositive Exponents

It is important to engender a real understanding of the meaning of nonpositive integer exponents. Students can, of course, be told that the meaning refers to the inverse of a number and commit this to memory. That is not particularly good teaching. A novice teacher ought to get into the habit of letting students understand concepts rather than merely accepting them as they are told.

Students who have just begun to understand the nature of positive integer exponents will probably respond to the question, "What does 5^n mean?" by saying something like "the product of n factors of 5." When asked what the nature of n

is, they will probably say it is a positive integer. Try motivating them to consider the nonpositive integers: 0 and the negative integers.

Consider $\dfrac{x^5}{x^5}$ (where $x \neq 0$), which equals $x^{5-5} = x^0$. Therefore, $x^0 = 1$. However, the following is a meaningless statement: "x used as a factor 0 times is 1." So, to be consistent with the rules of exponents, we *define* $x^0 = 1$; then, it has meaning.

In a similar way, a student cannot verbally explain what x^{-4} means. What would it mean to have "x used as a factor -4 times"? Using the rules of exponents, we can establish a meaning for negative exponents. Consider $\dfrac{x^5}{x^8} = \dfrac{1}{3}$. By our rules of operations with exponents, we find that $\dfrac{x^5}{x^8} = x^{5-8} = x^{-3}$. Therefore, it would be nice for $x^{-3} = \dfrac{1}{x^3}$, so we can define it this way, and our system remains consistent.

You might also show that these definitions enable an observed pattern to continue. Consider the following:

$$3^4 = 81$$
$$3^3 = 27$$
$$3^2 = 9$$
$$3^1 = 3$$

Then, continuing this pattern of dividing by 3 each time, we diminish the exponent on the left side by 1.

$$3^0 = 1$$
$$3^{-1} = \frac{1}{3}$$
$$3^{-2} = \frac{1}{9}$$
$$3^{-3} = \frac{1}{27}$$

When we get $\dfrac{x^k}{x^k} = x^{k-k} = x^0$, we can now consider what value 0^0 should have. Using the same idea, we get $0^0 = 0^{k-k} = \dfrac{0^k}{0^k}$, which is meaningless because division by $0^k = 0$ is undefined. Similarly, we cannot define 0^{-k}, for this yields $\dfrac{1}{0^k}$, which is undefined.

Thus, students can conclude that the base cannot be 0 when the exponent is 0 or negative. Therefore, the definitions $x^0 = 1$, $x \neq 0$, and $x^{-k} = \dfrac{1}{x^k}$, $x \neq 0$, become meaningful. Be sure that the students understand the subtleties of this development. It will serve them well with future mathematical phenomena.

Introducing the Notion of a Function

The concept of a function is an integral part of higher mathematics. We begin its introduction in the schools so that students will be able to use the concept to explain mathematical phenomena. It is important that students obtain a genuine understanding of what a function is and the type of functions we use. Sometimes, the intuitive "route" to understanding is the best. One such example follows.

In mathematics, finding concrete analogues to represent abstract concepts is not always easy. One example of use of a physical model to explain an abstract concept is in the development of the notion of a function. We use the model of a bow shooting arrows at a target. The arrows represent the domain, and the target represents the range. The bow (and its aiming) is the function. Because an arrow can only be used once,[2] we know that the elements in the domain can be used only once. The bow can hit the same point on the target more than once; therefore, points in the range can be used more than once. This is the definition of a function: a mapping of all elements of one set onto another, with the elements of the first set used exactly once. Some points on the target may never be hit by an arrow, yet all the arrows must be used. Analogously, some elements in the range may not be used, but all elements in the domain must be used. Conversely, through a mapping (or a "pairing") of all elements in the domain, some elements in the range may not be used.

When all points on the target (the range) are hit,[3] then the function (or mapping) is called an *onto function*.

When each point on the target is used only once, then the function is called a *one-to-one function*.

When each point on the target is used exactly once (i.e., once and only once), then the function is called a *one-to-one onto function* or a *one-to-one correspondence.*

Using the analogy of a bow shooting arrows to a target to represent the concept of a function enables the learner to conceptualize this abstract notion in a way that should instill permanent understanding.

Intuition Versus Justification

In the study of geometry, as with most other branches of mathematics, we instruct students not to assume anything just from a diagram or from what you think ought to be the case without justifying your conjecture. This is not to say that students should be discouraged from making "educated guesses"; educated guesses are good. But they must remember that these are just conjectures and must be justified before using the results of the guess. Sometimes, it pays for the teacher to take a little time from the standard syllabus to drive home this point. In this section, we provide some useful, and we dare say entertaining, examples to show students that they cannot rely completely on their intuition, although it may be a good guide to the conclusion they seek.

Geometry is often referred to as the visual part of mathematics. We tend to believe many things as we see them. For example, when asked to compare the two segments in Figure 6.16, the one on the right looks longer. In Figure 6.17, the bottom segment also looks longer. In actuality, the segments have the same length.

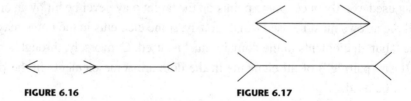

FIGURE 6.16   FIGURE 6.17

In Figure 6.18, the crosshatched segment appears longer than the plain one, and in Figure 6.19 the narrower and vertical stick appears to be longer than the other two even though to the left they are shown to be the same length. A further optical illusion can be seen in Figure 6.20, in which $\overline{AB}$ appears to be longer than $\overline{BC}$. This is not true as $\overline{AB} \cong \overline{BC}$.

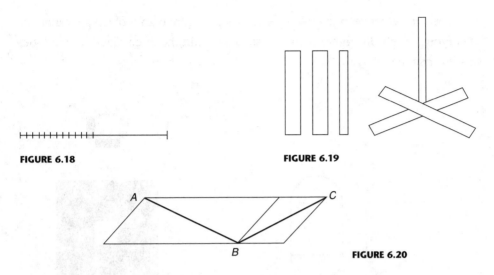

FIGURE 6.18

FIGURE 6.19

FIGURE 6.20

In Figure 6.21, the vertical segment clearly appears longer, but it is not, while in Figure 6.22. The horizontal segment appears longer, but it is not.

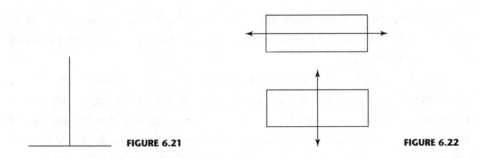

FIGURE 6.21

FIGURE 6.22

The curve lengths and curvature of the diagrams in Figures 6.23 and 6.24 are deceiving. Such optical tricks are important to point out to students so that they do not rely solely on their visual observations.

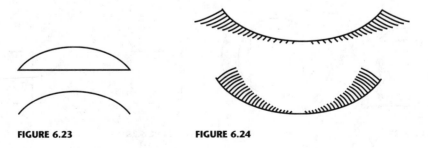

FIGURE 6.23

FIGURE 6.24

The square between the two semicircles in Figure 6.25 looks bigger than the square on the left. In Figure 6.26, the square within the large black square looks smaller than that above it.

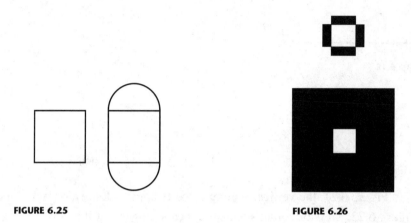

FIGURE 6.25   FIGURE 6.26

We see further evidence of fooling the senses in Figure 6.27, in which the circle inscribed in the square (left) appears to be smaller than the circle circumscribed about the square (right).

Figures 6.28 to 6.30 show how relative placement can affect the relative appearance of a geometric diagram. In Figure 6.28, the center square appears to be the largest of the group. In Figure 6.29, the center circle on the left appears to be larger than the center circle on the right. The center sector on the left in Figure 6.30 appears to be larger than the center sector on the right. In all of these cases, the two figures that appear not to be the same size are in fact the same size.

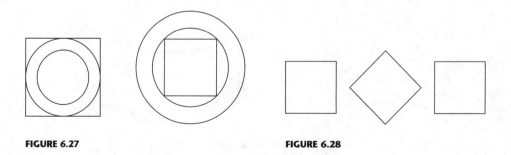

FIGURE 6.27   FIGURE 6.28

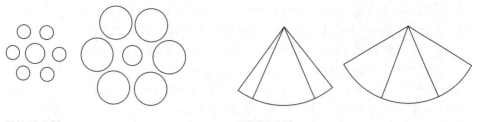

FIGURE 6.29   FIGURE 6.30

Such optical tricks are useful to put the geometry students on guard and make them more discriminating learners. There are also notions in geometry that just do not seem to "make sense." We offer one here as an illustration.

Consider a rope tied along the equator of the earth, circumscribing the entire earth sphere. Now, lengthen this enormously long rope by 1 meter. It is no longer tightly tied around the earth. If we lift this loose rope equally around the equator so that it is uniformly spaced above the equator, will a mouse fit beneath the rope?

We are looking for the distance between the circumferences of these two circles. Because the size of the circles is not given, suppose the small (inner) circle is extremely small, so small that it has a radius of length 0 and is thus reduced to a point. Then, the distance between the circles is merely the radius of the larger circle (Figure 6.31). The circumference of this larger circle is $2\pi R = C + 1$, or $2\pi R = 0 + 1 = 1$, where C is the circumference of the earth (now, for the sake of this problem, reduced to 0) and $C + 1$ is the length of the rope. The distance between the circles is $R = \dfrac{1}{2}\pi = 0.159$ meters, which would allow a mouse to fit comfortably beneath the rope.

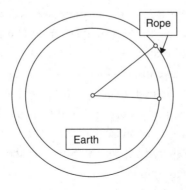

FIGURE 6.31

This unit is intended to demonstrate that, even in geometry, not everything is intuitively obvious, and that there are geometric "facts" that not only seem to be wrong, but also do not necessarily make sense without careful inspection.

The next two lesson suggestions are basic to the study of probability, yet are often overlooked by teachers who are more eager to move along in the syllabus than to set up a solid foundation in probability for their students. We believe these two lessons, which might be a slight digression for some, are essential in motivating students to probability and at the same time give them the basic understandings needed to master the subject.

Building Confidence in Probability

When students are introduced to probability they are told to believe that the chances of getting a head from the toss of a coin is $\frac{1}{2}$. A good teacher will allow the students to experiment with, say, 100 tosses and see that they are rather close to getting 50 heads and 50 tails. But, as the study of probability progresses and the events are not so obvious, there should be a demonstration that what we correctly calculate should be right even though it may not be intuitively obvious. To do this, you may wish to show how some probability calculations are contrary to intuition. Have the class consider the famous birthday problem.

Begin by asking the class what they think the chances (or probability) are of two classmates having the same birth date (month and day only) in their class of about 30 students. Students usually begin to think about the likelihood of 2 people having the same date out of a selection of 365 days (assuming no leap year). Ask them to consider the "randomly" selected group of the first 35 presidents of the United States. They may be astonished that there are two with the same birth date: James K. Polk (November 2, 1795) and Warren G. Harding (November 2, 1865). The class will probably be surprised to learn that for a group of 35, the probability that 2 members will have the same birth date is greater than 8 out of 10.

Student may wish to try their own experiment by visiting 10 nearby classrooms to check on date matches. For groups of 30, the probability that there will be a match is greater than .7, or in 7 of these 10 rooms there ought to be a match of birth dates. What causes this incredible result? Students should now be curious to learn how this probability is computed.

Continue with the lesson. What is the probability that one selected student matches her own birth date? Clearly, it is certainty, or 1. This can be written as $\frac{365}{365}$.

The probability that another student does not match the first student is $\frac{365-1}{365} =$ $\frac{364}{365}$. The probability that another student does not match the first and student is $\frac{365-2}{365} = \frac{363}{365}$. The probability of all 35 students not having the same birth date is the product of these probabilities:

$$p = \frac{365}{365} \cdot \frac{365-1}{365} \cdot \frac{365-2}{365} \cdot \ldots \cdot \frac{365-34}{365}.$$

Because the probability q that two students in the group have the same birth date and the probability p that two students in the group do not have the same birth date is a certainty, the sum of those probabilities must be 1. Thus, $p + q = 1$. In this case,

$$q = 1 - \frac{365}{365} \cdot \frac{365-1}{365} \cdot \frac{365-2}{365} \cdot \ldots \cdot \frac{365-33}{365} \cdot \frac{365-34}{365} \approx .8143832388747152.$$

In other words, the probability that there will be a birth date match in a randomly selected group of 35 people is somewhat greater than $\frac{8}{10}$. This is unexpected when

NUMBER OF PEOPLE IN GROUP	PROBABILITY OF A BIRTH DATE MATCH
10	.1169481777110776
15	.2529013197636863
20	.4114383835805799
25	.5686997039694639
30	.7063162427192686
35	.8143832388747152
40	.891231809817949
45	.9409758994657749
50	.9703735795779884
55	.9862622888164461
60	.994122660865348
65	.9976831073124921
70	.9991595759651571

FIGURE 6.32. Probability values.

one considers there were 365 dates from which to choose. Students may want to investigate the nature of the probability function. Figure 6.32 presents a few values to serve as a guide. Students should notice how quickly "almost-certainty" is reached. Were one to do this with the death dates of the first 35 presidents, one would notice that two died on March 8 (Millard Fillmore and William H. Taft), and three presidents died on the July 4 (John Adams, Jefferson, and Monroe). Above all, this demonstration should serve as an eye-opener about relying on intuition too much.

Demonstrating the Need to Set Up a Sample Space in Probability

This lesson might be best done in small groups. To begin, you will need four red chips and four black chips for each group of students. When students begin their study of probability, they look for formulas to resolve every situation. Rarely do they set up the sample space to see what is actually taking place. This activity places the students in a game situation in which their intuition works against them. Unless they actually set up the sample space, they will not be able to resolve the inequity of the game.

Begin by placing 1 red chip and 2 black chips in an envelope. Give the students the following rules for the game they are about to play:

1. They will draw 2 chips from the envelope, without looking.
2. If the colors of the 2 chips are different, then the teacher scores a point. If they are the same, then the student scores the point.
3. The first player to score 5 points is the winner.
4. After each draw, the chips are returned to the envelope, and the envelope is shaken.

Ask the students if they think the game is a fair one (that is, each player has an equal chance of gaining a point). After a discussion of their answers, play the game several times until the students realize that the game is not fair. (The teacher should win the game most of the time.) Now, ask them what single chip they would add to make the game fair. Most of the students will suggest adding a second red chip to the envelope. At this point, introduce the idea of setting up the sample space as follows:

Situation 1: 1 red chip and 2 black chips. The possible draws would be

RB_1 RB_2 $\mathbf{B_1B_2}$

Thus, the student has only 1 of 3 chances of scoring a point, for a $\frac{1}{3}$ probability. The original game is unfair.

> *Situation 2:* Adding 1 red chip, we have 2 red chips and 2 black chips. The possible draws would be
>
> R_1B_1 R_1B_2 **R_1R_2**
> R_2B_1 R_2B_2 **B_1B_2**

Surprise! The student has only 2 of 6 chances of scoring a point, for a $\frac{1}{3}$ probability. The game is again unfair.

> *Situation 3:* Adding another black chip to the original chips, we have 1 red chip and 3 black chips. The possible draws would be
>
> R_1B_1 R_1B_2 **R_1B_3**
> B_1B_2 B_1B_3 **B_2B_3**

This time, the student has 3 of 6 chances of scoring a point, for a $\frac{1}{2}$ probability. The game is now fair. The use of the sample space easily reveals that the students' intuition does not yield a correct resolution of the problem, thus making the concept of a sample space "indispensable."

Introducing the Law of Sines

Suppose you are planning a lesson on the introduction to the Law of Sines. You would like to develop or derive the law, and you would like to have ample time to apply the law to "practical" examples as well as the drill that typically follows the introduction of the law. To fit this into a normal 50-minute lesson, you might relegate a more serious inspection of the derivation to a homework assignment and simply introduce the law of sines and its applications to the triangle, or you may search for a concise derivation of the law of sines, such as the following.

Consider the triangle ABC with median $\overline{AM}$ in Figure 6.33. The area of $\triangle ABM = \frac{1}{2}(AB)(BM)\sin B$, and the area of $\triangle ACM = \frac{1}{2}(AC)(CM)\sin C$. Because the areas of these two triangles are equal, and $BM = CM$, it follows that $AB \sin B =$

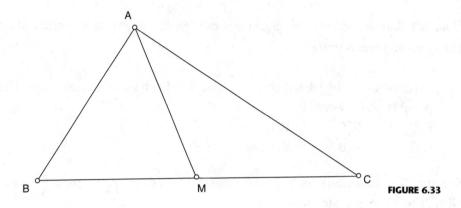

FIGURE 6.33

AC sin C. This is the Law of Sines:

$$\frac{AB}{\sin C} = \frac{AC}{\sin B}.$$

With this simple proof or derivation of the law of sines, the time for applications is then maximized. There are many clever ways to introduce the topic, such as presenting a geometric problem that requires the Law of Sines for solution. However, the trick is to get past the derivation quickly (and elegantly), which is what we have provided.

In this chapter, we provided a number of uncommon ways to introduce some key concepts in mathematics; we hope that we have opened the door for you to search for other such nonroutine ways to make your teaching more exciting. Although there are many sources for such novel approaches, we recommend *101 Great Ideas for Introducing Key Concepts in Mathematics* (Posamentier & Hauptman, 2006).

How to Use Questions Effectively— Or the Art of Classroom Questioning

Beyond having a clever presentation to develop a concept in mathematics, appropriate questioning is a valuable tool for effective instruction and assessment. It helps you know if your students are paying attention and if they understand what you are teaching. One mistake many teachers make is to ask questions in a one-on-one mode all of the time. Asking one student for an answer automatically tells the rest of the class that they do not have to pay attention—after all, they are not being put on the spot. When you question this way, all you are really learning is whether one student knows the answer. What about the rest of the class? Are they learning anything? Are they involved in the discourse of the lesson? Do they understand what is happening? Effective, clear, and critical questioning is an art. According to the National Council of Teachers of Mathematics' (NCTM) *Curriculum and Evaluation Standards for School Mathematics* (1989), the teacher's role is to "initiate and orchestrate [this kind of] discourse by posing questions and tasks that elicit, engage and challenge each student's thinking" (p. 35).

The NCTM's *Professional Standards for Teaching Mathematics* (1991) lists five reasons for asking questions in the mathematics class:

> Helping students work together to make sense of mathematics.
> Helping students to rely more on themselves to determine whether something is mathematically correct.
> Helping students to learn to reason mathematically.
> Helping students learn to conjecture, invent and solve problems.
> Helping students to connect mathematics, its ideas and its applications.
> (pp. 3–4)

To accomplish these requirements, you must learn to ask "good" questions.

How Do You Ask "Good" Questions?

Learning to ask good questions requires practice and preparation. You may decide to prepare several questions in advance for each lesson you plan to teach. Concentrate on questions that encourage thinking. Examples are as follows:

- What would happen if we replace x by 7 in the expression $\frac{(2x+7)}{x-7}$?
- Is an equilateral triangle also isosceles?
- How is your travel time affected if you increase your average speed by 5 miles per hour on the 100-mile trip from New York City to Philadelphia?

Some Dos and Don'ts of Questioning

The following are some kinds of questions you should and should not ask to maintain a successful discourse in your classroom.

Don't answer your own question. If the students see that you will give them the answer when no one responds, then it won't take long before there will be no responses at all so that you will give them the correct answer. They figure that if the teacher gives the answer, then it must be the correct response.

Don't ask yes/no questions. A question that can be answered with a simple yes or a no will hardly tell you anything about your students' knowledge. After all, they do have a 50 percent chance of being correct even if they do not have the slightest idea of what a square is.

Don't ask: Is the figure ABCD a square?

Do ask: What kind of polygon is the figure ABCDEF?

Don't ask a question to embarrass a student. We have all experienced a classroom in which a particular student is not paying attention to the lesson and is daydreaming. You will not gain much if you call on this student for an answer. The response will usually be "Huh?" or a sullen "I don't know." In either case, about all that is accomplished is to alienate that student.

Do wait after asking a question before you call on a student. Give the class time to think about your question and decide on an answer. It is advised that you wait at least three seconds before calling on someone. The appropriate duration of the wait time depends on the difficulty of the question. By pausing, you indicate to the students that everyone has the time to respond and think it through, not just the students who always volunteer. To a teacher, this period of silence feels much longer than it actually is. One thing you can do is to count mentally "one Mississippi, two Mississippi, three Mississippi" as you wait for a response.

Don't call on a student before you ask the question. If you preface your question with a student's name, then the rest of the class does not have to think at all. It is one student who is immediately put on the spot.

Don't ask: Barbara, what is the value of $3x + 4x$ when $x = 5$?

Do ask: What is the value of $3x + 4x$ when $x = 5$ . . . (pause) . . . Barbara?

Don't label the difficulty of your questions. Don't say "Here's an easy question!" If the student answers it correctly, then she might think "It was an easy one, so it was no big deal." If the student can't answer the question, then he will be extremely discouraged.

Don't encourage chorus answers. Asking the question of the entire class will only lead to a chorus of answers. But, how many of the students really understand what you are asking? How can this help you find out about any particular student?

Don't ask: Class, how much is $12x - 7x$?

Do ask: How much is $12x - 7x$ . . . (pause) . . . Dan?

Do ask open-ended questions. Open-ended questions encourage thinking. An open-ended question is one that has a variety of correct answers or has one correct answer but a wide variety of approaches to arriving at the answer. These kinds of questions encourage students to think of more than one way to approach a problem.

Don't ask: What is the measure of an exterior angle of the triangle in Figure 6.34?

Do ask: Could the triangle in Figure 6.34 exist? Explain your answer.

Don't ask: Which is larger, $+7$ or -7?

Do ask: Which is larger, $(-x)$ or $(+x)$?

Here is another example of an open-ended question:

How many different ways can you write a natural number using only addition?

To write 1, there is only 1 way: 1

To write 2, there are 2 ways: $1 + 1$ or 2

To write 3, there are 4 ways: $3, 1 + 2, 2 + 1, 1 + 1 + 1$

To write 4, there are 8 ways: $4, 3 + 1, 1 + 3, 2 + 2, 2 + 1 + 1, 1 + 2 + 1, 1 + 1 + 2, 1 + 1 + 1 + 1$.

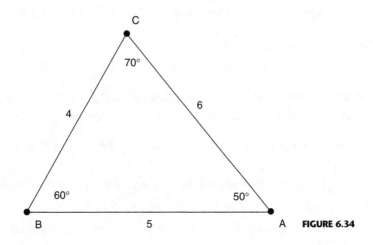

FIGURE 6.34

What would you expect to be the number of ways to write 5? To write 6?

Don't ask questions with multiple parts. A student might be able to answer the first part of a question with multiple parts but not the second or vice versa. Because the student does not know the answer to both parts, the student will not volunteer.

> *Don't ask:* Which triangles should we prove congruent, and how will that help us to prove that AB // CD?
>
> *Do ask:* Which triangles should we prove congruent? After that part has been answered: How do we use the congruent triangles to prove AB // CD?

Don't ask elliptical questions. An elliptical question is a question that is vague because the teacher forgot to address the specifics of the problem.

> *Don't ask:* What about these angles?
>
> *Do ask:* Which angle of the triangle has the greatest measure?

Don't ask leading questions. A leading question is one that pulls or tugs the answer you want from the students.

> *Don't ask:* Triangle ABC is equilateral, isn't it?
>
> *Do ask:* What kind of triangle is triangle ABC?

Don't ask personal questions. You and the students are all part of a community of mathematics learners. We all work together. A personal question that uses the words *me* or *I* helps create an artificial barrier between the students and the teacher and hinders the thought processes we are trying to encourage.

> *Don't ask:* Give me a solution set for $7x + 5 = 33$
>
> *Do ask:* Give us the solution set for $7x + 5 = 33$ . . . (pause) . . . Ann?

Use questions that compare and contrast items. This encourages active thinking and requires the student to make decisions beyond a mere guess.

> *Don't ask:* What is the relationship between the perimeter and the area of a square?
>
> *Do ask:* Compare and contrast the area and the perimeter of a square.
>
> *Don't ask:* How do you add or multiply fractions?
>
> *Do ask:* Compare and contrast adding and multiplying fractions.

The questions you ask in your class will keep the lesson moving. At the same time, they will help you diagnose any problems that arise as the students explain their work. Many people have said that teaching mathematics is simply asking the right questions.

Responding to a Student's Response

Once you have asked your question and elicited a response from one or more students, what do you do next? How you react when a student answers a question is a critical part of the teacher-student discourse. "How did you get that?" or "Why?" are questions that will probably frighten your students so that they cannot answer. It may be better to use a response such as:

- Share your thinking with the rest of us.
- Tell us in your own words how you did that.
- What made you think of that?
- Mark, can you explain in your own words what Anne did?

Remember, you are trying to increase the students' thinking abilities and communications skills, so having them explain in their own words is an excellent technique. Students find it easier to explain things using their own thoughts and words. In fact, you should encourage students to ask questions. The process of formulating a question often clarifies whatever it is the student does not understand. Help your students to formulate thought-provoking questions.

Above all, you should not repeat student answers, except for emphasis. If the students expect you to repeat any answer you get from them, then why should they listen to each other? They probably won't; they will expect that only what you, as the teacher, say will be of value. This will stifle interactive learning in the classroom.

Listen to your own questions with a critical ear. Be careful of what you ask and how you ask it. If you are not sure about the questions you are asking, consider writing them out when you plan your lessons. One helpful technique is to tape record a lesson to help you analyze your questioning techniques.

7

DRIVING THE LESSON WITH CHALLENGING PROBLEMS

The flow of your class is determined by how adeptly you handle the beginning, middle, and end of each lesson. Keep your class active from bell to bell to maximize learning and reduce boredom.

Getting the Lesson Started

The tone of your class will be set during the first few minutes of your lesson. If nothing valuable happens, then the students will decide that the first 5 or 10 minutes of class are wasted. Always get your class under way promptly. You can make your start-up activity a transparency for the overhead projector or a file from your computer projector. You can prepare it in advance and save it for future use.

Motivating the Lesson

Students need to feel motivated to get right into the lesson. Getting middle school and high school students interested in doing mathematics can be a difficult task. Motivation is an internal feeling that must be stimulated externally by the teacher to get the student to respond. You can use motivation in many ways. Let's tie together the motivational ideas and some examples of start-up activities that lead into lessons you might be teaching.

Motivation Through Irritation

One way to stimulate your students' thinking is what is sometimes called *motivation through irritation*. That is, to start class you present something that appears (on the surface) to be easy to do. However, after moving through the first part or parts of the activity, the students find themselves confronted with something they do not know how to handle. The innate desire to complete the activity acts as a stimulus for what you will teach that day. Consider the following examples of motivation through irritation.

1. You intend to introduce a lesson involving the trigonometric functions of angles of 90° or more. The students have already learned the values for the trigonometric functions of angles less than 90°. The following start-up activity would be appropriate when the students enter your room:

Problem

Find the value of each of the following without using your calculator:

$$\sin 30° = ?$$
$$\cos 30° = ?$$
$$\tan 180° = ?$$
$$\sin 150° = ?$$
$$\cos 240° = ?$$

The first two are quite easily done with a knowledge of the 30°-60°-90° right triangle. However, the last three items will cause the "irritation" as the students find themselves confronted with trigonometric functions of angles of more than 90°. They can no longer draw a right triangle and find the tangent, sine, and cosine. You will have to teach them how to approach the functions of these angles. It is your lesson for the day.

2. The following problem makes an excellent introduction to a lesson on the Pythagorean theorem (see Chapter 6 for a more complete treatment of this lesson).

Problem

Mr. Adams has a circular table top (width 2 inches) with a diameter of 12.5 feet. He must bring the table into his dining room through a door that is 5 feet wide and 12 feet high. Can he get it through the door?

Teacher's Note: Even if we "tilt" the table on the diagonal, will it fit through the door? Yes; the length of the diagonal of the door is 13 feet. Notice that we can ignore the thickness of the table for this problem because the table is so thin.

Motivation by Impossibility

There are times when some things can be shown to be impossible by seemingly correct mathematical procedures. Each of these usually brings with it an important message. These can often provide motivation for a topic to be taught.

1. This motivational challenge, which appears impossible at first glance, is an excellent start-up activity for a lesson on the pitfalls of division by 0. It involves showing the students a proof that $1 = 2$ and seeing if they can find out what is wrong with it:

Problem
Begin by letting $a = b$.
Now, multiply both sides of this equality by a to get $a^2 = ab$.
Subtract b^2 from both sides to get $a^2 - b^2 = ab - b^2$.
Factor both sides: $(a + b)(a - b) = b(a - b)$.
Divide by the common factor $(a - b)$ to get $a + b = b$.
Because $a = b$, we can substitute to get $(b + b) = b$ or $2b = b$.
Then, by dividing by b, we get $2 = 1$.

How can this be?

Teacher's Note: The "error" lies in the fifth line, where we divided by the common factor $(a - b)$. Because we started by assuming $a = b$, we are in effect dividing through by 0. This leads to the odd result that 1 appears to equal 2.

2. Your lesson for the day in an algebra class is an introduction to the concept of imaginary numbers and the value of $i = \sqrt{-1}$. It is important that your students realize that much of the work is done by definition. For example, the students have already learned that $\sqrt{a} \cdot \sqrt{b} = \sqrt{ab}$ (or $\sqrt{a} \cdot \sqrt{a} = a$) for positive real numbers. The following problem, then, appears to have a contradiction:

Problem
Find the value of $\sqrt{-4} \cdot \sqrt{-4}$.

We apply this rule and get: $\sqrt{-4} \cdot \sqrt{-4} = \sqrt{(-4)(-4)} = \sqrt{16} = 4$.

But $\sqrt{-4} \cdot \sqrt{-4} = \left(\sqrt{-4}\right)^2 = -4$. How can that be true?

Teacher's Note: You will have to define $\sqrt{-4} = \sqrt{-1}\sqrt{4} = 2i$. It follows that $(2i)(2i) = 4i^2 = -4$.

You can now support this introduction with a more complete discussion on the use of i for imaginary numbers.

Motivation Through Challenges

A nice motivation can be created by an easy-to-understand problem that is not so easy to solve, yet, the solution (i.e., the easy one) hinges on a mathematical concept that is to be presented or reviewed in the ensuing lesson.

1. Once you have taught the class the theorem that *tangents to a circle from a common external point have the same length,* you can confront them with the following seemingly difficult problem:

Problem

In Figure 7.1, $\overline{PQ}$, $\overline{PR}$, and $\overline{TV}$ are all tangent to circle O at points Q, R, and S, respectively. If the length of tangent PQ is 8, what is the perimeter of triangle PTV ?

Intuitively, the students may feel that "something is missing," that it is impossible to solve the problem with only the given information, and that the

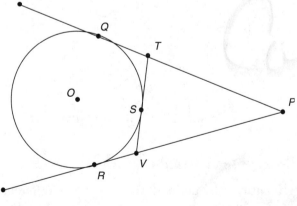

FIGURE 7.1

problem cannot be done. However, they need only know that tangent segments to a circle from a common outside point are equal.

Teacher's Note: Because $\overline{TQ}$ and $\overline{TS}$ are both tangent from point T, they are equal in length, and we can replace TQ by TS. Similarly, $SV = VR$. Thus, triangle PTV consists of $PT + TS + SV + PV$. Because $PQ = PR$, the length of the perimeter of the triangle is equal to the lengths of the two tangent segments from P, or $8 + 8 = 16$.

2. Here is another challenging geometry problem that can serve as either a lead-in to a lesson on the area of a circle or a review after the formula has been taught. If the formula has already been taught to the students, then they should be able to solve the problem, even though the results appear to be impossible.

Problem

Given five concentric circles shown in Figure 7.2, each radius is one unit larger than the previous one. Which is larger, the outer ring (the area between the largest two circles) or the shaded region?

Teacher's Note: It may surprise you (and your students) to realize that the areas shaded are exactly the same. Each has an area of 9π square units.

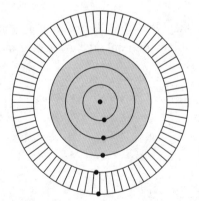

FIGURE 7.2

Motivation Through Intellectual Curiosity

Most students are intrinsically curious. There are many different activities they can examine that will provide interesting and unusual results. In most cases, the students can be motivated to find out why they work, rather than simply accepting that they do work. Number problems, in algebra especially, can be used at every level if we ask the students to explain mathematically why they "work."

1. Here is one example of a number activity, that can be used to start a class and will lead to a lesson involving prime numbers and composites. It also provides practice in evaluating an expression for different values of a variable.

Begin by telling the class about the history of prime-producing functions. Make certain that they understand what a prime number is.

Problem

We know that mathematicians have been searching for a prime-producing function for years. A prime-producing function is a function that produces only prime numbers when values are substituted for the variable. To this day, none exists. Yet, we think we have found one! You don't think so? Well, try this one. We claim that $n^2 - n + 41$ is a prime-producing function. You still don't think so? Why don't you try substituting values for n and see what happens?

For $n = 1$, we obtain $1^2 - 1 + 41 = 41$ (which is a prime number).
For $n = 2$, we obtain $2^2 - 2 + 41 = 43$ (which is a prime number).
For $n = 5$, we obtain $5^2 - 5 + 41 = 61$ (which is a prime number).
For $n = 10$, we obtain $10^2 - 10 + 41 = 131$ (which is a prime number).

You can try some other values of n for yourself and see if the function does indeed yield prime numbers.

Teacher's Note: The function $n^2 - n + 41$ will produce only prime numbers for values of n less than 41. At 41, the function yields 41^2, which is obviously not a prime.

2. Another activity involving prime numbers and composites to challenge the students' curiosity is to ask them if there are more prime numbers between 1 and 100 or between 101 and 200. Have them make a guess and explain why they think the way they do. They can then make use of the historical "sieve of Eratosthenes" to find out.

Have them write the numbers from 1 through 200 on a piece of paper. Begin by crossing out 1 because it is neither prime nor composite. Now, circle 2. Cross out all multiples of 2. The next number not crossed out is 3. Circle it. Now cross out all the multiples of 3 not already crossed out. The next number not crossed out is 5. Circle it and cross out all multiples of 5. Continue in this manner until all the numbers have either been circled or crossed out. The circled numbers are the primes. Count how many there are between 1 and 100, and between 101 and 200. Students may want to make a conjecture. This will lead nicely into a lesson on prime numbers.

3. An excellent hands-on, introductory activity to a lesson on the volume of a cylinder is the following: Provide groups of your students with a sheet of $8\frac{1}{2} \times 11$-inch paper. Ask them to form a cylinder by "rolling" the paper and then using tape to connect the edges. Some students will roll the paper until the 11-inch edges meet, forming a tall, thin cylinder with a height of 11 inches and a base circumference of $8\frac{1}{2}$ inches. Others will roll the paper until the $8\frac{1}{2}$-inch edges meet, forming a short, squat cylinder with height of $8\frac{1}{2}$ inches and a base circumference of 11 inches. Ask them which cylinder holds the larger amount (volume) or whether they are the same? The answers will vary. At this point, you might wish to use beans or rice or some other easily accessible material to fill each cylinder to see which holds more. However, the "why it works" will depend on a lesson using the formula for the volume of a cylinder, $V = \pi r^2 h$. Of course, this depends on finding the radii of the two base circles (1.35 and 1.75 inches, respectively.) This is an excellent opportunity for your students to use their calculators because the problem involves division by π.

Motivation Through Unusual Situations

Sometimes, you can motivate your students by presenting them with an unusual situation involving skills they may already have learned. The unfamiliar setting of the problem can often motivate them to utilize some of these skills. The problems often asked on college entrance exams can provide some excellent unusual situations.

1. Here is a problem involving exponents that may not look familiar to your algebra students but is probably well within their abilities. It is a good lead-in to a review of the laws of exponents and the solution of a pair of equations in two variables solved simultaneously.

Problem

Given $2^x = 8^{y+1}$ and $9^y = 3^{x-9}$.

Find the values of x and y.

Although this appears to be a totally unfamiliar situation (after all, your students have not studied equations with exponents raised to different bases), it can be solved as follows:

We can change both equations to equations having the same base:

$$2^x = 2^{3(y+1)}$$
$$3^{2y} = 3^{x-9}$$

Because the bases are now equal in each equation, so are the exponents. This leads to the pair of equations

$$x = 3(y + 1)$$
$$x - 9 = 2y$$

Solving these equations simultaneously yields $x = 21$ and $y = 6$.

2. Another unusual situation appears in the following problem. It is an excellent lead-in to a lesson that demonstrates that the "best" solution to a problem is not always the most obvious.

Problem

The sum of two numbers is 28 and their product is 5. What is the sum of their reciprocals?

Some of your students might try setting up a pair of simultaneous equations:

$$x + y = 28$$
$$xy = 5$$

Solving for x and y this way would eventually require the quadratic formula and would take a long time to solve. However, a much more interesting and efficient solution exists. If the numbers are x and y, then the sum of their reciprocals can be written as:

$$\frac{1}{x} + \frac{1}{y}$$

The sum of these fractions is

$$\frac{x + y}{xy},$$

but $x + y = 28$ and $xy = 5$, so the answer is simply $\dfrac{28}{5}$.

3. Here is an excellent start-up activity that can be used to demonstrate that a mathematical conjecture does not constitute a proof. This is a nice introduction to a lesson in a geometry class, introducing a rationale for why proofs are needed.

Problem

As shown in Figure 7.3, when points on a circle are joined, regions are formed. When 2 points are joined, we obtain 2 regions. For three points, we obtain 4 regions. For 4 points we obtain 8 regions and for 5 points, we obtain 16 regions. how many regions would you expect if we join six points?

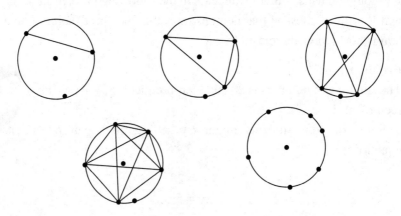

FIGURE 7.3

Many students will form a table as follows:

NUMBER OF POINTS	NUMBER OF REGIONS
2	2
3	4
4	8
5	16
6	?

Many students will recognize what seems to be a simple pattern and guess that there will be 32 regions. A careful drawing will show that there are really only 31 regions for 6 points. It is now "obvious" that they cannot simply use a conjecture to establish formulas; proofs are needed. For more on this, see Chapter 6.

Teacher's Note: The actual function that relates the number of points n to the number of regions is $f(n) = \dfrac{1}{24}(n^4 - 6n^3 + 23n^2 - 18n + 24)$. Although the algebraic proof is beyond most high school courses, it can serve as a motivator for advanced study.

4. When you begin to speak of number sequences and your lesson about this topic will be aimed in a particular direction, it may be nice to make students aware of some oddities in this arena. There are many important sequences of numbers in mathematics that your students should recognize whenever they appear. One of these is the Fibonacci sequence. In this sequence, each term after the first two ones is the sum of the previous two terms. This start-up activity combines some of the properties of the Fibonacci sequence with the use of an algebraic proof. (For more on Fibonacci numbers, see Posamentier & Lehmann, 2007.)

Ask your students to write any two numbers they wish directly under one another and begin to form the Fibonacci sequence by adding the two terms. Then, add Terms 2 and 3 to get Term 4. Continue until 10 terms are on the list. Ask the students to add the 10 numbers. Then, ask them to multiply the 7th number by 11. Incredibly, they will get the same answer. For example, suppose they choose 3 and 7. Then, the sequence would appear as:

Term 1	3	
Term 2	7	
Term 3	10	(which came from $3 + 7$)
Term 4	17	(which came from $7 + 10$)
Term 5	27	(which came from $10 + 17$)
Term 6	44	(which came from $17 + 27$)
Term 7	71	(which came from $27 + 44$)
Term 8	115	(which came from $44 + 71$)

Term 9   186   (which came from $71 + 115$)
Term10   301   (which came from $115 + 186$)
Sum $= 781 = 71 \cdot 11$

After mystifying them with this bit of mathematical magic, they will be interested to know why it works.

Let the two numbers selected be a and b. Then, the Fibonacci-like sequence formed is:

Term 1	a
Term 2	b
Term 3	$a + b$
Term 4	$a + 2b$
Term 5	$2a + 3b$
Term 6	$3a + 5b$
Term 7	$5a + 8b$
Term 8	$8a + 3b$
Term 9	$13a + 21b$
Term 10	$21a + 34b$
Sum =	$55a + 88b$

which is $11 \times (5a + 8b)$, the 7th term.

5. The concept of numbers and their factors is extremely important, especially in the middle school. Students should recognize that factors occur in pairs, and that the factors are commutative. The following is an interesting and unusual problem to use as a start-up activity when introducing the concept of factors in the middle grades. It not only uses the concept of factor pairs, but also shows the class that a problem may have more than one correct answer.

Problem

Alice and some friends are seated at a round table. Alice's mother brings in a plate of 25 cookies. Alice takes the first cookie then passes the plate to the next person. This person also takes a cookie and passes the plate on. The plate is passed around the circle of friends. Each person takes one cookie when the plate reaches them, until all cookies are gone. Alice has taken the first cookie and the last one. She also may have taken some in between. How many people could be seated at the table?

Teacher's Note: One approach is to "discard" the 25th cookie. Now, each person has taken the same number of cookies. Because no cookies are broken, the number of people (and the number of cookies) must be whole numbers. Have the students use their guess-and-test strategy to figure out the answers. The answers are the factors of 24, excluding 1 person and 2 people because the problem stated Alice and her friends. Thus, the answers are:

3 people, 8 cookies each (and Alice gets 9 cookies)

4 people, 6 cookies each (and Alice gets 7 cookies)

6 people, 4 cookies each (and Alice gets 5 cookies)

8 people, 3 cookies each (and Alice gets 4 cookies)

12 people, 2 cookies each (and Alice gets 3 cookies)

24 people, 1 cookie each (and Alice gets 2 cookies)

Remember, these start-up activities are designed to interest the students, to get them settled down, and to motivate them toward to topic of the day. They are not meant to take the entire class period or to replace the intended lesson. They are merely motivational introductions to specific lessons. You should begin to collect these and build an arsenal of such ideas so that you can use them when appropriate. Catalogue them so that you have them at ready reference. As you can see from our examples, some of these can be used for various lessons; others are specific to one topic.

Concluding the Lesson

Just as the first few minutes of class are important, so are last few minutes. Just as a good story ends on a climactic "high note," you can attempt to make the final impression of your lesson a lasting one. Consider using "mathematical tidbits"—in a carefully measured fashion—to get the students interested and excited about the general feeling for mathematics.

What are the criteria for these mathematical tidbits? They should be fun to do and should grab the students' interest. They should take no more than 5 to 10 minutes to complete. They should be used to convince the students that mathematics can have unusual and enjoyable aspects and is powerful and beautiful.

A word of caution: Don't simply copy the suggestions we offer in this chapter (although you can, if you wish). Instead, use them as models to create similar activities for your own students. You may have to change the difficulty level, the language, the setting, or even the numbers. Begin to collect these ideas and create a file of mathematical tidbits that you can use and modify in coming years.

1. Here is an idea that can be used in either middle school or high school. It deals with money and provides some practice in subtraction with regrouping. At the same time, it lets the students discover number patterns as they try to answer the question.

Marlene's Dilemma

Marlene went into the store and spent $8.15. She gave the clerk a $10.00 bill and received $1.85 in change. She noticed that her change and the amount she had spent used the same digits but in different order. Marlene wondered if there were any other sums she might have spent so that the digits in her change and in the amount spent were the same when she handed the clerk a $10.00 bill. Can you find them?

POSSIBLE CHOICES

SPENT	CHANGE	SPENT	CHANGE
$1.85	$8.15	$5.45	$4.55
$2.75	$7.25	$6.35	$3.65
$3.65	$6.35	$7.25	$2.75
$4.55	$5.45	$8.15	$1.85

Some students may include $9.05 and $0.95. This could prompt a discussion on the necessity for a zero in the dollar position.

2. Early in their mathematics instruction, students are taught how to round numbers. However, sometimes the interpretation of the problem and the meaning of the remainder will cause students to ignore these rules. Here is an activity that presents the students with four situations in which the interpretation of the remainder needs some careful consideration rather than merely resorting to a rule. This is a good activity for a middle school or junior high school class, although it has been used successfully with high school students as well.

Interpret the Remainder

(a) The school is sending 505 students to the football game next Saturday and wants to rent buses. Each bus holds 33 students How many buses will the school need? _____

What will you do with the remainder?

(1) Round up   (2) Round down   (3) List the remainder as it is

(b) The houses in a housing complex are being hooked up to the new cable TV system. There are 175 houses, and 4 technicians are sent to hook them up. How many houses should each technician connect? _____

What will you do with the remainder?

(1) Round up   (2) Round down   (3) List the remainder as it is

(c) Andrea is having a pizza party at the local roller blading rink. Each pizza costs $9.00. Andrea has $48.00 to spend on pizza. How many pizzas should she order? _____

What will you do with the remainder?

(1) Round up   (2) Round down   (3) List the remainder as it is

(d) Eight people went to a local restaurant for dinner. The bill came to $105.00, including the tip and the tax. How much should each person contribute if they divide the bill equally? _____

What will you do with the remainder?

(a) Round up   (2) Round down   (3) List the remainder as it is

The following are possible answers:

(a) The remainder of 10 means that there will be 10 students left after we fill 15 buses. Even though the remainder is less than half of the divisor (33), we must round the number up to 16 buses.

(b) The remainder is 3 when we divide 175 by 4. Thus, we round up to 44, but only for 3 of the technicians. The answer is that they will connect 44, 44, 44, and 43 houses.

(c) We round down even though the remainder is more than half. Andrea can order 5 pizzas ($5 \times \$9.00 = \$45.00$), and she will have $3 left.

(d) We will leave the remainder as is. $\$105 \div 8 = \$13$ and a remainder of 13¢. Thus, each person should pay $13.13.

3. Students often "see" different meanings when viewing the same items. Much depends on their previous knowledge as well as their mathematical backgrounds. This mathematical tidbit allows the students free rein to select whichever item is different from the rest in their opinion. A second advantage to this opener is that the students must express—in words—the reason for their selection. This provides practice in explaining their thought processes in writing. A similar activity can easily be designed for any grade level. There can be more than one correct response.

Which Doesn't Belong?

In each of the following, there is one item that is different from the rest. Select the item that is different and give the reason why you chose that item.

(a) 47,474	24,662	1,331	424
(b) 1	2	3	11
(c) 1 foot 6 inches	18 inches	1/2 yard	1 2/3 feet
(d) $\sqrt{4}$	$\sqrt{9}$	$\sqrt{11}$	$\sqrt{225}$
(e) 3–4–5	5–12–13	$\sqrt{3} - \sqrt{4} - \sqrt{5}$	30–40–50

The following are possible answers:

(a) Some students may select 1,331 as the only odd number. Others may select 24,662 because it is the only choice that is not a palindrome—that is, a number that can be read the same backward or forward.

(b) Students may select 1, because it is the only number that is not a prime. Others may select 2 as the only even number.

(c) Some may select ½ yard as the only measurement written in words. Others may select 1⅔ feet because that is the only choice not equivalent to 18 inches.

(d) Some students may select $\sqrt{11}$ as the only item that is irrational. Others may select $\sqrt{4}$ as the only one to yield an even result. Others may select $\sqrt{225}$, which is the only choice to yield a two-digit result.

(e) Some students may select $\sqrt{3} - \sqrt{4} - \sqrt{5}$ as the only set that is not a Pythagorean triple. Others may choose 30–40–50 as the only one with an even number for the hypotenuse.

4. This tidbit can be used with students in senior high school or upper-level middle school. It is an activity that requires some thought and some reasoning.

No School This Year

What is wrong with the reasoning in the following example presented by Andy to his mathematics teacher?

NUMBER OF DAYS OF NO SCHOOL		
Saturdays and Sundays	52×2	= 104 days
Sleep (8 hours per day $\times$ 365 days)	$365 \times 1/3$	= 122 days
Summer vacation	2 months	= 60 days
Holidays		= 20 days
Days not in school		= 306 days
Days in school = $365 - 306 = 59$ days		

The following is a possible explanation: There is obviously some overlapping in the union of the various sets given. For example, there are Saturdays and Sundays included in the summer vacation time, as well as in the sleep category. This example is of particular importance in that it makes students aware of being critical readers—important not only in reading math problems, but also in reading today's newspapers, which are full of tables and charts to make their point. These are sometimes not accurate for the same reason as our example is misleading.

5. This tidbit can be developed to fit the mathematical abilities of any grade. The two shown as models use activities within the scope of students in the upper middle school grades or senior high school. They involve units of measure, arithmetic computation, as well as fractions, exponents, simple geometry, and percent. The activity is self-checking because each of the digits from 0 through 9 should occur exactly once. The answers are given in parentheses after each question.

Check Yourself

In each of the following, the digits from 0 through 9 occur in the answers exactly once. Do the problems and check yourself to see if the 10 digits do actually occur only once in each group.

1. (a) What is the lowest common denominator for 3/4 and 2/3 ?   (12)
   (b) What is the second multiple of 30?   (60)
   (c) How many degrees are there in one-half of a right angle?   (45)
   (d) What is the prime number between 35 and 40?   (37)
   (e) How much is $10^2 - 2$?   (98)

2. (a) How many inches are there in 1 yard?   (36)
   (b) What is the sum in cents of 2 dimes, 3 nickels, and 6 pennies? (41)
   (c) Change 100/2 to a whole number.   (50)
   (d) What is the product of 9×3?   (27)
   (e) Wow! The blades that cost $178 are on sale at 50% off.

   What would they cost now?   (89)

6. To some students, the position and size of triangles can cause problems. Some even refuse to recognize that a figure is a polygon if its orientation is unusual. In this activity, students are challenged to find how many triangles there are in the given illustration (Figure 7.4). There are triangles that overlap in the diagram.

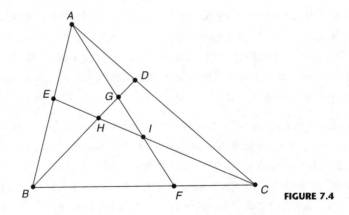

FIGURE 7.4

The answer shows that there are 17 triangles of various sizes and shapes in the figure. A good strategy for counting the triangles is to redraw the figure and count triangles that appear with each additional line segment (i.e., that depends on the new segment for part or all of a side).

7. This activity provides a challenge for the brighter students in your class.

They are asked to write the natural numbers from 1 to 20 using only four 4s each time. They may add, subtract, multiply, or divide; use square roots; and use parentheses. They may also use one 4 as an exponent or can put two or more 4s side by side as in 44 or 444. You might challenge the class to see how far they can go beyond 20 using only four 4s.

There are several ways to do most of these. Here are some possibilities.

$$1 = \frac{4+4}{4+4} = \frac{\sqrt{44}}{\sqrt{44}}$$

$$2 = \frac{4 \cdot 4}{4+4} = \frac{4-4}{4} + \sqrt{4}$$

$$3 = \frac{4+4+4}{4} = \sqrt{4} + \sqrt{4} - \frac{4}{4}$$

$$4 = \frac{4-4}{4} + 4 = \frac{\sqrt{4 \cdot 4 \cdot 4}}{4}$$

$$5 = \frac{4 \cdot 4 + 4}{4}$$

$$6 = \frac{4+4}{4} + 4 = \frac{4\sqrt{4}}{4} + 4$$

$$7 = \frac{44}{4} - 4 = \sqrt{4} + 4 + \frac{4}{4}$$

$$8 = 4 \cdot 4 - 4 - 4 = \frac{4(4+4)}{4}$$

$$9 = \frac{44}{4} - \sqrt{4} = 4\sqrt{4} + \frac{4}{4}$$

$$10 = 4 + 4 + 4 - \sqrt{4}$$

$$11 = \frac{4}{4} + \frac{4}{.4}$$

$$12 = \frac{4 \cdot 4}{\sqrt{4}} + 4 = 4 \cdot 4 - \sqrt{4} - \sqrt{4}$$

$$13 = \frac{44}{4} + \sqrt{4}$$

$$14 = 4 \cdot 4 - 4 + \sqrt{4} = 4 + 4 + 4 + \sqrt{4}$$

$$15 = \frac{44}{4} + 4 = \frac{\sqrt{4} + \sqrt{4} + \sqrt{4}}{.4}$$

$$16 = 4 \cdot 4 - 4 + 4 = \frac{4 \cdot 4 \cdot 4}{4}$$

$$17 = 4 \cdot 4 + \frac{4}{4}$$

$$18 = \frac{44}{\sqrt{4}} - 4 = 4 \cdot 4 + 4 - \sqrt{4}$$

$$19 = \frac{4 + \sqrt{4}}{.4} + 4$$

$$20 = 4 \cdot 4 + \sqrt{4} + \sqrt{4}$$

8. Faced with summing a series, most students would just plow right into the problem, using whatever means they learned to sum series. If this did not look promising, then many would just begin to add the terms. This is a good lead-in to a number of topics.

Consider the problem of finding the sum of the following series:

$$\frac{1}{1 \cdot 2} + \frac{1}{2 \cdot 3} + \frac{1}{3 \cdot 4} + \cdots + \frac{1}{49 \cdot 50}$$

Students should be allowed about 2 minutes to read and "digest" the problem. After you see them trying to add the fractions

$$\frac{1}{2} + \frac{1}{6} + \frac{1}{12} + \frac{1}{20} + \frac{1}{30} + \cdots,$$

you should stop them and "impress" them with some of the following nifty methods:

One way to begin is to see if there is any visible pattern. We investigate one possibility:

$$\frac{1}{1 \cdot 2} = \frac{1}{2}$$

$$\frac{1}{1 \cdot 2} + \frac{1}{2 \cdot 3} = \frac{2}{3}$$

$$\frac{1}{1\cdot 2}+\frac{1}{2\cdot 3}+\frac{1}{3\cdot 4}=\frac{3}{4}$$

$$\frac{1}{1\cdot 2}+\frac{1}{2\cdot 3}+\frac{1}{3\cdot 4}+\frac{1}{4\cdot 5}=\frac{4}{5}$$

From this pattern (in which the factors of the last fraction's denominator give us the numerator and denominator of the sum), we will make a guess that the series that goes to $\dfrac{1}{49.50}$ has the following result:

$$\frac{1}{1\cdot 2}+\frac{1}{2\cdot 3}+\frac{1}{3\cdot 4}+\frac{1}{4\cdot 5}+\cdots+\frac{1}{49\cdot 50}=\frac{49}{50}$$

Another pattern for this series can be obtained by representing each fraction in the series as a difference in the following way:

$$\frac{1}{1\cdot 2}=\frac{1}{1}-\frac{1}{2}$$

$$\frac{1}{2\cdot 3}=\frac{1}{2}-\frac{1}{3}$$

$$\frac{1}{3\cdot 4}=\frac{1}{3}-\frac{1}{4}$$

$$\vdots$$

$$\frac{1}{49\cdot 50}=\frac{1}{49}-\frac{1}{50}$$

Adding these equations, the left side gives us our sought-after sum, and on the right side almost all the fractions drop out, leaving $\dfrac{1}{1}-\dfrac{1}{50}=\dfrac{49}{50}$.

These surprising illustrations of useful patterns will get a reaction from your students, "Oh, I would never be able to do this on my own," but this should be an unacceptable response for "practice makes perfect." At any rate, used properly, it could be a fine lead-in to a lesson.

9. You may wish to show your students an oddity and then have them use algebra to understand it. By beginning your lesson with the following, you can eventually show your students the usefulness of algebra for it will be through algebra that their curiosity will be quenched.

Have the students work individually at their seats on the following instructions, which you can give them orally.

Select any three-digit number with all digits different from one another. Write all possible two-digit numbers that can be formed from the three digits selected. Then, divide their sum by the sum of the digits in the original three-digit number.

Students should all get the same answer, 22. There ought to be a big resulting "Wow!"

For example, consider the three-digit number 365. Take the sum of all the possible two-digit numbers that can be formed from these three digits: $36 + 35 + 63 + 53 + 65 + 56 = 308$. The sum of the digits of the original number is $3 + 6 + 5 = 14$. Then, $308/14 = 22$.

To analyze this unusual result we begin with a general representation of the number:

$$100x + 10y + z.$$

We now take the sum of all the two-digit numbers taken from the three digits:

$$(10x + y) + (10y + x) + (10x + z) + (10z + x) + (10y + z) + (10z + y)$$
$$= 10(2x + 2y + 2z) + (2x + 2y + 2z)$$
$$= 11(2x + 2y + 2z)$$
$$= 22(x + y + z)$$

which, when divided by the sum of the digits $(x + y + z)$, is 22.

These illustrations show the value of algebra in explaining simple arithmetic phenomena. Make sure this leads in to your lesson and that the following material does not appear dull in comparison to this lesson beginning for this would make using this tidbit counterproductive (see Posamentier et al., 2006).

8

REASONING AND PROBLEM SOLVING

The thrust of the mathematics taught in schools today has undergone a major directional shift. Some decades ago, learning algorithms to add, subtract, multiply, divide, and solve algebraic equations was emphasized. Problem solving typically focused on solving algebraically specific types of "word problems," such as uniform motion problems, age problems, mixture problems, and so on. When the National Council of Teachers of Mathematics (NCTM) published *An Agenda for Action: Recommendations for School Mathematics of the 1980s* (1980), their primary recommendation was that problem solving must be the focus of school mathematics in the 1980s. When the same organization published the *Curriculum and Evaluation Standards for School Mathematics* in 1989, the requirements for all grades, K–12, were problem solving and reasoning. NCTM's *Principles and Standards for School Mathematics* (2000) continued this thrust toward competency in problem solving and reasoning.

For a long time, the word exercises appearing in most textbooks after a specific topic had been taught were felt to meet the requirement for teaching problem solving. However, these exercises usually did not require much thought. If the word problem occurred on a page that showed how to solve a pair of equations simultaneously, then students needed that method to solve the adjoining exercises. Now, most teachers agree that problems, by their very nature, should not be a stimulus that elicits an automatic or "mechanical" response from students. Students should be required to do more than apply a specific algorithm to solve a problem; rather, they should identify the processes to apply to the unfamiliar situation. Problems are no longer described by type but must encompass a wide variety of interests and areas. Problem solving and reasoning have become major goals of

131

the mathematics curriculum, along with the traditional algorithms. By putting the algorithmic skills into a problem setting, the students obtain the practice they need in a setting that they recognize as useful.

Yet, mathematics instruction is not based on the usefulness of the applications. Your enthusiasm must motivate your students to see the cleverness of some problem-solving techniques. This further demonstrates the power and beauty of mathematics. It may not be easy to impart to your students that what they learn in math class has a far greater effect on them than the ability to apply a topic to real-world situations. They learn reasoning, logical thought processes, and many problem-solving strategies also clearly applicable to everyday situations.

The widespread use of the calculator frees teachers to place more emphasis on problem solving and reasoning and less on some basic arithmetic skills. With a calculator, even students who have not yet mastered the fundamentals of arithmetic may participate in problem-solving activities without feeling inadequate. *Every child can be, and ought to be, a successful problem solver.* And success in problem solving leads to success in skill development, which leads to success in problem solving, which leads to . . . well, you get the idea.

Place your skill development lessons into problem settings. For example, instead of asking students to find the circumference of a circle with radius r, ask them to discover which is greater, the height of a typical can of tennis balls (holding three balls) or the distance around that same can (Figure 8.1). (The height is $3d$; the distance around is πd or approximately $3.14d$.)

To teach problem solving and reasoning successfully, your classroom atmosphere should be a totally nonthreatening environment. Any student can feel free to

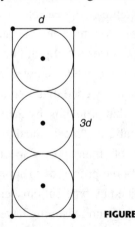

FIGURE 8.1

make a contribution to the discussion without any fear of ridicule or being "put down." Accepting the student's contribution (even if it is not completely correct) and making use of it to lead the discussion in the right direction ensures the student's future participation and offers encouragement to join in the ongoing discussion. Telling the class, "Let's see if we can expand on Mary's answer," makes Mary feel that she has made a contribution and gives you a point of reference to continue. As we said, all students are capable of becoming problem solvers. In fact, as students become more interested in problem solving, they often become more interested in the entire subject of mathematics. Your enthusiasm and your sensitivity to the students' thought processes set a proper tone in the class doing problem-solving activities.

Teaching Problem Solving

Heuristics

Some people feel that simply giving students lots of problems to solve will help them to become better problem solvers. We have not found this to be completely true. It is true that students need practice in problem solving, much as they do with any mathematical skill. In his landmark 1945 book, *How to Solve It,* George Polya mentions that when we approach a problem, we typically ask ourselves if we have ever encountered a similar problem in the past and, if so, how did we attempt to solve it. This process of association can be a first attempt at finding an appropriate strategy for the particular problem at hand. For this reason, we recommend providing students with a number of problem-solving strategies and then a procedure to follow to decide when to apply them. For your students to become good problem solvers, you ought to lead them to follow a set of guidelines, or heuristics. Polya introduced a set of basic heuristics:

- Understand the problem.
- Devise a plan.
- Carry out your plan.
- Look back.

Today, most textbook series contain a set of heuristics based on Polya's list. We use the following four steps: read the problem, select a strategy, solve the problem, and look back.

Read the problem (understand the problem). Reading the problem not only means reading it, of course, but also digesting the material presented and understanding what is going on. In other words, the student identifies *the question* ("What am I being asked to find?") and *the facts* ("What have I been given?").

Select a strategy (devise a plan). The student considers the many strategies commonly used in problem solving and selects those that are appropriate to the task at hand. Among them are

- Intelligent guess and test it.
- Look for a pattern.
- Work backward.
- Reduce and expand.
- Account for all possibilities.
- Simulate the action (act it out).
- Make a table (or make an organized list).
- Consider extreme cases.
- Write an equation.
- Draw a diagram.
- Use logical reasoning.
- Adapt another point of view.
- Solve a simpler analogous problem.

These strategies are not the only ones available. In fact, a student often needs to use several strategies in solving a single problem. Students should become familiar with these strategies and practice using them in solving problems.

Solve the problem (carry out your plan). In this step, the student uses arithmetic, algebraic, and geometric skills and the selected strategy to solve the problem. This includes finding the correct answer.

Look back. In this final step, the student checks the results to make certain there have been no computational errors and checks the reasonableness of the answer. Does the answer makes sense? Does it use the appropriate units of measure? Has the actual question been answered? Sometimes, the solution to the equation used in the process is not yet the final answer to the question asked.

This set of heuristics will be similar to the one found in your class textbook. Feel free to add more strategies or to delete some that you feel are not appropriate. Remember, it is your classroom, and you must modify the instructional program to best suit the class. It is also likely that even two classes at the same grade level may require modifications to accommodate the precise composition of the class.

Given that many students do not succeed at problem solving because they fail to read the problem or to understand what they are reading, the first heuristic in our set is particularly important. Do not assume that your students can read a problem in a meaningful manner. You might present the following problem to your students to solve to emphasize the necessity for reading the problem carefully.

Problem
The perimeter of a rectangle is 72 feet, and the length of the rectangle is 8 feet more than three times the width. Find the perimeter of the rectangle.

Some students will draw a diagram or write an equation. Even then, many will still get it wrong. How many of you missed the message in this illustrative example? Yes, the answer is in the first part of the statement of the problem, where the perimeter is given. Students must learn to read carefully. We have given this problem to many groups of math teachers, and they also missed this. We simply wanted to point out how some people jump into a problem-solving situation without *really* reading the problem statement carefully.

Each of the strategies can be taught using model problems. Remember, however, that some students might decide to solve a problem using an approach or strategy different from yours. Their solutions will look different. This should be encouraged. An old maxim states it is better to solve one problem in four ways than to solve four problems in one way. We use several problems to demonstrate possible strategy selection for use with your students.

Students should be accustomed to the solve the problem by considering the heuristics. After all, this is the part of the plan that they have been doing ever since they arrived in school. Encourage them to work carefully and try to avoid arithmetic errors. It is important that the students understand that the answer they get must be correct. Although we are right to emphasize the problem-solving process as well as the students' thought processes, in mathematics, the correct answer is absolutely essential. Notice that we are differentiating between the words *solution* and *answer*. The solution is the entire process, from the initial encounter with the problem until it is completed and finished. The answer is something that appears as a result of the solution process.

The final step in our heuristic plan is an important one. In the look back part, the students must examine their work carefully, making sure that there are no computation errors. They must make certain that they have actually answered the question they were asked and used the appropriate units of measure.

Above all, make sure that your students write explanations of how they solved each problem. This will improve their communication skills as well as their problem-solving skills. There is nothing wrong with students talking to themselves. Often, by doing so they will be forced to organize their thoughts—to make them coherent—and in the process crystallize their thinking. This can, of course, also occur when they talk among themselves.

It has become more common to require students to write a brief paragraph explaining how they solved the problem and what they were thinking in the process. The type of exposition here differs from other contexts and by its very nature must be precise and without much "color." This last step of the heuristic plan becomes even more important as the students write their explanation of what they did and how they did it. They must write convincingly how they solved the problem and must justify that their method is correct.

The key to teaching problem solving is the teacher. The way your classroom runs and the attitude you show toward problem solving will determine your success. If you simply put a problem on the board and rush to show the class how to do it, then little will be accomplished. The students will not gain thinking skills. One excellent technique is to put your students into small groups to solve problems. Research shows that our students benefit from working with peers. The discussion is more open, it is more lively, and everyone gets more opportunity to speak. The exchange of thought and ideas is beneficial to everyone.

Finally, you must recognize that problem solving takes time. You cannot expect students to read a problem and jump right in to solve it. If they can, then it really was not an appropriate problem.

Applying the Heuristics

Let's see how these heuristics can be applied to solving some problems.

Problem

Your mother has asked you to wash the dishes after dinner during the entire month of June. You can choose from either of two plans:

Plan 1: She will give you $70 for the month.

Plan 2: She will give you 1¢ on June 1, 2¢ on June 2, 4¢ on June 3, 8¢ on June 4, and so on, paying you twice as much each day as the day before.

Which plan would you select and why?

Read the problem. Have the students read the problem aloud. Ask them to identify what the problem is asking and what information they are given. *The problem asks* which plan we would choose and why. *The facts are* that one plan pays exactly $70 for the month, and the other doubles the amount paid each day, beginning with 1¢. The month of June contains 30 days.

Select a strategy. We will make a table to organize the data information. Then, we will examine the results of each plan.

Solve the problem. The first plan will pay me $70 for the month. The second plan is shown in Figure 8.2. We can stop here because it is readily apparent that the second plan will pay much more than the first plan. (If your students wish to carry the table out through the 30th day, then they will find that they would receive

DATE	PAY FOR THE DAY ($)	TOTAL AMOUNT RECEIVED ($)
1	.01	.01
2	.02	.03
3	.04	.07
4	.08	.15
5	.16	.31
6	.32	.63
7	.64	1.27
8	1.28	2.55
9	2.56	5.11
10	5.12	10.23
11	10.24	20.47
12	20.48	40.95
13	40.96	81.91
14	81.92	163.83

FIGURE 8.2

a total of $10,737,128.33 under the second plan.) We would select Plan 2 because it pays much more money than Plan 1.

Look back. Is our arithmetic is correct? Yes; we kept doubling the amount each day. We did answer the question that was asked by selecting Plan 2 as our choice. Notice that we made use of the strategy to make a table. This enabled us to organize our work in an easily handled fashion.

Problem

A farmer sent his son and daughter into the field to count the number of his cows and chickens. As typical teenagers, they came back with the following information: "I counted 160 legs," said his daughter. "And I counted 50 heads," said his son. The farmer, as smart as his children, was able to figure out quickly how many cows and how many chickens he had. How many of each did he really have?

Read the problem. *The problem asks* us to find out how many cows and how many chickens there were. *The problem tells* us that there were 160 legs and 50 heads. It also tells us there were cows (which have 4 legs each) and chickens (which have 2 legs each).

Select a strategy. If we were approaching this problem in a middle school, then we might decide to use the guess-and-test strategy. To do this accurately, however, we need to keep track of our guesses and their results. Thus, we need a table.

Solve the problem. Because there were 50 heads, there must have been 50 animals altogether. Let's make our first guess 20 cows and 30 chickens (Figure 8.3).

NUMBER OF COWS	NUMBER OF COW LEGS	NUMBER OF CHICKENS	NUMBER OF CHICKEN LEGS	TOTAL LEGS
20	80	30	60	140

FIGURE 8.3

This is not a good guess because there are too few legs. Let's increase the number of four-legged animals and decrease the number of two-legged animals, which will give us more legs. Let's guess 25 cows and 25 chickens (Figure 8.4).

NUMBER OF COWS	NUMBER OF COW LEGS	NUMBER OF CHICKENS	NUMBER OF CHICKEN LEGS	TOTAL LEGS
20	80	30	60	140
25	100	25	50	150

FIGURE 8.4

That is better, but still not right. Let's guess 30 cows and 20 chickens (Figure 8.5).

NUMBER OF COWS	NUMBER OF COW LEGS	NUMBER OF CHICKENS	NUMBER OF CHICKEN LEGS	TOTAL LEGS
20	80	30	60	140
25	100	25	50	150
30	120	20	40	160

FIGURE 8.5

That's it! There were 30 cows and 20 chickens in the field.

Look back. Our arithmetic is correct. We answered the question. We put in the correct units (cows and chickens). Notice that you might select a different strategy, especially if you were teaching in a high school in which the students had learned how to solve a pair of equations simultaneously. You might select the strategy to write an equation: Let x = the number of cows. Let y = the number of chickens. Then,

$$x + y = 50$$
$$4x + 2y = 160$$

Multiplying the first equation by 2, we can subtract from the second equation:

$$4x + 2y = 160$$
$$2x + 2y = 100$$
$$2x = 60$$
$$x = 30$$

Substituting in the original equation,

$$x + y = 50$$
$$30 + y = 50$$
$$y = 20$$

The farmer had 30 cows and 20 chickens.

Any time you have a problem that can be solved by using a pair of equations solved simultaneously, it can also be solved by the guess-and-test strategy.

Problem

Find two prime numbers which sum to 141.

Read the problem. *The problem asks* us to find two prime numbers. *What do we know?* They have a sum of 141. *Sum* in this problem means to add.

Select a strategy. One solution that will occur quickly to many students is to write a list of prime numbers and search for a pair with a sum of 141. This guess-and-test strategy can be tedious. Let's try to use logical reasoning.

Solve the problem. For any two numbers to have an odd sum, one of the numbers must be even, the other odd. However, we know that there is only one even prime number, namely, 2. Thus, the other prime number must be 139. The two prime numbers are 2 and 139.

Look back. Is our arithmetic correct? Yes. Did we solve the problem? Yes. Did we state the answer to the question asked? Yes.

Problem

Joanna wants to buy some candy from a vending machine. Each candy item costs a different amount of money. The machine has four slots: one accepts only nickels, one accepts only dimes, one accepts only quarters, and one accepts only pennies. The machine will accept, at most, one coin for each of the slots from among a quarter, dime, nickel, or penny. How many different candies can the machine offer?

Read the problem. *What are we asked to find?* We need to find the number of different candies the machine can offer. *What do we know?* The machine accepts at most one coin of each type. It may accept fewer. The four types of coins are the quarter, dime, nickel, and penny. Each candy item costs a different amount of money.

25¢	10¢	5¢	1¢	VALUE ¢
1	1	1	1	41
1	1	1	—	40
1	1	—	—	35
1	—	—	—	25
1	1	—	1	36
1	—	1	1	31
1	—	—	1	26
1	—	1	—	30
—	1	1	1	16
—	1	1	—	15
—	1	—	1	11
—	1	—	—	10
—	—	1	1	6
—	—	1	—	5
—	—	—	1	1

FIGURE 8.6. Solution 1 list.

Select a strategy. Many students will begin by making an organized list of all possible combinations of coins in some systematic manner. It should be obvious, however, that this list will be confusing to make, and they might easily miss one or more of the combinations. Let's try the problem in two ways: First, we'll make an organized list, then we'll look at this problem from another point of view.

Solve the problem. For Solution 1, we make an organized list (Figure 8.6). By systematically placing a 1 on the chart to indicate the insertion of that coin and leaving blank where no coin is inserted, we get a list that shows there are 15 ways that a candy can be priced.

For Solution 2, examine the possibility for each coin slot in succession. We notice that we have exactly two choices for each coin slot: We either put in a coin or don't. Thus, for the quarter slot, there are two possibilities: put a quarter in or don't. This is similar for the nickel slot, the dime slot, and the penny slot. Thus, there are two possibilities for each slot, or a total of $2 \cdot 2 \cdot 2 \cdot 2 = 16$ possibilities. Of course, this includes the case in which no coins are put into any of the slots. And, Joanna can't get candy for free. So, there are exactly $16 - 1 = 15$ possible combinations that the machine can offer.

Notice the elegance of this second solution. It requires some thought but provides an alternative to the list, which might have been difficult for some students to make. Both methods yield the same answer (as you would expect).

Look back. Is our arithmetic correct? Yes, $2 \cdot 2 \cdot 2 \cdot 2 = 16$ and $16 - 1 = 15$. Did we remember to remove the one situation with no coins? Yes. Did we answer the question that was asked? Yes, we found the number of different possible combinations.

Problem

Find the sum of the numbers in the 20th row of the following array. Here we are given the first five rows:

$$
\begin{array}{ccccccccc}
 & & & & 1 & & & & \\
 & & & 3 & & 5 & & & \\
 & & 7 & & 9 & & 11 & & \\
 & 13 & & 15 & & 17 & & 19 & \\
21 & & 23 & & 25 & & 27 & & 29
\end{array}
$$

Read the problem. *What are we asked to find?* We need to find the sum of the numbers in the 20th row. *What do we know?* We are given the numbers in Rows 1 through 5.

Select a strategy. We can continue writing the array until we arrive at Row 20. Then, we can add these numbers. But, it looks like there will be a large set of numbers to write and to add. Let's try to look for a pattern.

Solve the problem. Because we are not interested in the individual numbers in the 20th row but their sum, let's see what the sums are for the rows we already have (Figure 8.7).

ROW	SUM
1	1
2	8
3	27
4	64
5	125

FIGURE 8.7

The row sums appear to be the cube of the row number. Therefore, we may assume that the pattern carries through for the 20th row as well; the answer will be the cube of 20, or $20^3 = 8,000$.

Look back. Did we answer the question? Yes, we gave the sum of the numbers in Row 20. Is our arithmetic correct? Yes: $20 \cdot 20 \cdot 20 = 8,000$. A word of caution: Although in most cases it can be assumed that the pattern will carry forward to the 20th row, it is not ensured. Consider the sequence of numbers 1, 2, 4, 8, 16; the next number can be either 32 or 31, depending on the pattern you are planning to follow. In the case of 32, we are merely taking successive powers of 2; in the case of 31, we are counting the number of regions that a circle can be cut into with a successive number of straight lines, no three of which are concurrent (see p. 119).

Problem

There are two new health clubs in town, and they are offering special packages to attract new members. The Firm-It-Up Health Club will charge $25 a month plus $5 for each visit. The Trim-Tone Health Spa is offering a plan for $5 a month plus $10 a visit. If both clubs offer the same facilities, which club should Gladys join?

Read the problem. *What are we asked to find?* The problem asks us to find which club Gladys should join. *What do we know?* The Firm-It-Up charges $25 a month plus $5 a visit. The Trim-Tone charges $5 a month and $10 a visit. Both clubs have the same facilities.

Select a strategy. The data in this problem suggest that we make a table to organize the data.

Solve the problem. Let's make a table showing how much each gym will cost Gladys. As in Figure 8.8, if Gladys plans to visit the gym more than four times a month, she should join the Firm-It-Up Club; it is the better buy. For exactly four visits, the gyms will cost the same. For fewer than four visits, she should join the Trim-Tone Health Spa.

NUMBER OF VISITS PER MONTH	0	1	2	3	4	5	6	7
Firm-It-Up	$25	$30	$35	$40	$45	$50	$55	$60
Trim-Tone	$5	$15	$25	$35	$45	$55	$65	$75

FIGURE 8.8

Look back. Did we answer the question? Yes, we gave the three possibilities. Is our arithmetic correct? Yes.

As a suggestion, once the table has been made, the students can create a graph of the two situations using the data to plot the points. The graph quickly reveals that the cost is the same for four visits, and the Trim-Tone Health Spa accelerates at a much faster rate. This is an excellent visual approach to the problem.

Problem

If the area of parallelogram *EFGB* is 20, what is the area of parallelogram *ABCD* if *A* is on $\overline{EF}$ and G is on $\overline{CD}$ (Figure 8.9)?

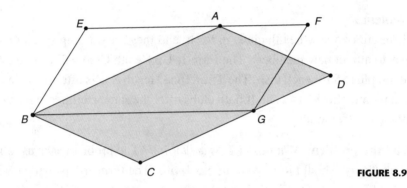

FIGURE 8.9

Read the problem. *What are we asked to find?* We are given one parallelogram's area and asked to find that of the other. *What do we know?* We know that both figures are given as parallelograms, and that a vertex of each is on the side of the other. We also know that they share the point *B*.

Select a strategy. Selecting a strategy is a difficult task here. We are accustomed to searching for congruent (or similar) triangles and that usually gets us to our desired conclusion. The use of computer drawing programs such as Geometer's Sketchpad might help us conceptualize a solution to this problem. With this program, we can move points according to the property that they were supposed to have. Let's use extremes to analyze the problem.

Solve the problem. Here, for example, the point *A* is not determined, and more precisely than that, it is on the side *EF*. We can use the using extremes strategy and assume that the point *A* is on the endpoint of the side *EF*, namely, on the point *E*. Similarly, the point *G* could coincide with the point *C*, and still all the restrictions of the given problem are being held. In that case, the two parallelograms coincide and therefore have the same area, 20.

Look back. Did we violate any of the given stipulations for the positioning of the two parallelograms? No. Did we answer the question asked? Yes.

There is a second solution that uses an auxiliary line. The skill of determining which auxiliary line to draw, or even to determine if one is necessary, comes with practice and is worth noting. Draw the line segment *AG* and have your students focus on triangle *BAG*. A quick look should indicate that this triangle is exactly half the area of each of the two paralellograms, thus making the two parallelograms equal in area. (Note that the triangle and each of the parallelograms share a common base and altitude.)

Problem

In Figure 8.10, the triangle *ABC* has its three interior angle bisectors drawn, meeting the sides at the points *D, E,* and *F.* If the angle *ABC* = 120°, find the measure of the angle *FED.*

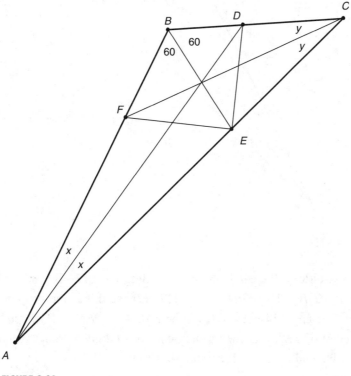

FIGURE 8.10

Read the problem. *What are we asked to find?* We are looking for the measure of the angle *FED*.

What do we know? We have angle bisectors. We should know what properties they have besides the obvious one. We should know that any point on the angle bisector is equidistant from the sides of the angle.

Select a strategy. Selecting a strategy is perhaps the most difficult part of this challenging problem. We are accustomed to looking for congruence or similarity. Neither will play a role here. Let's use working backward as a beginning. We know the property of the angle bisectors, so let's try to use it here (Figure 8.11).

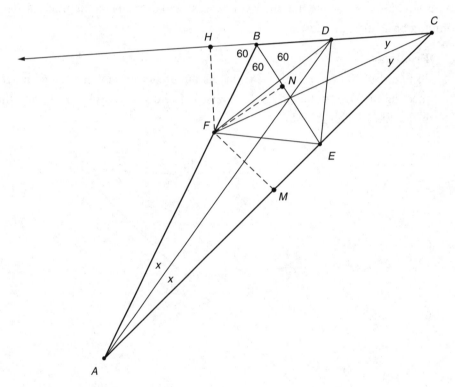

FIGURE 8.11

Solve the problem. We can begin by extending $\overline{CB}$ to *H*. Because $\angle HBF = 60°$, $\overline{BF}$ bisects $\angle HBE$. Therefore, $HF = FN$ because this is the property of the angle bisector. For angle bisector *CF*, $HF = FM$. Thus, $FN = FM$, establishing $\overline{FE}$ as the bisector of $\angle BEA$. Using an analogous procedure, we can show that $\overline{DE}$ bisects $\angle BEC$. We can then conclude that $m\angle FED = 90°$.

Look back. This problem was unusual and yet important to show students. It is unlikely that most students would solve it at first try because its technique is out of the ordinary. It does not rely on congruence or similarity and yet ought to be shown to students because it is rich in other types of reasoning. We were able to use the only property that was actually given to us (that of the angle bisector), yet we needed auxiliary line segments. Just as with the preceding problem, the use of an auxiliary line is something that comes with experience and should be used expeditiously. Students should not think that they should attempt to put such lines into a diagram as soon as a solution is not immediately forthcoming. This makes such problems of particular value because students can see the "sense" behind introducing lines to a diagram.

Some of these problems are appropriate for a middle school class and some for a high school class. The level of difficulty will determine your use of each problem and how far you would carry the discussion. Most important, you must make sure you focus solidly on the purpose of presenting each problem. Loss of focus can be a distractor from the normal curriculum work. There can be many reasons to present such problems:

- They can be a motivator for an ensuing topic in the curriculum.
- They can demonstrate (dramatically) a problem-solving strategy that will be needed for a future theme to be studied by the class.
- They can be a part of a problem-solving effort you are planning to provide for the class throughout the term, yet interspersed strategically.

Whatever their purpose, it is key that you show the appropriate enthusiasm for the elegant solutions exhibited. This will be a cue for the students to remember them for future use.

Where to Find Problems

To teach problem solving, you will need a collection of problems. We would suggest that you start a problem file. You can begin your collection with the problems discussed in this chapter. Get a package of 5×8 inch file cards. Simply write the problem on the face of a card. On the back, you can write the solution or solutions or the strategies you wish to use. You might even place a brief note of the mathematical skills needed. This enables you to decide when to use this problem. Clearly, some may want to store the problems electronically. However, remember to prepare the files so that they can be readily identified and accessed. Problems can be used by themselves to teach a strategy, or they can be used as a topic introduction to start a lesson or as a review of a topic either at the end of a lesson or at the end of a unit.

Use your textbook verbal problem exercises to create your own problems. That is, reword the problems so that they are more interesting to your students but keep the same mathematical underpinnings. For example, the following is a typical motion problem from an algebra textbook:

Problem

Two bicycle riders start from the same place at the same time. One rides at a rate of 9 miles per hour; the other rides at a rate of 6 miles per hour. If they travel in the same direction, in how many hours will they be 12 miles apart?

Now, let's see how you might revise it to make it more interesting for your students:

Reworded Problem

Derek Jeter and Alex Rodriguez are planning to ride their bicycles in the Annual Charity Marathon. They plan to start together from the starting line and ride the race together. However, they forgot that Derek rides at 9 miles per hour, and Alex rides at 6 miles per hour. They notice that they are getting farther and farther apart, so they stop after they are 12 miles apart. How many hours were they riding?

It is the same problem, but the words make it more interesting to the youngsters. (You don't have to use Derek Jeter and Alex Rodriguez. Use any local or national sports figures or movie stars whose names your students will recognize.)

Every time you see a good problem, copy it. You can find problems in the books we list in the References and Resources. The *Mathematics Teacher* and *Teaching Mathematics in Middle School* are two excellent journals of the NCTM. Each contains a set of problems every month; many of these problems will make excellent additions to your problem deck. If you attend a professional meeting, then some of the speakers will suggest problems to use. Online access to various Web sites will also provide you with some problems. Keep adding to your deck. It will grow rapidly and become a valuable resource for you.

Problem of the Week

Some teachers have instituted a "problem of the week" contest in their classes. Each Monday morning, a problem is placed in an appropriate position somewhere in the classroom. Students are encouraged to take the problem home, solve it, and then bring back their solutions. The problem is solved in class on Friday with everyone taking part. With your department head's permission, you might want to set up a Problem of the Week section on the department's bulletin board, and each week list the successful solvers along with the solution. You will find many students try to solve the problem.

Rewards can be given for a correct solution. In some schools, the mathematics department has purchased pencils with the school name and the phrase "POW—Problem of the Week" to give as rewards to the first 10 students who submit a correct and complete solution each week. Those who submit the most solutions by the end of the semester should be recognized in a school publication or rewarded in some analogous way.

Many students will take the Problem of the Week home and solve it with a parent's help, which is fine. It is another way to involve the parents in their child's work. Of course, you should insist that each student explain her solution in writing or orally to see that the student does, indeed, understand it. You can find sources for such problems in a variety of places (see References and Resources).

Review of the Process

Let's review the steps, or heuristics, for teaching students how to solve problems.

There are many heuristic models in use today. Most mathematics textbook series have one. Many have four steps, as we have used in this chapter. When you teach the use of this heuristic model, there are several thoughts and questions for you to consider. Notice that the questions are given in the first person, so that the teacher is included in the problem-solving process.

Read

What is this problem about? Have the students read the problem several times. Then, ask someone to explain what is happening in the problem, but in his own words. Sometimes, you may have to ask them to talk about the meaning of key words, such as sum, difference, greater than, and the like. Having students explain the problem in their own words ensures that the problem is understood.

What are the facts we are given? Have the students actually list the given information. As they do this, many students will begin to see the relationships that exist among the various items of data in the problem. Ask the students to locate and explain any key words.

What are we asked to find? Students must decide which question they are to answer.

Do we have sufficient information to solve the problem? The students should look carefully at what has been given to decide if something is missing. If so, this is a good time to ask them what information they need and why they cannot resolve the problem situation.

Is there anything extra in the problem? The students should decide if all the information given is necessary in solving the problem. Is anything superfluous? Often, there are extra pieces of information intended as distracters.

Select a Strategy

Have we ever seen a problem like this one? If the students recognize the problem as one they have seen before or of a type that they have encountered before, then they can try to use the same method of attack as previously used to solve the problem.

If we have, what method or strategy worked last time? If not, which of our strategies might we try? The students begin their search for an acceptable strategy, one that will solve the problem. They may have to examine the entire list of strategies that they have been taught. You can ask questions to lead them to the most effective strategy.

Solve the Problem

Where do we start (with the solution)? The students need a starting point. It may be as simple as asking if they add, subtract, multiply, or divide. Or, it might be necessary to change strategies.

Do we need more than one strategy? If the students are bogged down with a single approach, then you might suggest that they add a second strategy and approach the problem from a different perspective.

Look Back

Have we indicated what our answer is? Rather than leaving it to the reader to guess at the answer, be certain that the answer is clearly marked and clearly indicated.

Have we answered the question that the problem asked? The students must be certain that they have actually answered the original question. Often, they find a value for a variable and give that as their answer when that is not the answer to the actual question asked, but rather the step just before the answer is reached. You should ask the students what the original question was and whether they have answered it.

Have we put the correct units into our answer? Although one may argue that the question "How many inches...?" requires only a number as the number of inches, the students should get into the habit of putting the correct units into their answer.

Is our arithmetic correct? Have the class go back and check their work. Make certain that they have done it correctly. Students sometimes become careless in this part of the process and regard it as a mere formality. It definitely is not. The work should be carefully checked for accuracy.

Does our answer make sense? An answer, for example, of 340 feet for the length of a desk hardly makes sense. Perhaps the answer was really 3.4. If the answer does not make sense, then go back and check the work again.

Are we able to explain our work? As more and more tests include problem solving and open-ended questions, the students must be able to communicate what they did and why they chose to do it that way. Be certain that the students can explain their work clearly. Whereas in the past many tests required a specific procedure to solve a problem, there is an increasing trend to allow any method of solution as long as the students can explain *what* they have done and *why* they used that method.

9

THE RESPONSIBILITY OF ASSESSMENT

It is the responsibility of every teacher to determine the extent to which students are learning. *Principles and Standards for School Mathematics* (National Council of Teachers of Mathematics, 2000) states that assessment "should support the learning of important mathematics and furnish useful information to both teachers and students" (p. 11). Assessment should be thought of in two ways: evaluative and diagnostic. Both are of equal importance, especially to the teacher.

Evaluative Assessment

Although there are many ways to determine if students comprehend concepts, testing has always been the primary means of evaluation. With the renewed emphasis on benchmark testing, it is crucial for teachers to master the art and craft of assessment so that they may evaluate each student's progress and gauge the effectiveness of their own teaching. In addition, teachers must prepare their students for these ever-increasing benchmark examinations. Constructing a "good test" requires thoughtful planning and careful design. A poorly designed examination can be a frustrating and wasteful experience for both the student and the teacher. It also engenders ill will, anger, resentment, and distrust. It is important to embrace the notion that a good examination should make students feel good about their learning and reward them for their diligence in preparing homework and studying regularly.

Always keep in mind that each exam is an opportunity to gain valuable insight into how your students are thinking about mathematics, and to assess your approach in presenting these concepts to them. To do this, however, you must take many factors into account before designing the examination. Remember, too, that testing is only one way to assess student progress.

> It is important to consider that over the course of a year, teachers can build in many opportunities to assess how students are learning, and then use this information to make beneficial changes in instruction. This diagnostic use of assessment to provide feedback to teachers and students over the course of instruction is called formative assessment. It stands in contrast to summative or evaluative assessment, which generally takes place after a period of instruction and requires making a judgment about the learning that has occurred (e.g., by grading or scoring a test or paper). (Boston, 2002)

Diagnostic Assessment

It is important that you determine how well you have taught your lessons and how well your students are grasping the concepts and skills that you have presented. What are their weaknesses? Do they understand the concepts? Are they reasoning through the problems? Did you teach the concepts in a clear, understandable manner? How can you help each student? These questions are all part of an ongoing process of classroom assessment. By answering them, you can become a better teacher.

When most teachers think of assessment, they are thinking about summative or evaluative assessment, commonly known as the *classroom test*. The other evidentiary tools of student progress include classroom participation, the nature and quality of student questioning and discourse. Evaluating students based on their class work, homework, and group work is also an effective way to assess student progress. Thus, it is important to use a variety of assessment tools to determine what students have learned and have not learned, in other words, to diagnose their weaknesses and identify their strengths.

In "Assessment Crisis: The Absence of Assessment FOR Learning," Richard J. Stiggins (2002) states, "If we wish to maximize student achievement in the U.S., we must pay far greater attention to the improvement of classroom assessment. Both assessment *of learning* and assessment *for learning* are essential. One is in place; the other is not." Stiggins highlights the need for formative or diagnostic assessment to take a leading role in guiding instruction. Even evaluative testing can be diagnostic as long as the teacher interprets the results of the examination to modify instructional practices. Providing students with more support when necessary, and retesting them, is an ideal situation.

Second-opportunity assessments are a good way to send a clear message that we value the mathematics that we are teaching even if students do not demonstrate proficiency on their first assessment. Of course, we want students to demonstrate mastery on the first try, but simply moving on without providing remediation and the opportunity for further assessment does not provide a solid foundation for future success in mathematics. This second-opportunity assessment does not have to take the same form as the first assessment. Its purpose is to encourage the student to learn the material and demonstrate mastery. This will strengthen the skills of the community of learners and fortify the foundations of the learning community.

It is unrealistic to expect students to succeed when you have identified conceptual weaknesses in the building blocks for learning but have not corrected them. By appropriately identifying learning outcomes as realistic goals that are set in collaboration with students, you can evaluate progress in a systematic fashion and provide support if necessary. Stiggins (2002) asks, "How can we use assessments to help all our students want to learn? How can we help them feel able to learn?"

Designing the Classroom Test

There are a few overriding principles that should govern the administration and grading of an exam. First, students are to be evaluated based on their proficiency with concepts and skills. Your purpose is not to compare students with each other but to assess their individual progress toward clearly defined concepts and performance indicators. Of course, grades can eventually be used to compare students, but you are not filling a quota or limiting the number of As and Bs, as has been the practice in many schools (and universities) for centuries. Students are competing against themselves in an effort to demonstrate mastery of concepts and skills.

As stated, the teacher-made classroom test is still the major evaluative assessment device used in most classrooms, and it is crucial that you learn how to construct a good one. The major issues to consider before constructing an exam are discussed next. First, be clear (to yourself) which mathematical concepts and skills you are testing. That is, what do you want your students to have learned from the unit being tested? Then, consider the following:

1. The exam format (layout, answer on test paper or elsewhere, etc.).
2. The varying levels of difficulty of the test items (is the class gifted, average, or heterogeneously grouped?).
3. The types of test items (multiple choice, extended response, proofs, questions requiring a calculator, etc.).
4. The placement of the questions (ordering the test items by difficulty, by subject, etc.).
5. The scoring rubric and the awarding of partial credit (alternate solutions considered).
6. The use of technology (if any).
7. The possibility for extra credit problems (you may want to challenge those students who complete the exam with time to spare).
8. The time constraints under which the students must work.

The first step in designing a test is to determine which mathematical concepts and skills are to be tested. In addition, you want to determine how you can differentiate various levels of understanding and mastery. Your goals and objectives for the exam can be narrow and focus on a few concepts and skills or address a wider range of topics. If you are not clear about your objectives for this exam, then it will be difficult for you to articulate what students should study and how they should prepare for the text. You should also take into consideration the grading of the examination as you consider its design. All tests must be graded carefully and returned the next day or at the latest the day after that if the results are to be used in a thoughtful and meaningful way to improve instruction. Adolescents have a tendency to lose interest in correcting their mistakes after a few days.

Now that you have determined the topics to be covered on the exam and the timeline for its grading and its return to your students, you must decide on the types of questions that you might ask. Although the timely grading of the examination is important, this is not meant to imply that you should design a test solely consisting of multiple-choice and short-answer questions that can easily be graded and returned. Multiple-choice and short-answer test items have been promoted as "objective" because the scorer (sometimes a machine) cannot make a judgment about the correctness of an answer but simply must mark it right or wrong. Although this may be true, many claim that multiple-choice tests are designed to be "tricky," with "distractors" designed to trap students. Yet, distractors play a role in ensuring that the student understands the concept. In addition, the lack of partial credit makes them unforgiving and usually not suitable for a classroom test. Teachers cannot learn as much about their students from multiple-choice test items as they can from extended-response questions, answers to which clearly show a student's work. Thus, with multiple-choice questions, the benefits of easy scoring and a quick turnaround time are offset by these negative factors. For example, consider the following question:

The area of a triangle with sides that are 3, 4, and 5 cm is (a) 6 cm²; (b) 12 cm²; (c) 17 cm²; (d) 15 cm².

Notice that the student must know the formula for the area of a right triangle and recognize that the triangle here is a right triangle. If the student knows the correct formula but chooses an incorrect answer such as (b), then you may not know the reason for the student's choice. Was the student using the formula for perimeter? Or, was there an arithmetic error, such as forgetting to divide by 2? Or, does the student not know the correct formula to use?

Barry Cherkas (1993) devised a way to award partial credit on a multiple-choice test; credit is based on the quality of the choice of the distractor. He refers to this practice as *humanizing the multiple-choice test*. It should be noted that this is a particularly difficult examination to design. It typically can only be constructed after using the same question in an extended-response format with a similar audience and then determining and selecting the most appropriate distractors. A more rudimentary method for awarding partial credit on multiple-choice tests is to require that the students show all their work. This may seem to counterbalance the notion of a multiple-choice test because the teacher must now carefully examine each question and solution; however, it can provide valuable feedback to teachers about their students' progress.

The extended-response question requires the student to demonstrate some thought and mastery of the concept and to convey this understanding in writing to the scorer. It provides the best opportunity for students to display evidence of their understanding of the major concepts. The following are some extended-response questions that allow the teacher to assess students' understanding of specific concepts and theorems in geometry related to angle measurement in an isosceles triangle.

Problem

1. The measure of the exterior angle at the base of an isosceles triangle is 130°. Find the measure of the vertex angle of this triangle. (Show all work.)
2. The measure of the base angle of an isosceles triangle exceeds the measure of the vertex angle by 27°. Find the measure of the vertex angle of the triangle. (Show all work.)
3. The vertex angle of an isosceles triangle has a measure of 56°. Find the vertex angle of the isosceles triangle formed by the base angle bisectors and the base of the given triangle. (Show all work.)

Here is a question involving middle school algebra:

Problem

John's father is 45 years old. He is 15 years older than twice John's age. How old is John?

Each of the questions could easily be presented in multiple-choice format. However, because of the calculations and the algebra embedded in these problems, the teacher would not be able to determine if an incorrect answer was caused by a simple calculation error or a more serious conceptual error. Thus, the opportunity for diagnostic assessment would have been squandered by employing the multiple-choice design. Presenting these questions as extended-response questions allows the teacher to determine clearly the students' understanding of the associated theorems and concepts. In addition, by examining the student responses, the teacher can better design materials to support remediation of concepts and skills if appropriate.

The Scoring Rubric

Do not let the term *scoring rubric* scare you. In reality, teachers have been using scoring rubrics for years without using the name. That is, we have always given partial credit for what was correct when students solved an extended-response question that did not result in the correct answer. All a rubric does is make certain that everyone knows what each part of the answer is worth so that there is consistency in grading. Consider the following question:

Solve $x^2 - 4x + 1 = 0$ by completing the square. (12 points)
(a) Subtract 1 from both sides of the equation: $x^2 - 4x = -1$
(b) Take one-half the coefficient of x and square it: $(-2)^2 = 4$
(c) Add this to both sides of the equation: $x^2 - 4x + 4 = -1 + 4$
(d) Express the left side as a perfect square: $(x - 2)^2 = 3$
(e) Take the square root of each side: $x - 2 = \pm\sqrt{3}$
(f) Add 2 to both sides of the equation: $x = 2 \pm\sqrt{3}$

The suggested rubric for the question is as follows:

a. Student successfully forms the appropriate perfect trinomial square. (6 points)
b. Student forms an incorrect perfect trinomial square. (3–4 points)
c. Student converts perfect trinomial square to $(x - 2)^2 = 3$. (2 points)
d. Student successfully takes the square root of both sides of the equation and gets two solutions (Step e). (2 points)
e. Student finds both solutions (Step f). (2 points)

Notice that this question contains many concepts and skills, each of which must be carried out flawlessly to determine the solution set (see a similar example in Chapter 5). However, the question must have a scoring rubric that is designed to reward students for understanding the mathematically rich, multistep process and to penalize them gently for less-egregious errors in calculation. When you mark an exam, always follow the scoring rubric. And when you return the exam to your students, give them a copy of the rubric that was used. There are several reasons to do this:

1. The importance of each step in the process should be quantified. Students can use this information to concentrate on the major concepts and refine their skills. When you return examinations to your students, this is the time when they are most curious regarding what they got wrong and why. Take advantage of this "dynamic" and provide the scoring key and rubric to them.

2. Assessment should be transparent. Students should feel like they have been treated fairly and equally. It is often difficult to make adolescents believe that they have been treated equally without supplying evidence. The rubric ensures that everyone getting the same things right and wrong will receive the same scores. Students should feel comfortable knowing what they got wrong, why it was wrong, and the consequences for having gotten it wrong. Incidentally, reinforcement of work done correctly is also important.

3. The rubric provides a clearly defined road map for successfully completing the problem. Ideally, we would like every exam item to be reviewed in class. However, there are circumstances that may prevent this. By distributing the scoring rubric, we enable students to learn how to complete each problem in a step-by-step, systematic fashion, on their own if necessary.

Let's look back at the three geometry problems presented on page 157. Consider the first one:

Problem

1. The measure of the exterior angle at the base of an isosceles triangle is 130°. Find the measure of the vertex angle of this triangle. (Show all work—15 points.)

Here is a scoring rubric for this problem:

a. Draws a triangle and represents the given angle measurement. (4 points)
b. Finds the measure of the supplement to the exterior angle (the base angle). (3 points)
c. Uses the base angles theorem to find the measure of the other base angle. (3 points)
d. Uses the sum-of-the-angles-of-a-triangle theorem to find the measure of the vertex angle. (5 points)

Let's consider the next problem.

Problem

2. The measure of the base angle of an isosceles triangle exceeds the measure of the vertex angle by 27°. Find the measure of the vertex angle of the triangle. (Show all work—15 points.)

Here is a scoring rubric for this problem:

a. Draws a diagram of a triangle and represents the measures of the vertex angle and the base angles algebraically. (6 points)
b. Uses the algebraic representation of the vertex and base angles to write an equation that represents the sum of the angles of a triangle. (4 points)
c. Solves the equation and finds the measure of the vertex angle. (5 points)

Again, the rubric provides the teacher and the students with a step-by-step method for a solution to this problem and indicates the value for each step along the way.

Problem

3. The vertex angle of an isosceles triangle has a measure of 56°. Find the vertex angle of the isosceles triangle formed by the base angle bisectors and the base of the given triangle. (Show all work—20 points.)

Here is a scoring rubric for this problem:

a. Draws the original triangle and the angle bisectors of the base angles. Identifies the intersection of the angle bisectors and identifies the newly created isosceles triangle with sides that are segments of the angle bisectors and the base (Figure 9.1). (8 points)
b. Determines the degree measure of each of the base angles of the original triangle and the degree measure of each of the base angles formed by the angle bisectors of the original base angles. (7 points)
c. Determines the degree measure of the angles formed by the base of the original triangle and the angle bisectors of the base angles. (5 points)

When handing back a test, you may want to ask selected students to write their solutions on the board. Alternatively, students can write their solutions on transparencies or prepare solutions on their laptop computers. You can preselect students to share their solutions as you grade the set of exams, ensuring that students of varying abilities have an opportunity to display their work. If you encounter a clever solution to a problem, then you can have that student share her solution with the class as well. On a well-designed exam, a majority of the students should get most of the questions correct. Thus, it may only take a short while for students to

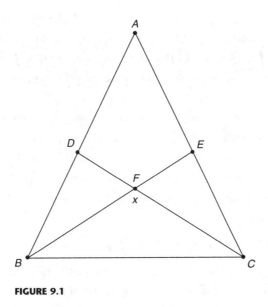

FIGURE 9.1

see their errors and make corrections to their work. Test review and analysis should not consume an entire period. You can have students correct their mistakes at home. This activity, along with the distribution of the scoring rubric, supports the notion that assessment should be formative. In some instances, you may wish to hand out model solutions to the class.

One way to take advantage of the increased motivation that accompanies the return of graded tests is to create second-opportunity assessments for each student. For example, if you have given a geometry test containing the three items in the problem examples, you might identify five or six similar problems for each of the three questions. Should a student lose 10 points for missing out on a major concept in Question 1, you may employ a second-opportunity assessment that will allow that student to "buy back" 5 or 6 of those points by successfully completing a number of exercises similar to those the student got wrong. Again, keep in mind that the goal of assessment is to inform teachers and students of student progress with an eye toward improving instruction and redefining goals for student performance. If this test revealed a weakness that could not be overcome with dedicated practice problems, then a more aggressive academic intervention strategy may be more appropriate. Regrettably, teachers sometimes send the message that the assessment signifies the end of a learning cycle. The assessment is an important benchmark in the learning cycle but certainly not the end of it. Rather, formative assessment is an opportunity for teachers, students, and parents to reflect on student progress, teaching strategies, student work ethics, and support services with the goal of identifying those aspects that are working well and pinpointing those aspects that need improvement.

The results of a test provide an important opportunity for you to assess your teaching. If the majority of your students get a particular problem wrong, then you have to examine the problem carefully. Was it too difficult? Or, perhaps you hurriedly taught the concepts and failed to assess student progress throughout the lesson. In any case, both good and disappointing test results should serve as a means to assess your teaching.

Selecting and the Ordering of Questions

The first thing to do when preparing a classroom math test is to make a list of what you expect students to know about the topic tested (i.e., the instructional objectives). This is the time when you determine the *relative* importance of the various skills and concepts that have been discussed and presented in class.

Once you have decided which topics are to be tested, you must decide how you wish to test them. Some concepts or skills can be tested with simple, short-answer test items. You may still wish to require students to show their work to allow for partial credit and, more importantly, to allow you to examine their work and gain insight into their understanding. Other topics may require extended responses to determine mastery of the concepts. Try to create a mental inventory of the concepts and skills that can be assessed with short-answer test items and those that require extended responses. The typical assessment places the short-answer questions at the beginning of the exam and the extended-response items after these. Avoid asking unusual or tricky questions that do not truly test the concepts covered in class. Tricky questions tend to give inferences that are not directly tied to the material presented in class. You are not out to trap the students but to give them an opportunity to demonstrate how much of the work they have really mastered. For example, consider the following test item to assess students' knowledge of the Pythagorean theorem.

Problem

At 12:00 noon, a jogger heads due north from the town of Mathville at a constant pace of 1 mile every 6 minutes. At 1:00 p.m., a bicyclist heads due east at the rate of 16 miles per hour. If they both continue at a constant rate, then how many miles apart will they be at 6:00 p.m.?

Although this problem may seem relatively benign and is a solid problem-solving exercise, there are many characteristics about it that students may find tricky and may overlook during the pressure of a classroom test. This problem is unsuitable for testing a student's knowledge of the Pythagorean theorem. The units of measure are different, and a student might miss this; the bicyclist is traveling in miles per hour; the jogger is traveling in miles per minute. This could easily be overlooked or misinterpreted. Keep your questions simple, not convoluted; be sure the questions test the concept you are examining and do not have distractors in the questions themselves.

It is important to prepare the questions on a test in such a way that they create a smooth flow for the test taker. Much like a television quiz show, the first few questions should be the easiest to help the students relax, get into a rhythm, and develop confidence. Think back to the standardized tests that you have taken in your lifetime, and you will recall that every "professionally designed" test begins with easy problems and concludes with the most challenging ones. This technique for test design is employed to follow the natural learning curve that we employ daily in our classrooms. A good test should reflect your classroom work and not be a series of surprises.

Timing the Test

Creating a test is a daunting task for even the most experienced teachers. After you have decided on the content to be covered on the exam, you may find that it is difficult to include everything on the test. The most common mistake made by inexperienced teachers is creating exams that attempt to test too many concepts and skills, often repetitively. Occasionally, an exam is constructed that is simply too long. Regrettably, the discovery that an exam may be too long usually takes place during its administration. To avoid a catastrophe like this, we recommend that you have your test previewed by one or two veteran teachers who can share their opinions. Simply asking for an opinion from your supervisor or a few colleagues should provide sufficient feedback to ensure that your test is meaningful, and that success or failure does not depend solely on the student's ability to work quickly. Remember, you are testing concepts, problem solving, and skills. It is inappropriate to make this a speed drill. A mathematical problem should require a student to ponder one or two methods of solution and choose one that will deliver the solution efficiently. An exercise is simply a mathematics problem for which the method of solution is already known. Obviously, problem solving is desirable over completing exercises. (See Chapter 8 for a further discussion of problem solving.) Skills, which are important, can usually be mastered through the completion of a series of exercises. Problem solving, however, requires careful analysis and thought and is an art form that should be woven into the fabric of mathematics instruction and beyond.

Other things to consider in timing your exam include the amount of writing the students will be required to do to answer the questions. Will they be required to draw intricate diagrams (especially in geometry)? Will calculators be required for sections of the exam? If so, will the students be required to justify their solutions in addition to using the calculator? These factors can affect the timing of the examination. In a well-designed exam, all students should have adequate time to complete the questions and have at least 5 minutes remaining to check their work.

One way you can create a "buffer" to deal with the time issue is to include an extra credit problem on the exam. Those students who complete the exam quickly have an additional problem to work on. It should be mentioned here that an extra credit problem should not be worth many points, perhaps only 5 points extra on a 100-point examination. Students should have a clear priority in completing the exam and checking their solutions before attempting the extra credit problem. The purpose of the extra credit problem is to keep students engaged in the examination and not to overly reward students for working quickly.

Because you are designing the assessment, be mindful that you already know the method of solution and, in many cases, the actual answer. You should sit down with a blank piece of paper and take the exam as if you were a student. That is, read the examination paper as your students will, draw the diagrams, and write out the detailed solutions. A general rule for timing an exam is that you should be able to complete an exam that is 45 minutes long in about 8–15 minutes, depending on the amount of writing required. If it takes you longer than 8–15 minutes to complete it, then the exam may be too long.

Preparing Your Students for the Test

It is natural for teachers to want their students to perform well on a test. When your students perform well on your assessments, it reaffirms the effectiveness of your professional practice and rewards students who have studied diligently. It is extremely important to make it clear which topics, concepts, and skills are to be assessed. Although the students do not need to know the exact questions on the test, they are entitled to know the nature of the questions and the criteria for success. The NCTM Assessment Standards (1995) include the Openness Standard, which states, "Before their learning is assessed in a formal way, all students are informed about what they need to know, how they will be expected to demonstrate that knowledge, and what the consequences of assessment will be." You should prepare your students for their tests by following these guidelines:

1. *Announce the test a few days ahead of time.* This will allow the students to plan their studying accordingly. Remember, mathematics is not the only subject that they are taking. There are many demands made on a student's time from other academic classes and extracurricular activities. It is desirable to allow students to have a weekend to prepare for a test.

2. *Give homework assignments that include review material* (see Designing the Homework Assignment in Chapter 5). You can also provide your students with a copy of last year's examination on the same topic or create a comprehensive review sheet for the exam. Providing a comprehensive review sheet is an effective way of motivating students to prepare for an examination. The added benefit of the comprehensive review sheet is that many students will attempt to master every question on the sheet. Of course, your exam will only be a subset of the concepts and skills contained on the comprehensive review sheet, but it is hoped your students will have mastered all of its items, so that you have further extrinsically motivated learning.

3. *Clearly articulate what will be covered on the test.* You can do this by indicating page numbers from the textbook or the relevant homework assignments. Designing tests that are based on a series of homework assignments supports the Openness Standard of the NCTM and benefits students by providing a snapshot of their weaknesses. Furthermore, we want students to view homework not only as a task that does not end with the completion of the assignment but also as a tool that prepares them for their tests and their success in more advanced topics in mathematics.

4. *Inform students about the format of the exam.* The practice helps to minimize anxiety, an unnecessary distractor for the test. For instance, you may indicate

that there are 10 short-answer responses and two extended-response problems. In addition, you should inform them about the policy on the use of calculators for the exam. Some exams are administered in two parts; calculator active and non-calculator active. Tell them what they must bring to the test, including pencils, straightedge, compasses, calculators, and so on.

5. *Consider making some time after school for individual tutoring for students with specific questions or weaknesses.* Encourage students to monitor their progress through their success with the homework assignments. It is important that the student receive support in advance of the test. Use of a buddy system is another way to provide all students with an opportunity to have some questions answered. Assigning buddies with a common lunch period is an effective way for students to provide one another with support. There is no better way to solidify knowledge of concepts than to teach them.

Informing Students of Their Grades

After you have administered an examination and graded it in a timely fashion, you have to inform students of their grades. The process of returning examinations should include some opportunity for communication between the teacher and the student. Students may have questions about how the test was scored. One technique is to return their examinations along with a copy of the solutions and scoring rubric.

With younger students, it is advisable to ask a parent, guardian, or another adult to sign each test paper (to verify that they have seen it) so that they can be kept up to date on their child's progress and to enlist their help in providing support as necessary. The report card should not be the first time parents learn of their child's successes or difficulties in mathematics.

Improving Their Test Scores

Several support mechanisms exist to help struggling students. Many schools have a tutoring center for student remediation. Some parents are willing to seek private tutors for their children. You may wish to compile a list of recommended private tutors based on positive feedback that you receive from parents and students. This is more desirable than asking parents to find a competent tutor on their own.

Most parents are uninformed when it comes to finding an effective mathematics tutor. Private tutors who are recommended by you will be familiar with school policy and more likely to support your methods as well as your homework, testing, and grading policies.

Many school districts have a policy that forbids teachers to accept compensation for tutoring a student who attends their school. In addition, you should never tutor a student in your class for compensation. This would present a conflict of interest.

Assessing Your Assessment

Every teacher should take a moment to reflect on the success of a class on a given test. Significant response trends can reveal a poorly worded, ambiguous question. They can also detect a serious flaw in your presentation of the material. Teachers should perform an item analysis[1] of each question on their test to determine if the question was fair. Suppose that, in a class of 32 students, 20 of them get a particular question wrong. Effective test design should not allow for a significant percentage of a class to be incapable of answering a question. You must analyze and determine the characteristics of this question that prevented students from responding to it successfully. Was the question worded properly? Was the question exceptionally tricky, or did it have excessive distractors? Was this topic and similar questions included in the homework assignments? Was this topic (and the page numbers) included in the advance notice of the test? After careful analysis, you may conclude that you have to reteach the topic, especially if it is a prerequisite for other topics.

Another valuable way to evaluate your assessment instrument is to ask the students for their impressions of the test before it is returned to them. Students will be quick to share with you their feelings of preparedness for an exam from a variety of perspectives:

1. Did the test cover the expected topics?
2. Were problems on this test closely related to the homework assignments preceding the examination?
3. Were the test items of the same level of difficulty as those given for homework or done in class?

4. Were those topics adequately taught?
5. Was the test properly timed?

If the answer to any of these five items is no, then the students may rightfully feel that they were assessed (tested) unfairly. You can distribute an anonymous survey to gauge students' feelings about the test items, their appropriateness, and your instruction prior to the exam. You will find that students are willing to accept accountability for their success and failure if you have followed the recommendations contained in this chapter. You can share the results of this survey with the class. Some students who are not successful may wish to place the blame for their failure on you or some other external factor. Conducting and sharing the results of the survey with the class informs particular students that their peers found the test fair and appropriate. This form of shared responsibility will give your class a good feeling about your constant desire to provide fair evaluations.

The Class Did Poorly—Should You Curve Your Exam?

One of the most discouraging events for any teacher is grading a class set of exams only to learn that the class did poorly. This is a sensitive situation that requires a tactful solution. You may have to deal with frustrated students, parents, and, perhaps, administrators. If you feel confident that you have complied with the five items listed in the preceding section, then you should not curve the test scores. If you have inadvertently contributed to this situation, then adjusting the scores is appropriate. Here are some possible models to adjust (curve) test scores.

Many teachers curve their grades by changing the scoring rubric after an exam has been administered. One way to make an adjustment is to be more generous with partial credit on extended-response questions. Of course, this option is not available if the test is comprised primarily of short-answer questions. One method for adjusting grades on a short-answer exam is to employ a dynamic scoring model. Let's consider a multiple-choice exam that contained 25 items. Assume each item was originally worth four points. After administering the exam, you notice that your best students, who typically score at the top of the class, have done poorly. You can now adjust the scoring by creating a table that deducts points according to the model in Figure 9.2.

NUMBER OF WRONG RESPONSES	POINT DEDUCTION
1–2	2 points each
3–5	2 points for the first two wrong; 3 points for the remaining wrong responses
6+	13 points subtracted for the first 5 wrong; 4 points subtracted for each additional wrong response

FIGURE 9.2. Scoring adjustment.

This adjustment results in shifting the grades slightly higher. Some prefer this model to other curving models that provide the greatest rewards for the least proficient. This model rewards everyone but is not skewed to overly reward those with the greatest weakness. This scoring model may counterbalance the unforgiving nature of multiple-choice questions that allow for no partial credit. Figure 9.3 shows how this curving model actually affects typical scores on the 25-question exam.

Another model, which is much simpler, uses the square root times 10. This model takes the square root of each grade and multiplies it by 10 to arrive at the adjusted score. For example, a score of 81 would be adjusted to a 90, a score of 64 would be adjusted to an 80, and a score of 42 would be adjusted to a 65. Notice that this model disproportionately rewards students with the lowest scores.

NUMBER CORRECT OUT OF 25	ORIGINAL SCORE, %	ADJUSTED SCORE, %
25	100	100
24	96	98
23	92	96
22	88	93
21	84	90
20	80	87
19	76	83
18	72	79
17	68	75
16	64	71
15	60	67
14	56	63

FIGURE 9.3. Effect of model on scores.

The second-opportunity assessment can also serve as a way to curve test scores. This model gives students another chance to demonstrate proficiency and rewards them for doing so.

Another effective model is to offer students the opportunity to take a supplemental examination, on the same material, after school. The results of this test can be averaged with the earlier exam to curve the grade.

You will notice that discarding an exam was not presented as an option. It is rarely desirable to nullify the results of an entire exam. This sends a message to the class that they control the destiny of the assessment, and that if they collectively do poorly, they will not be held accountable. Discarding an exam should be reserved only for the most extreme situations, like the occurrence of fire drills during the test or whenever the integrity of the exam has been compromised through a security breach or cheating.

Testing Students of Varying Ability Levels

Although differentiated instructional models are promoted as a way to provide instruction to students with varying skill degrees within a class, formal assessment of these students is challenging. The question of equity presents itself when a talented-and-gifted child is placed with a group of average students. Should a gifted learner be expected to do more on the assessment? Before creating your policy, talk with your supervisor and other experienced teachers to see if a school or district policy already exists. One assessment model that you can consider is to test these children on the same core concepts as the entire class and then provide an additional assessment component that can be used to judge progress on their advanced studies.

Handling Absentees on Test Days

The most effective strategy for dealing with exam day absenteeism is to prevent it. One method is to require a parent or guardian to phone the school the morning of the absence. The adult should also leave a contact number so that you can schedule the make-up exam early in the day or during a free period on the student's first day back in school. This reduces, but does not eliminate, the opportunity for communication between students. Whenever possible, you should not allow students to miss your math class to take a make-up exam. Make-up tests should not be the same test that was originally administered. Although it is a burden to prepare a new exam for a few absentee students, it is the only way to make the assessment process equitable.

Comprehensive Assessment

Much of what we teach has changed from skill-oriented instruction to an emphasis on problem solving and reasoning. It stands to reason, then, that assessment must also change to enable you to examine the thought processes of your students. In this chapter, we referred to formative assessment and summative assessment. We use the term *comprehensive assessment* to encompass both types because this provides a comprehensive view of how well students are doing. Although the classroom test is still the mainstay of your assessment program, there have been great strides in using alternative methods for assessing student progress. Many books refer to these as *alternative assessments*. However, this is sometimes a bit of a misnomer because they are not used as alternatives to testing but in addition to tests. You should become acquainted with various assessment devices and use them as well as regular examinations whenever appropriate. You can find much written material on comprehensive/alternative assessment. Some of the more prominent ones are discussed next.

Informal Observations

Teachers have always made use of informal observations. When you are teaching your class, you are always watching your students. Just seeing the look on a student's face that says, "Aha! I get it!" is an informal observation. Similarly, the frown on a student's face that says, "I don't understand," is another informal observation. What makes this type of assessment noteworthy is what the teacher does with it. If a student's look indicates that the student does not understand something, then you can seize the moment and reteach the material. If a student gives an unusually thoughtful answer to a question or asks a thought-provoking question, then you should make a brief note of it. You can make this note on your seating chart or in your student record book. The note might take the form of simply a + or − symbol. Or, you can write a brief note, such as, "Johnny asked a terrific question today," and note the date as an informal observation. Similarly, a note such as "Mary really did a good job with the homework problem" and the date is another observation. At the end of the marking period, these brief observations can help you obtain a more complete picture of your students than simple use of their tests scores alone.

Portfolios

Portfolios are not new. For years, professionals such as fashion models, architects, and artists have used them. In the field of mathematics education, they are relatively new. A portfolio is a collection of a student's best work as decided on by the student with your guidance. For example, you might ask students to select three of their best homework assignments for inclusion in their portfolios. Or, you could include a book report on a famous mathematician. You can even have the students include an unusual solution to a difficult problem-solving exercise. If the students have worked on and presented a group project, then the summary of their work can be included. The students should feel free to include anything else they think should be there to show off their work.

Physically, the portfolio is a manila folder, cardboard folder, large envelope, or even a loose-leaf notebook into which the student puts her work. The portfolio is usually kept in the student's possession so that it can be shared with parents at home. Although you should examine the portfolio and make suggestions to the students, grading a portfolio is discouraged. Imagine how a child might feel on receiving a grade of C for what he considers his best work.

The main purpose of the portfolio is to demonstrate progress as the school year progresses. In many secondary schools, the portfolio moves along with the student as the student progresses through the grades. In this way, teachers can examine the student's past work. In fact, there are even some colleges that are now examining student portfolios as one criterion for admission.

Notebooks

Every student must keep a mathematics notebook and bring it to class every day. Although it need not be an actual notebook (many teachers prefer the students to use a section of a loose-leaf binder for mathematics), each student should have an ongoing record of what has been taught throughout the year. You should have the students begin each day's notes by putting the date of the lesson in the margin. The students then take careful notes on what is taught. The class work and problems done in class should be in the notebook. This provides the students with an excellent vehicle when they study for an exam.

At least once in each marking period you should collect the student notebooks and grade them. You should look for answers to the following questions when you grade a notebook.

1. Is the notebook neatly done?
2. Are the notes complete? Completeness will vary from student to student. Some students only write down things they do not understand. Others try to incorporate every word that was said in class. Every student, however, should show some work for each day in class. They should show the activity that was used to start the lesson. They should write down the topic of the lesson taught that day. They might even wish to show how they worked on problems throughout the lesson.
3. Will the student be able to study from the notes? When students prepare for an exam, the first thing they should consult is the notebook. If they have taken good, complete notes, then they will be able to use the notebook for review. The class notes should provide an outline of what to study as they prepare for an exam.

Journals

The student journal is a relatively new phenomenon in mathematics classes. As there has been an increase in the area of problem solving and reasoning, it has become more important than ever for teachers to examine students' thought processes. The journal provides an opportunity for students to express their thoughts as they solve problems. This "thinking about your own thinking" is referred to as *metacognition*. When they review for an exam, students can use this self-investigation of their thinking to help them recall how they approached and solved problems. You can supply the topics for them to write about in their journals. Consider the following suggested topics:

1. How would you explain solving a specific type of verbal problem to someone who missed today's lesson?
2. Explain how you solved the following problem. Show your work and explain your thinking.

3. How does working with real numbers differ from working with imaginary numbers?
4. What was the most interesting thing you learned in today's lesson?
5. Did you find last night's homework difficult? Why or why not?

You should notice a distinct pattern in all of these forms of comprehensive assessment. As we increase the amount of problem solving, thinking, and reasoning required of our students, as we ask them to explain what they did and why they did it, it becomes important for them to increase their communication skills. The ability to offer written explanations of their work and their thinking is now an integral part of most external tests. It is imperative that they express themselves clearly and succinctly in their explanations to others. As you make use of these additional forms of assessment, you will obtain a more complete picture of how well your students are doing.

10

BEYOND THE CLASSROOM: EXTRACURRICULAR ACTIVITIES AND KEEPING UP WITH THE PROFESSION

The math teacher's responsibility does not end with classroom instruction. Many pursue additional venues to motivate and enrich their students beyond the classroom. In this chapter, we describe some of the ways you might engage youngsters in extracurricular activities aimed at broadening their perspectives about the subject matter. We also discuss the professional responsibilities you might take on to advance your own intellectual growth and instructional effectiveness.

Extracurricular Activities

Setting up a Peer-Tutoring Center

Mathematics learning should be supported both inside and outside the classroom. Setting up a peer-tutoring center is one way that students can contribute to their learning community. Invite students who demonstrate mastery of the subject matter to volunteer in the peer-tutoring center. Encourage students who need additional support to attend. The peer-tutoring arrangement benefits both the tutee and the tutor. The student tutors gain a more thorough understanding of a topic when they prepare to present it to others. Peer-tutoring centers encourage student collaboration and foster personal growth. Some schools require school service for graduation. Volunteering to work in the peer-tutoring center is a useful way to have students meet that requirement.

Of course, any peer-tutoring center must be supervised by a teacher. The teacher's roles in the peer-tutoring center are to ensure that students and tutors are appropriately matched and to be available to provide help for the most challenging problems that may arise during the tutoring sessions.

Before peer tutoring begins, it is important to train the student tutors. They should be acquainted with the resources available to them as well as some teaching techniques. Caution student tutors against simply doing the problems for the tutee. Stress to them that instead, they should observe the tutee attempting the problem and focus on identifying and correcting conceptual or procedural errors.

The structure of the tutoring center depends primarily on the number of student tutors available and the number of students seeking help. If the number of tutors matches the demand for tutoring, then one-on-one tutoring is ideal. Because demand for tutoring fluctuates, especially the day before an exam, it is advisable to develop a flexible peer-tutoring model that can accommodate the needs of both individual students and larger groups of students.

In the one-on-one tutoring arrangement, a tutor will work with a single student to reinforce the concepts and skills presented in class. In this arrangement, the tutor can review the class notes and homework problems and provide detailed explanations for both. The tutee should be encouraged to ask questions to clarify any remaining issues before moving on.

Realistically, there may be times when a group of students would be assigned to a student tutor. The peer-tutoring supervisor must carefully group students of similar abilities so that a student tutor is not overwhelmed with providing differentiated instruction. The student tutor, with the help of the supervising teacher, must assess the needs of the group members and select problems that are meaningful to all students in that group.

Creating a Math Club

Many students are interested in learning additional mathematics topics. A math club enables motivated students to pursue these interests. Math clubs can sponsor a variety of afterschool activities to support student interest in mathematics. Some math clubs invite speakers from local colleges and universities to give talks on interesting topics. Math clubs can be organized to

- Provide peer tutoring.
- Publish a mathematics magazine.
- Maintain a math bulletin board with math news, career opportunities, and concise topics that can be used to enrich students.
- Write and distribute a challenging problem of the week throughout the school (or post it on the math bulletin board or Web site).

- Produce a schoolwide mathematics assembly program.
- Engage in any activity that creates interest in mathematics.

The math club can sponsor trips to noneducational sites where mathematics is used, such as architectural firms, brokerage houses, insurance companies, accounting firms, casinos, and even race tracks.

The formation of a math club should be carefully planned. The faculty advisor must have a clear idea of the club's activities so that students can be recruited for participation. It is recommended that a student steering committee be formed to help plan the activities and advertise the formation of the club. The first meeting should be planned to make a great impression on potential math club participants. It is not always easy to impress students with the beauty of mathematics, even if they are good math students. Therefore, it is important that the faculty advisor and club leader plan a series of interesting and meaningful activities.

Math clubs provide an opportunity for students to learn about topics that are beyond the scope of the syllabus. Some math clubs meet weekly to learn about an interesting topic in mathematics. Figure 10.1 lists possible topics for student term papers (or projects). This list is merely intended as a guide for generating additional topics.

Forming a Math Team

Creating a math team provides an opportunity to focus on some useful problem-solving activities that would hardly be possible in the course of regular classroom instruction. Preparing for math team competitions enables students of all abilities to sharpen their problem-solving skills and explore topics normally beyond the scope of the syllabus. A common misconception is that math team participation is only for the gifted and most advanced students. In fact, average math students can use the math team as a motivation for developing their skills.

Teachers can creatively adapt competition questions to make them appropriate for students of all abilities. Questions designed for a cohort of gifted students in grade 8 may be appropriate for a class of average students in grades 9 and 10.

Math teams can compete in many ways. The easiest way for a school's math team to compete against teams of similar ability levels is to join a math league. Most math leagues organize students by grade level or ability level and then mail competitions to the schools for administration on a given day. Some competitions may be held online. At the end of the year, winners in various categories are determined.

- Advanced Euclidean geometry
- Algebraic fallacies
- Algebraic models
- Algebraic recreations
- Ancient number systems and algorithms
- Arithmetic fallacies
- Arithmetic recreations
- Bases other than ten
- Binary computer
- Boolean algebra
- Calculating shortcuts
- Cavalieri's theorem
- Checking arithmetic operations
- Conic sections
- Continued fractions
- Cryptography
- Crystallography
- Curves of constant breadth
- Cylindrical projections
- Desargues's theorem
- Determinants
- Diophantine equations
- Divisibility of numbers
- Duality
- Dynamic symmetry
- Elementary number theory applications
- The Euler line
- Extension of Euler's formula to N dimensions
- Extension of Pappus's theorem
- Fermat's last theorem
- Fibonacci numbers
- Finite differences
- Finite geometry
- The five regluar polyhedra
- Flexagons
- The four-color map problem
- The fourth dimension
- Fractals
- Game theory
- Gaussian primes

- Geodesics
- Geometric dissections—tangrams
- Geometric fallacies
- Geometric models
- Geometric stereograms
- Geometric transformations
- Geometry of bubbles and liquid film
- Geometry of a catenary
- Geometry constructions (Euclid)
- Gergonne's problem
- The golden section
- Graphical representation of complex roots of quadratic and cubic equations
- Groups
- Higher algebra
- Higher-order curves
- Hyperbolic functions
- The hyperbolic paraboloid
- Intuitive geometric recreations
- Investigating the cycloid
- The law of growth
- Linear programming
- Linkages
- Lobachevskian geometry
- Logarithms of negative and complex numbers
- Logic
- Magic square construction
- Map projections
- Mascheroni's constructions
- Mathematics and art
- Mathematics and music
- Mathematics of life insurance
- Matrices
- Maximum-minimum in geometry
- Means
- Methods of least squares
- The metric system
- Minimal surfaces
- Modulo arithmetic in algebra

- Monte Carlo method of number approximation
- Multinomial theorem
- Napier's rods
- Networks
- The nine-point circle
- Nomographs
- The number pi, phi, or e
- Number theory proofs
- Paper folding
- Partial fractions
- Pascal's theorem
- Perfect numbers
- Polygonal numbers
- Prime numbers
- Probability
- Problem solving in algebra
- Projective geometry
- Proofs of algebraic theorems
- Properties of Pascal's triangle
- Pythagorean theorem—triples
- Regular polygons
- The regular seventeen-sided polygon
- Relativity and mathematics
- Riemannian geometry
- Solving cubics and quartics
- Special factoring
- Spherical triangles
- The spiral
- Statistics
- Steiner constructions
- Tessellations
- Theory of braids
- Theory of equations
- Theory of perspectives
- Three-dimensional curves
- The three famous problems of antiquity
- Topology
- Unsolved problems
- Vectors

FIGURE 10.1. Topics for math projects.

You might also investigate if there is a local, regional, county, or statewide math league you can join. If not, consider developing one with some nearby schools.

Math team competitions can consist of many components. There is individual competition, team competition, relay competition, and a team power question. Each of these phases of a mathematics competition is an exciting way for students to engage in mathematics. The individual competition typically consists of 8 to 10 short-answer questions that students answer in about 15 to 20 minutes. They can either be open-ended or multiple-choice questions. Some contests are composed of multiple-choice questions exclusively. The American Mathematics Competition, administered at three levels (grades 8, 10, and 12), consists of 25 multiple-choice questions that must be answered in 75 minutes. Math Counts, an organization dedicated to middle school mathematics, sponsors a national competition that has team and individual components.

Math League Press (Mathematics League, 2006) creates competitions for students beginning with grade 4 and continuing throughout high school. All of the competitions are designed to be administered in a single class period. Contests from one grade level may be appropriate for learners in previous or subsequent grades.

There are two types of team competitions. Some contests simply take the aggregate of individual scores to arrive at a team score. In other team competitions, a group of students must answer a series of questions within a given time frame. Unlike the individual competition, the organization and teamwork play an important role in this type of contest. Because time will be a factor in the success of the team, the appropriate assignment of problems usually determines the team's success. This type of team competition is usually for high school students mature enough to work unsupervised in groups.

A relay competition is an exciting phase of a mathematics competition in which students work in groups of three. The first person seated in the row solves a problem and passes the answer to the person sitting behind her. That student must use the answer to solve a different question. This answer is then passed to the third person, who must use it to solve an entirely different question. This is a timed activity, and the final person in the relay submits the final answer after three or six minutes. Correct answers submitted after three minutes are awarded twice the value of the correct answers submitted after six minutes. The number of students in the relay can vary, and the relay can be adapted for use in the mathematics classroom.

Another interesting component of some math competitions is the *power question*. A power question is presented to the team and is a series of laddered exercises that become progressively more challenging. Typically, a power question involves students investigating a given topic and providing proofs or answering questions about this topic. Power questions are usually challenging and require a level of sophistication well beyond the norm.

Student Preparation of Math Research Papers

Math standards throughout the country call for increased writing in mathematics. Students are challenged to think and communicate mathematically; similarly, they are asked to write about mathematics. Although mathematics is a tool that can be used to model almost everything in our world, the mathematics that is presented in the classroom is prescribed and somewhat limited in scope. Students can benefit by exploring interesting topics that lie outside the boundaries of their curriculum. These topics can include vignettes from the history of mathematics, examination of a problem from a variety of perspectives, use of technology to investigate famous problems, exploration of topics not in the curriculum yet "reachable" by most students, and much more.

Students who are involved in writing research papers are asked to read several sources on a given topic and then synthesize the information into a comprehensive and cohesive research report. Students may introduce a topic through an application or by some historical anecdote. Then, they present material on the topic at a level appropriate for their grade. For example, a student who chooses to write about primitive Pythagorean triples might discuss their nature, write about their properties, and present ways to generate them. For instance, beginning with natural numbers m and n, $m > n$, and setting $a = 2mn$, $b = m^2 - n^2$, and $c = m^2 + n^2$, it can be shown that $a^2 + b^2 = c^2$. Students can then investigate the properties of the terms a, b, and c and determine under what conditions they will form a primitive triple. They may choose to use a spreadsheet to generate integer values for m and n and then, using the generation scheme, find a, b, and c. A formal proof of their conjectures may follow.

Students preparing math research papers should find ways to expand the scope of their investigation to include related topics. When studying Pythagorean triples, students may wish to extend their investigations to include higher powers. This would lead to Fermat's last theorem. Although there are no integral solutions for the equation $a^n + b^n = c^n$, where $n > 2$ and a, b, and c are positive whole numbers, there are solutions to a related equation $a^3 + b^3 + c^3 = d^3$ (3, 4, 5, 6). In addition, there are solutions to $a^4 + b^4 + c^4 = d^4$ (although they are large numbers). With the use of technology, students can explore relationships involving large numbers.

The Internet can be a valuable resource for students; however, you must caution them to use only juried sources (those that are subject to editorial review) to ensure accuracy. There are many Web sites devoted to mathematics, and students should be encouraged to search the Internet to discover interesting topics to research. Another good source for student research projects is mathematics journals. For example, *The Mathematics Teacher* has many articles that can inspire student math research investigations.

Students who prepare math research papers should be allowed to present their work to the class or to the math club. Students can prepare transparencies or use a PowerPoint presentation. Student presentations should be about 10–15 minutes long and should be entertaining and informative. If any of these brief overview presentations generate interest, then a longer presentation might be in order. Give students in attendance an opportunity to ask questions of the presenter. There are numerous benefits to having students present their work. The practice hones a student's ability to present cogent summaries of their work, provides alternatives to the more usual teacher-centered sessions, and offers the students opportunities to articulate their thoughts—a life-learning objective.

Encourage students to enter their work in local or statewide math fairs. In a math fair, students present their research and answer questions related to it. Prizes are awarded for outstanding research papers. Outstanding projects can be submitted to the Intel Science Talent Search and the Siemens-Westinghouse Competition in Math, Science, and Technology. These are national competitions that offer generous scholarships for winning research papers. If no local math fair exists in your region, then you might consider organizing one.

Making Parents a Part of the Learning Process

Because most secondary mathematics teachers typically spend just 45 minutes a day with any given student, it is important to enlist the assistance of parents. Parents are usually willing to support their child's teacher, but they first need to know what their supportive role ought to be. In some cases, they will also be eager to know precisely what you are teaching because many parents, unfortunately, may be unfamiliar with the material or may have a preconceived notion of their weakness in mathematics and may feel themselves to be inadequate partners, incapable of supplying support. Informing students and parents of your home-work, testing, and grading policies is a good start. Some teachers like to send home a "student contract" during the first week of school that outlines these policies as well as expectations for all students. This could be a first step in which parents can play a supportive role to ensure that their child continues to meet the requirements of your course. For example, if you usually assign homework every day, you should inform parents so that they can monitor their children's work habits. It is wise to contact a parent whenever a student seems to be having diffi-culty with the material taught. There may be some extenuating circumstances con-tributing to a student's troubles. Student difficulties in mathematics identified early enough can be overcome with relatively simple measures. Parents can be a tremendous asset in helping to arrange support.

If a parent determines that his child does not understand the underlying con-cepts to complete a homework assignment, then you might, in consultation with the parent, suggest some extra help. This might include scheduling some time for the student to meet with you for individual instruction, participating in a peer-tutoring program, or possibly getting outside private tutoring. When caught early enough, such interventions could be brief rather than remaining as an ongoing "crutch" throughout the school year. Students tend to perform better when they are aware that the teacher has established communication with their parents. Such communication with parents should not be reserved only for remediation. You also ought to call the parent of the student who is excelling. Positive reinforcement can have a favorable lasting effect.

Improving Your Professional Practice

Professional Development

Successful and effective teachers are always engaged in activities that improve their teaching skills. This includes searching for ways to incorporate the latest technolog-ical advances into their instruction. We encourage you to attend seminars, lectures, and workshops that will expose you to and prepare you to use some new instruc-tional techniques. Although some technology workshops can be thinly veiled sales pitches, you can still make these workshops a part of your information-gathering process. Comparing products that will best meet your needs and those of your students is part of the general professional development expected of teachers. Publishing companies also sponsor professional development workshops geared toward improving your teaching skills. Although some of the materials may be directed to their textbooks, the materials may be general enough so that they can easily be adapted for use with your current textbook. Attending professional workshops places you in the company of other dedicated teachers and provides you the opportunity to share best practices.

Professional development sessions also give you an opportunity to hear from educators brought in to share expertise that would otherwise be hard to find. Professional connections that can be nurtured on an ongoing basis may also result from attendance at these sessions.

Taking Graduate Courses in Mathematics

Expanding your knowledge of mathematics will serve you well in the classroom. Some states have continuing education requirements for newly licensed teachers but do not require further study for tenured, veteran teachers. However, districts usually offer salary increases for further study in the academic area you teach as well as in pedagogical courses that could improve your teaching effectiveness. Regardless of your situation, enrolling in appropriately selected graduate-level courses in mathematics and mathematics education should prove to be a stimulating and rewarding experience. Colleges and universities often offer a wide variety of courses for mathematics.

As a graduate student in mathematics, you have the opportunity to empathize with your students by experiencing what it feels like to be a student—especially if the courses you take are somewhat challenging.

Subscribing to Mathematics Journals

There are many ways to stay current with new trends and approaches in teaching mathematics. The easiest way to keep abreast of these trends is to subscribe to mathematics education journals. In the United States, there are more than 30 mathematics journals designed for math teachers. The three most prominent are *The Arithmetic Teacher* (elementary) (recently renamed *Teaching Children Mathematics*), *Mathematics Teaching in the Middle School,* and *The Mathematics Teacher* (high school). These monthly journals are published by the National Council of Teachers of Mathematics (NCTM) and provide valuable suggestions for improving instruction. They also offer some enrichment ideas, expanding on topics in the curriculum to give teachers a deeper understanding of the material they are teaching, and offer some practical applications of the curriculum topics. Many state math teacher organizations publish a journal that will provide similar support.

Another source to consider is the Consortium for Mathematics and Its Applications (COMAP), a nonprofit organization dedicated to improving mathematics education. COMAP has developed curriculum materials that use mathematics to explore and model real-world phenomena. The organization has journals and other publications dedicated to elementary, middle, and high school teachers as well as undergraduate materials that may be suitable for use with math clubs or honors classes.

The Mathematical Association of America publishes three monthly journals at the undergraduate and graduate levels: *The College Math Journal, Mathematics Magazine,* and *American Mathematics Monthly.* Although most of the articles are not suitable for the majority of high school students, it is important for teachers to stay sharp and current with their math skills. Teachers have a constant obligation to enrich their instruction and can achieve this partly by staying current with their profession.

Building a Math Library

It is important for mathematics teachers to build a personal resource library that includes a wide variety of math textbooks as well as an assortment of books on the history of mathematics, recreational mathematics, contest problems, problem solving, and pedagogy. The sooner you begin to assemble your library, the sooner you can motivate your students by including interesting topics from these sources. You can start to build your personal library by obtaining examination copies of textbooks from publishers. Textbooks differ in their approach to presenting and developing concepts. Having a variety of math textbooks enables you to select the approach best suited for your students and for your teaching style. Having a few textbooks on the same subject will also prove useful when you prepare examinations. Constructing tests by selecting items from different textbooks gives you more flexibility in choosing test questions and can save you a significant amount of time.

Because engaging students is key to their learning, it is important for teachers to have a variety of ways to motivate them. Recreational mathematics is an excellent way to capture student interest. Typical textbooks do not provide enough material to thoroughly enrich your classes—both gifted students and regular achievers—so it becomes incumbent on you to develop a collection of books and other print materials that can offer you topics and ideas appropriate to enrich your instruction. Your personal library will be an invaluable source for finding interesting additions to your lesson plan.

Attending Math Conferences

Each year the NCTM and other organizations sponsor an annual and several regional mathematics teacher conferences. These conferences are usually composed of a keynote address, followed by a series of workshops and brief presentations on relevant topics, ranging from didactic issues to explorations of relevant mathematical topics for teachers at the various grade levels. In addition to the extensive workshop menu, publishers of mathematics textbooks, educational materials, supplementary books, and technological support material exhibit their products. Publishers freely distribute examination copies of their textbooks, which could provide you with an opportunity to see options for future instructional programs; this also allows you to expand your personal mathematics library. Technologies can be previewed, and teachers can have hands-on trials with the latest innovations in software, calculators, and computers. Teachers derive great satisfaction from attending conferences, and many school districts value your participation and will subsidize your travel expenses to attend. It is highly recommended that you attend as many conferences as your schedule permits.

Accessing Grant Funding Opportunities

Many grants are available to educators. Funding sources for these grants include the federal government, state governments, local governments, colleges and universities, foundations, unions, and corporations. Teachers ought to seek out all possible grant opportunities. These grants can support tutoring centers and mathematics libraries and even be dedicated to improve a teacher's professional competence through self-study. Grants such as the Presidential Awards for Excellence in Mathematics and Science Teaching can recognize outstanding mathematics teachers and reward them for being "models for their colleagues and leaders in the improvement of mathematics education" (National Science Foundation, n.d.). The NCTM, through their Mathematics Education Trust (MET), has a number of grants that support increasing content knowledge of teachers at all levels. These grants support "teacher-initiated projects designed to enhance the teaching and learning of mathematics" (NCTM, n.d., Grants and Awards). In addition to consulting your school or district grants officer, you might use the Internet to search for educational grants in mathematics teaching.

In the same manner that we want our students to become lifelong learners, teachers should continue to improve their teaching skills and knowledge of mathematics. Professional development should be viewed as an ongoing activity that can be accomplished in many ways, some more obvious than others. By reading journals, attending conferences, enrolling in graduate classes, and seeking other ways to keep current with the profession, you will grow as a professional, be more effective, and have a more rewarding experience in the classroom.

APPENDIX: WHAT A MATH TEACHER HAS TO KNOW ABOUT SPECIAL EDUCATION

JAN WEATHERLY VALLE

THE CITY COLLEGE OF NEW YORK–CUNY

Since the 1975 passage of Public Law 94-142 or the Education for All Handicapped Children Act (renamed in 1990 as the Individuals with Disabilities Education Act, or IDEA), the federal government has mandated a free and appropriate public education (FAPE) for *all* children, including those children identified as having disabilities. Moreover, the law stipulates that children with disabilities be educated in the least restrictive environment (LRE)—meaning that children with disabilities should be educated with their peers in community schools to the maximum extent possible.

In light of the requirements of IDEA, most teacher education programs require mathematics teacher candidates to take one or two courses in special education (e.g., a survey course in disability categories or a course in behavior management). More progressive teacher education programs offer dual-certification programs in which teacher candidates are prepared to teach general *and* special education students.

Despite consistent movement toward more inclusive mathematics classrooms, a common misperception persists—even among some veteran teachers—that students identified with disabilities remain the primary responsibility of special education faculty. In fact, you may hear some colleagues make comments such as "I didn't go to school to be a special education teacher," implying that mathematics teachers can exercise choice over whether or not to address the instructional needs of students with disabilities. As a mathematics teacher, be aware that you are *legally responsible* for meeting the educational needs of students with disabilities in your classes.

Special Education Laws and You

The Individuals with Disabilities Education Act

IDEA guarantees a free and equal educational opportunity for students with disabilities. In brief, IDEA is monitored by the U.S. Department of Education and requires public schools to do the following:

- Seek out and provide appropriate instructional programs for all students with disabilities (regardless of the severity of the disability).
- Actively engage parents of students with disabilities as partners in educational decision making.
- Convene a team (including the parent, at least one *general education teacher* of the student, at least one special education teacher or special education service provider of the student, a representative who is qualified to implement or supervise curriculum for students with disabilities and is knowledgeable about the general education curriculum, an individual who can interpret assessment results, any other professional deemed appropriate by the parent or school, and the student, if appropriate) to create and implement an Individualized Educational Program (IEP) for every student deemed eligible to receive special education services.
- Educate students with disabilities in the LRE, which may include, but is not limited to, the *general education* classroom.

In light of these requirements, you can, as a mathematics teacher, expect to teach students with disabilities in your classes. As noted, an IEP is prepared for each student identified as having a disability (or disabilities). You are required to implement the objectives or modifications stated on the IEPs of all students with disabilities in your classroom. Remember, the IEP is a legal document that ensures the appropriate education of students with disabilities, regardless of whether the educational setting is the general classroom or a separate special education classroom. You and the special education teacher share responsibility for the education of your mutual students with disabilities.

Section 504 of the Rehabilitation Act of 1973

Section 504 of the Rehabilitation Act of 1973 (commonly referred to simply as Section 504 by school personnel) refers to a civil rights law that protects persons with disabilities from discriminatory practices. Compliance is monitored by the U.S. Office of Civil Rights. Regarding public schools, Section 504 guarantees that students with disabilities receive equal access to education. In other words, physical or instructional barriers to the curriculum must be removed to ensure students with disabilities access to the same educational opportunities as their nondisabled peers.

Equal access is achieved most often through the implementation of classroom modifications outlined in a Section 504 plan designed by parents and school personnel. Students who are eligible for a Section 504 plan include those with disabilities who do not meet the criteria for placement in special education services or those with disabilities who may be eligible for services but for whom the general education setting with accommodations and modifications is deemed most appropriate. Unlike IDEA, Section 504 does *not* provide special funds, teachers, services, classroom settings, or materials/resources.

Communities of Learners

Students come to school with myriad background experiences and learning style preferences. Learner variation should be expected rather than unanticipated. There is no such thing as learner uniformity regardless of whether a class includes students with disabilities. Moreover, you can expect some students without IEPs to share in common, to one degree or another, the kind of learning challenges typically exhibited by students with IEPs. For example, the following characteristic areas are associated with secondary students with *learning disabilities* (defined as a student with average-to-gifted intelligence who displays a significant discrepancy between ability and expected achievement, primarily thought to be the result of neurological processing difficulties) specifically in the area of mathematics:

- *Processing speed* (e.g., student reads, writes, and responds slowly; recalls math facts slowly; takes longer to complete homework and tests than typically expected; struggles to efficiently and accurately retrieve information stored in memory, such as math formulas and math facts).
- *Fine-motor coordination* (e.g., student writes numbers illegibly, has difficulty writing numbers in small spaces, copies math problems slowly or inaccurately from the chalkboard or text, avoids written work because it is arduous).

- *Conceptualization of mathematical ideas* (e.g., student appears not to grasp the "language" of mathematics, has difficulty expressing mathematical ideas in words or with other symbolic representations, does not readily grasp mathematical patterns and relationships, displays inflexibility regarding number sense, displays difficulty telling time).
- *Memory* (e.g., student has difficulty remembering instructions, particularly those requiring multiple steps; struggles with active working memory—the ability to hold two or more components in one's head while simultaneously working on another component; performs poorly on review tests or mixed probes; displays difficulty with sequential memory tasks).
- *Attention* (e.g., student has difficulty maintaining attention to steps in algorithms or problem solving, displays weak visual attention to detail in written work, struggles to sustain attention during instruction).

No doubt you have already encountered students who exhibit some combination of such characteristics who are not labeled as having any kind of disability or students who are labeled with disabilities other than a math learning disability (e.g., attention deficit hyperactivity disorder, Asperger's syndrome, speech/language delay/disorder, emotional/behavioral disorders). It is this fact that leads current critics of special education to argue that the educational needs of students are more similar than dissimilar, and regardless of whatever label may or may not be assigned, *all* students benefit from instruction designed to meet their respective learning needs.

The Secondary Mathematics Curriculum and Students with IEPs

Why Include Students with Disabilities in the General Education Classroom?

In the 30 years since the passage of Public Law 94-142 (Education Act for All Handicapped Children, renamed in 1990 as IDEA), the number of public school students identified as having disabilities and in need of special education services has grown exponentially. On the one hand, such growth reflects a more sophisticated understanding and response to the educational needs of students with disabilities. On the other hand, a high rate of segregated special education placements for students with disabilities has long been documented in spite of the law's insistence that students with disabilities be placed in the LRE.

Moreover, the traditional special education diagnosis-and-remediation approach, emphasizing behavioral and cognitive instruction, has received increasing criticism. Researchers contend, for example, that the kind of behaviorist approach to mathematics often practiced in special education classrooms (stressing drill and practice, memory, and automatization) reinforces impulsive rather than reflective processing; focuses on isolated skills and the end product ("the right answer"); discourages learner decision making and analysis; emphasizes numeric representation over pictorial, concrete, linguistic, or algebraic representations; and provides little valuable information about a student's thinking process. Likewise, information-processing theory as applied to mathematics instruction has been critiqued for placing the student with disabilities in the perceived role as an "astrategic learner" who needs to replicate the strategies of others to grasp mathematical concepts. Such academic concerns (as well as a host of other concerns) prompted stronger language within the 1997 reauthorization of IDEA—and most recently within the 2004 reauthorization—to ensure that students with disabilities have equal access to the general education curriculum to the maximum extent possible.

Integrating Students with IEPs into the General Education Classroom

Keep in mind that there is no single experience of disability in the same way that there is no single experience of race, class, or gender. Students with disabilities, like their nondisabled peers, come to you with multiple school experiences and multiple ways of responding to such experiences. You can anticipate, however, that it is likely that any student who has experienced failure or difficulty with mathematics—particularly over an extended period of time—may come to class armed with defense mechanisms, such as disinterest, disengagement, or various diversionary tactics. Thus, your most important challenge as a teacher is to create a supportive, safe, and genuine community of learners. To progress in mathematics, students must be comfortable enough to take risks, make mistakes, and learn from one another.

A safe and supportive classroom community sets the stage for implementing the six broad goals outlined by the National Council of Teachers of Mathematics (NCTM) that all students should work toward.

> **INTERVIEW**
>
> As a teacher of mixed students (general and special education), my goal is to build self-esteem.[1] The students have to feel like they can do it. It's that atmosphere of making students feel comfortable so they will take chances, even when they know they might be wrong. You have to create that environment. At home, you'll say anything to your family because you feel comfortable talking with them. At school, that's how it has to be. Students have to have the sense that they belong here—that I'm just like everyone else. I might have some issues, but I still *belong* here. My goal as a teacher is to teach math, but it is also to teach my students life skills. I want them to be better people. I want them to not just come out of class saying, "Yeah, we learned math." I want them to come out of class and say, "I got it. I understand what Mr. Johnson is saying—we have to help each other."

1. To value mathematics as an essential area of competency for all citizens.
2. To be able to reason mathematically as a way to deal competently with life's complex situations.
3. To learn to communicate about mathematics to peers in a group situation.
4. To be able to solve a wide variety of mathematical problems with confidence.
5. To develop and maintain attitudes regarding the importance of mathematics for all individuals.
6. To take 4 years of high school math.

The NCTM standards challenge traditional mathematics instruction in which students sit quietly in rows, listen to the teacher (the font of mathematics knowledge) outline the steps for getting the "right answer," and individually practice solving problems. To foster positive attitudes toward mathematics, confidence in solving mathematical problems, and the ability to talk about mathematics with others, the "new" mathematics classroom offers students opportunities to work in small groups to solve contextualized math investigations, emphasizes and encourages multiple ways to solve problems, and asks students to explain their mathematical thinking to one another.

Students who have received drill-and-skill mathematics instruction in special education classes (as well as nondisabled peers who come from traditional math classrooms) may find the group approach to mathematics bewildering at first. Keep in mind that some students may not understand how to use the language of mathematics to explain their thinking, how to work with others in a group, or even how to see themselves as mathematicians in their own right. Expect and plan for an adjustment period as students orient to new ways of thinking about and doing mathematics.

Traditional special education instruction has long focused on the assessment, identification, and remediation of skill deficits. Such instruction, grounded in the tenets of behaviorism, requires that a task be broken down into its component steps. The teacher presents each component in isolation. As the student gains mastery of each component, the components are "strung together" until the entire task is learned. In recent years, however, the efficacy of incremental part-to-whole instruction has been called into question. Critics argue that the task analysis approach to instruction can result in mastery of isolated components that do not necessarily translate into the skills needed to perform the complete task. In other words, students invest energy and time to learn skills that may be dissimilar or immaterial within the context of the whole task. Moreover, a student who struggles to master an isolated skill within a sequence (e.g., has difficulty committing multiplication facts to memory) may not be presented with the opportunity to develop conceptual knowledge because of the focus on mastering skills.

INTERVIEW

Let's say you're a 7th grade teacher and you are giving 3rd grade work to your 7th graders because they "need" it. Come on now—they might need skills, but there is a difference between teaching skills and teaching them a concept. We integrate both at the same time. If a student doesn't know basic facts, I'll slowly integrate that. I don't assume students have learned it from last year—unless I had them. If they are coming from another teacher, I can't assume that they were already taught. I don't penalize them for something I did not teach them. I integrate it. If I know that students have trouble with fractions, then I will integrate fractions into the problems and I will teach them while I am teaching the lesson.

> If I'm teaching mean, median, mode, for example, students who have a harder time getting information or the concepts—I give them whole numbers. And, the students who have already mastered the concept, they might get fractions and mixed numbers. Therefore, no one is being cheated in the middle. Everyone is gaining something. The goal is the same concept, but how they're getting the concept is what the goal is about.
>
> I started working this all out, and students are benefiting from it. Students are learning. Students who have had trouble in math in previous years are finally coming to class saying, "I get it!" and "I thought that I would never be able to learn math!" And, students who excel in math continue to excel.

Keep in mind that some students identified as having math learning disabilities are global rather than sequential thinkers. They can be capable of visualizing and grasping mathematical concepts and patterns but may struggle with paper-and-pencil math because of challenges with memory, attention, and fine motor skills. In fact, such students may remark that the process of writing down the sequential steps of a math problem on paper interferes with their intuitive understanding of the mathematical concept. Unfortunately, many secondary students identified as having math learning disabilities have not been afforded previous opportunities to engage meaningfully with mathematical concepts because of an overemphasis on successful and complete mastery of basic skills. Thus, these students understand mathematics as an exercise in memorization rather than reasoning.

To facilitate communication among students regarding mathematics (one of the six NCTM goals addressed in this chapter), provide ample opportunities for learning through social interaction. For example, students need to engage in collaborative dialogue, explanation and justification, and negotiation of mathematical meanings. Any student (special education or otherwise) whose primary exposure to mathematics has been worksheet driven—with an emphasis on getting the right answer—most likely will need support in learning and practicing the language needed to engage in mathematical conversation. You can help students focus on the process of mathematical thinking as well as facilitate communication skills by asking such questions as

- How did you figure that out?
- Can you walk me through your thinking?
- How could you make sure that you are really right about that?

INTERVIEW

I started out as a traditional teacher because that was the way I was taught myself. Students were having difficulty getting the information because I was teaching one way and one way only to everyone—assuming that everyone could learn everything at the same time. I had troubles in the classroom, and it reflected the way I was teaching. So, I really had to think about that as an educator.

I took courses and I read. I learned more about what it means for students who come with disabilities and how I need to address them. It's not about having the classroom quiet. It's not about everybody learning the same thing. It's about students who are happy and engaged because they're learning. I knew I needed to group students and let them talk about the process. And it got loud, and people would come by and look in the room and say, "What's going on?" But it wasn't the loudness of kids being disrespectful and disruptive. It was the loudness of learning going on!

It was hard for them at first because traditionally they had always stayed in rows. Some had had bad experiences in groups so they didn't want to go in groups. It was a slow, slow, slow process. It took time. It started with pairs. I had to get them just to be able to talk with each other. Then, we went to groups of three or four. I had to model for them. I also had my former students come in and model accountable talk for the class—to show them how it is done.

And, it was hard for me, too, because I had to give up my comfort zone. You are giving up something that you learned all your life, and you have to change. Change is hard. Change is difficult when you're taught one way and one way only. And, a lot of times teachers don't want to change because it's easier to do it the way they have been doing it—regardless of who's learning and who's not learning.

- How did you know that?
- What does that mean?
- Can you show me by using these manipulatives or drawing a representation?
- Can you teach me?
- Is this strategy working for you? Why do you think that?

INTERVIEW

I want students to say, "I didn't get it." But I want them to think about it. Ask students, "Why wouldn't it work?" Give them a chance. Scaffold them through it. Talk to them. Don't just say, "You didn't get the right answer—next!" Why did you think that way? What could you have done differently so that it would have worked? Talk them through it. It is the *questions* you need to focus on. It's not just about giving students problems and making sure they do it right.

Remember that your ultimate goal is to support all students to the point at which they can routinely pose such questions to one another as well as offer clear explanations that others can understand.

Students with and without IEPs benefit from the contextualization of mathematics in real-life scenarios. We cannot assume that students grasp the relevancy of mathematics to the world outside the classroom. Such connections need to be made explicit—even for secondary students—and with regularity.

INTERVIEW

When we study graphs, for example, I cut graphs out of magazines and newspapers, and I let students interpret them. What do you think this is saying? What do you think the poll meant when it said 40 percent of votes? And, this person had a total of a million votes, how many did this person get? What is that percentage? What does that mean when you see percentages?

These are the things I want students to come out with when they are in class. I told my students about an infomercial that I recently saw on TV. "You can order these fat pills for $30 for four payments. If you call right now, we'll give it to you for $20 for six payments!" Some students would say, "Wait a minute! That's the same price—that's the same price!" But other kids would say, "I'm gonna go with the $20 because 20 is less than 30." They can't see that it is $20 over six payments, $30 over four payments—and it is still the same thing. Someone at home who doesn't make that connection thinks, "I might as well go with the $20. I'll just have to pay two extra. But I'm only paying $20." These are the kinds of things I want them to be aware of.

I even took a field trip last year. I had never taken any group of kids anywhere before. The other math teachers said, "You are crazy! What are you doing? Math? We don't take kids on field trips!" I took my students to Chelsea Piers to bowl. I had them keep their scores for each frame. Then, I had them come together as a whole entire class with all the data together. We dispersed the data to groups. Each group was responsible for doing something—creating a stem and leaf block, creating histograms, creating percent of change from one frame to the next frame—and then we just talked about the overall experience. "Oh, it was fun, Mr. Johnson! We never got to go out of the building. I can see the relationship there. I see what statisticians do! They gather this information. They take a sample of the population. And they go out and they can say this is the percentage change—some increased, some decreased." And so they made the connections. It was a fun day of learning math.

Reasonable Accommodations or Modifications: IEPs and Section 504

Be aware that students identified as having a disability (or disabilities) under IDEA or Section 504 are guaranteed equal access to the general education curriculum. As outlined in this chapter, every student who receives special education services has an IEP, a document prepared by parents and school personnel. In addition to short- and long-range instructional objectives, there is a section of the IEP in which reasonable classroom accommodations or modifications are outlined specifically. These accommodations or modifications pertain to both the special and the general education settings and reflect the individual student's instructional needs. If that Section 504 does not include special services, the entirety of the Section 504 plan is devoted to accommodations or modifications.

The majority of special education students are included in general education classrooms for all or part of the school day. You can expect to have students with IEPs in most of your classes. At the beginning of each school year, make sure that you know which of your students have IEPs. You should be given this information by the special education faculty, administration, or school guidance counselor. However, be aware that it is your responsibility to access and act on this information.

(Ignorance is not an excuse under the law.) If you have not been given information about the special education students in your classes by the first week of school, then proactively seek this information from your administration.

It is also your responsibility to know which classroom accommodations or modifications are included in each IEP or Section 504 plan. If the special education faculty has not approached you with this information, then ask permission to view these documents. As the mathematics teacher of a special education student, you have the right (and responsibility) to read the student's IEP. Special education faculty should function as a resource for you. Do not be shy about asking for explanations or suggestions about how to implement the accommodations or modifications in your classroom. Most accommodations or modifications center around adapting the presentation of information, assignment requirements, and evaluation. The following are examples of accommodations or modifications that might be required for a student with disabilities to access the general education math curriculum:

Presentation of information
- Provide the student with visual models (e.g., list steps for solving problems on a class chart, keep a step-by-step model of the problem on the board or on a small note card for the student to keep at his desk, use an overhead projector).
- Provide opportunities for paired learning with another student or group of students.
- Provide hands-on learning opportunities.
- Provide preferential seating for the student.
- Give test/exam review summaries for students (and their parents).
- Provide a peer note taker, permission to tape record lecture, or copy of the teacher's lecture notes.

Assignment requirements
- Reduce and/or modify writing (e.g., provide printed problems rather than ask student to copy from a book, chalkboard, or overhead projector; provide worksheets with ample room between problems to write; provide the student with graph paper on which to write problems; break assignments into smaller segments; reduce the number of practice problems required).
- Extend the time required to complete written assignments.
- Allow the use of a calculator or math fact chart.

Evaluation
- Provide a separate testing site to eliminate classroom distractions.
- Provide extended or untimed testing.
- Allow open book/notes during tests.
- Give opportunities for retests and oral tests.
- Highlight instructions or key terms.

General education teachers sometimes express concern regarding the "fairness" of such accommodations or modifications for some students and not others. It may help to reconsider the meaning of fairness in the classroom. Remember that students with disabilities face learning difficulties that most other students do not. It is important to communicate to all students that fairness does not mean equal but rather giving each person what that person needs to learn. As a mathematics teacher, it is critical for you to understand that accommodations or modifications (required on IEPs and Section 504 plans) have been determined by school personnel and parents as necessary to a student's equal access to the general education. Thus, it is your legal obligation to adhere to the IEP or Section 504 plan. Neither document can be altered or deviated from without written consent from both the parents and school personnel.

INTERVIEW

Teachers have to think, "I'm not above these students." You have to talk to them. "I understand what you are going through. It's hard. But this is how we deal with problems." You have to let them understand that you are there for them.

Special ed and general ed have to be integrated. It has to be. I used to be one of those people—I will admit to this—who would say about students with IEPs, "That's not my job to teach them." Then, you think about it and say, "Wow. What if I had a child, and my child needed some special services, and the teacher said, 'I didn't go to school to do that!'" I would be devastated. So, we have to think about it. We have to think about the child!

A Final Note

Do not fear having students with disabilities in your classroom. You will find that students with disabilities will enrich your classroom community and teach you how to be a better teacher for all students. Remember that you are part of a team of school professionals committed to the success of students with disabilities. Ask questions, collaborate, observe, but most of all, talk to your students. Ask them how they learn best—and listen, *really* listen. You will find that they are your best resource.

NOTES

CHAPTER 2

1. A primitive Pythagorean triple has no common factor throughout.

CHAPTER 3

1. A SMART Board, or interactive whiteboard, is a large touch screen on which computer images are projected. The teacher can control the computer by touching the screen instead of using a mouse.

2. A 1940 compendium of the known proofs of the Pythagorean theorem is available from the NCTM (Loomis, 1968).

CHAPTER 5

1. *Ordered pairs* refers to having students assigned a collaborative partner with whom they can work if the teacher quickly wants to form small groups. Students can turn to these partners for assistance during a challenging exercise. Having small group procedures set up in advance gives the teacher many options and ensures that all students can remain actively engaged throughout the period.

CHAPTER 6

1. According to E. T. Bell in his famous book, *Men of Mathematics* (1937), Gauss in his adult years told of this story but explained that the situation was far more complicated than the simple one we currently tell. He told of his teacher, Mr. Büttner, giving the class a five-digit number, such as 81,297, and asking the class to add a three-digit number such as 198 to it 100 times successively; then, the students were to find the sum of that series. One can only speculate about which version is the true one.

2. Actually, a gun and bullets would be a better analogue than the bow and arrow because the bullet can *really* be used only once. For this illustration, make it clear to the students that the arrow, once shot, cannot be used again.

3. Obviously, in reality an infinite number of arrows would be required, so it must be appropriately simulated.

CHAPTER 9

1. An item analysis simply determines if an item distinguishes between the high and low scores on a test. That is, do the high scorers get a particular item correct, while the lower scorers get the item wrong?

APPENDIX

1. The interviews in this section are with John Johnson, 9th grade mathematics teacher, Thurgood Marshall High School, New York, NY.

REFERENCES AND RESOURCES

Altshiller-Court, N. A. (1952). *College geometry.* New York: Barnes & Noble.

Barnett, I. A. (1972). *Elements of number theory.* Boston: Prindle, Weber, & Schmidt.

Bell, E. T. (1937). *Men of mathematics.* New York: Simon & Schuster.

Berggren, L., Borwein, J., & Borwein, P. (1997). *Pi: A source book.* New York: Springer.

Boston, C. (2002). ERIC Clearinghouse on Assessment and Evaluation, College Park, MD. (ED470206, 2002-10-00).

Bruckheimer, M., & Hirshkowitz, R. (1977). Mathematics projects in junior high school. *Mathematics Teacher, 70,* 573.

Brumbaugh, D. K., Ashe, D. E., Ashe, J. L., & Rock, D. (1997). *Teaching secondary mathematics.* Mahwah, NJ: Erlbaum.

Cherkas, B. (1993, February). *Humanizing the multiple choice test with partial credit.* Melbourne, FL: Research Council for Diagnostic/Prescriptive Mathematics.

Chrystal, G. (1964). *Textbook of algebra.* New York: Chelsea.

Courant, R., & Robbins, H. (1941). *What is mathematics?* New York: Oxford University Press.

Coxeter, H. S. M., & Greitzer, S. L. (1967). *Geometry revisited.* New York: Random House.

Davis, D. R. (1949). *Modern college geometry.* Reading, MA: Addison-Wesley.

Diggins, J. E. (1965). *String, straight-edge, and shadow: The story of geometry.* New York: Viking Press.

Dudley, U. (1987). *A budget of trisections.* New York: Springer.

Elgarten, G. H. (1976). A mathematics intramurals contest. *Mathematics Teacher, 69,* 477.

Farmer, D. W., & Sandford, T. B. (1996). *Knots and surfaces: A guide to discovering mathematics.* Providence, RI: American Mathematical Society.

Gorini, C. A. (Ed.). (2000). *Geometry at work: A collection of papers showing applications of geometry.* Washington, DC: Mathematical Association of America.

Hall, H. S., & Knight, S. R. (1960). *Higher algebra.* London: Macmillan.

Holmes, J. E. (1970, October). Enrichment or acceleration? *Mathematics Teacher, 63*(6), 471–473.

House, P. A. (1980). *Interactions of science and mathematics.* Columbus, OH: ERIC Clearing House for Science, Mathematics, and Environmental Education.

Ippolito, D. (1999, April). The mathematics of the spirograph. *Mathematics Teacher, 92*(4), 354–357.

James, R. C., & James, G. (Eds.). (1976). *Mathematics dictionary* (4th ed.). New York: Van Nostrand Reinhold.

Johnson, R. A. (1929). *Modern geometry.* Boston: Houghton Mifflin.

Jones, M. H. (1983, October). Mathcounts: A new junior high school mathematics competition. *Mathematics Teacher, 76*(7), 482–485.

Karush, W. (1962). *The crescent dictionary of mathematics.* New York: Macmillan.

Krulik, S., & Rudnick, J. (1998). *Assessing reasoning and problem solving: A sourcebook for elementary school teachers.* Boston, MA: Allyn & Bacon.

Krulik, S., Rudnick, J., & Milou, E. (2003). *Teaching mathematics in middle school: A practical guide.* Boston: Allyn & Bacon.

Leonard, W. A. (1977). No upper limit: The challenge of the teacher of secondary mathematics. Fresno, CA: Creative Teaching Association.

Lichtenberg, B. K. (1981). Some excellent sources of material for mathematics clubs. *Mathematics Teacher, 74,* 284.

Loomis, E. S. (1968). *The Pythagorean proposition.* Reston, VA: National Council of Teachers of Mathematics.

Loy, J. (1997). The Pythagorean theorem. Retrieved August 2, 2006, from http://www.jimloy.com/geometry/pythag.htm

Madachy, J. S. (1979). *Madachy's mathematical recreations.* New York: Dover Paperbacks.

Magic Squares. http://www.magic-squares.de/general/squares/squares.html

Martin, G. E. (1998). *Geometric constructions.* New York: Springer.

Mathematics League. (2006). The Math League [home page]. Retrieved August 2, 2006, from http://www.mathleague.com

Morgan, F. (2000). *The math chat book.* Washington, DC: Mathematical Association of America.

Morgan, F., Melnick, E. R., & Nicholson, R. (1997, December). The soap-bubble-geometry contest. *Mathematics Teacher, 90*(9), 746–750.

National Council of Teachers of Mathematics. (1980). *An agenda for action: Recommendations for school mathematics of the 1980's.* Reston, VA: Author.

National Council of Teachers of Mathematics. (1989). *Curriculum and evaluation standards for school mathematics.* Reston, VA: Author.

National Council of Teachers of Mathematics. (1991). *Professional standards for teaching mathematics*. Reston, VA: Author.

National Council of Teachers of Mathematics. (1995). *Assessment standards for school mathematics*. Reston, VA: Author.

National Council of Teachers of Mathematics. (2000). *Principles and standards for school mathematics*. Reston, VA: Author.

National Council of Teachers of Mathematics. (n.d.). Grants and awards. Retrieved August 2, 2006, from http://www.nctm.org/about/grants.htm

National Council of Teachers of Mathematics. (n.d.). NCTM Illuminations Project [home page]. Retrieved August 2, 2006, from http://illuminations.nctm.org/

National Science Foundation. (n.d.). The Presidential Awards for Excellence in Mathematics and Science Teaching [home page]. Retrieved August 2, 2006, from http://paemst.org/Program.cfm

Newman, J. R. (1956). *The world of mathematics*. New York: Simon & Schuster.

Olds, C. D. (1963). *Continued fractions*. New York: Random House.

Posamentier, A. S. (2000a). *Making algebra come alive*. Thousand Oaks, CA: Corwin.

Posamentier, A. S. (2000b). *Making geometry come alive*. Thousand Oaks, CA: Corwin.

Posamentier, A. S. (2000c). *Making pre-algebra come alive*. Thousand Oaks, CA: Corwin.

Posamentier, A. S. (2002). *Advanced Euclidean geometry: Excursions for secondary students and teachers*. Emeryville, CA: Key College Press.

Posamentier, A. S. (2003). *Math wonders to inspire teachers and students*. Alexandria, VA: Association for Supervision & Curriculum Development.

Posamentier, A. S., & Hauptman, H. A. (2006). *101 great ideas for introducing key concepts in mathematics* (2nd ed.). Thousand Oaks, CA: Corwin.

Posamentier, A. S., & Jaye, D. (2006). *What successful math teachers do, 6–12*. Thousand Oaks, CA: Corwin.

Posamentier, A. S., & Lehmann, I. (2004). *π: A biography of the world's most mysterious number*. Amherst, NY: Prometheus Books.

Posamentier, A. S., & Lehmann, I. (2007). *The fabulous Fibonacci numbers*. Amherst, NY: Prometheus Books.

Posamentier, A. S., Smith, B. S., & Stepelman, J. (2006). *Teaching secondary mathematics: Techniques and enrichment units* (7th ed.). Upper Saddle River, NJ: Merrill/Prentice Hall.

Pythagoras Theorem. (n.d.). Retrieved August 2, 2006, from http://www.unisanet.unisa.edu.au/07305/pythag.htm

Sadovskii, L. E., & Sadovskii, A. L. (1996). *Mathematics and sports* (S. Makar-Limanov, Trans.). Providence, RI: American Mathematical Society.

Schaaf, W. L. (Ed.). (1978). *A bibliography of recreational mathematics.* Washington, DC: National Council of Teachers of Mathematics.

Smith, D. E., (Ed.). (1929). *Source book in mathematics.* New York: McGraw-Hill.

Stiggins, R. (2002). Assessment crisis: The absence of assessment FOR learning. *Phi Delta Kappan 88*(10), 758–765.

Third International Mathematics and Science Study (TIMSS). Available at http://nces.ed.gov./timss/

Weisstein, E. W. (1999). Franklin Magic Square. From *MathWorld—A* Wolfram Web Resource. Retrieved August 2, 2006, from http://mathworld.wolfram.com/FranklinMagicSquare.html

Wright, F. (1965). Motivating students with projects and teaching aids. *Mathematics Teacher, 58,* 47.

Resources for Extracurricular Activities

History of Mathematics

Ball, W. W. R. (1960). *A short account of the history of mathematics.* New York: Dover.

Bell, E. T. (1937). *Men of mathematics.* New York: Simon & Schuster.

Bell, E. T. (1979). *Mathematics, queen and servant of science.* Washington, DC: Mathematical Association of America.

Boyer, C. B. (1968). *A history of mathematics.* New York: Wiley.

Bunt, L. N. H., Jones, P. S., & Bedient, J. D. (1976). *The historical roots of elementary mathematics.* Englewood Cliffs, NJ: Prentice Hall.

Cajori, F. (1928). *A history of mathematic notations.* LaSalle, IL: Open Court.

Campbell, D. M., & Higgins, J. C. (Eds.). (1984). *Mathematics: people, problems, results.* Belmont, CA: Wadsworth.

Eves, H. (1976). *An introduction to the history of mathematics* (4th ed.). New York: Holt, Rinehart, & Winston.

Focus Issue on History. (2000, November). *Mathematics Teacher, 93*(8).

Gray, S. B., & Sandifer, C. E. (2001, February). The sumario compendioso: The new world's first mathematics book. *Mathematics Teacher, 94*(2), 98–103.

Hamburger, P., & Pippert, R. E. (2000, April). Venn said it couldn't be done. *Mathematics Magazine, 73*(2), 105–110.

Heath, T. L. (1963). *Greek mathematics.* New York: Dover.

Kaplan, R. (1999). *The nothing that is: A natural history of zero.* New York: Oxford University Press.

Kelley, L. (2000, January). A mathematical history tour. *Mathematics Teacher, 93*(1), 14–17.

Maor, E. (1994). *The story of a number.* Princeton, NJ: Princeton University Press.

Nahin, P. J. (1998). *An imaginary tale: The story of $\sqrt{-1}$*. Princeton, NJ: Princeton University Press.

Norwood, R. (1999, February). A star to guide us. *Mathematics Teacher, 92*(2), 100–101.

Posamentier, A. S., & Gordon, N. (1984, January). An astounding revelation on the history of π. *Mathematics Teacher, 77*(1), 52.

Posamentier, A. S., & Lehmann, I. (2004). *π: A biography of the world's most mysterious number.* Amherst, NY: Prometheus Books.

Posamentier, A. S., Smith, B. S., & Stepelman, J. (2006). *Teaching secondary school mathematics: Techniques and enrichment units* (7th ed.).Columbus, OH: Merrill/ Prentice Hall.

Resnikoff, H. L., & Wells Jr., R. O. (1984). *Mathematics in civilization.* New York: Dover.

Seife, C. (2000). *Zero: The biography of a dangerous idea.* New York: Viking Penguin.

Smith, D. E. (1929). *A source book in mathematics.* New York: McGraw-Hill.

Smith, D. E. (1953). *History of mathematics.* New York: Dover.

van der Waerden, B. L. (1963). *Science awakening.* New York: Wiley.

Wiggins, G., & McTighe, J. (1998). *Understanding by design.* Alexandria, VA: Association for Supervision and Curriculum Development.

Mathematical Recreations

Ball, W. W. R., & Coxeter, H. S. M. (1960). *Mathematical recreations and essays.* New York: Macmillan.

Barbeau, E. J. (2000). *Mathematical fallacies, flaws, and flimflam.* Washington, DC: Mathematical Association of America.

Bay, J. M., Reys, R. E., Simms, K., & Taylor, P. M. (2000, March). Bingo games: Turning student intuitions into investigations in probability and number sense. *Mathematics Teacher, 93*(3), 200–206.

Beasley, J. D. (1976). *The mathematics of games.* New York: Oxford University Press.

Benson, W., & Jacoby, O. (1976). *New recreations with magic squares.* New York: Dover.

Caldwell, J. H. (1966). *Topics in recreational mathematics.* London: Cambridge University Press.

Cipra, B. (1989). *Misteaks . . . and how to find them before the teacher does.* San Diego, CA: Academic Press.

Cundy, H. M., & Rollett, A. P. (1961). *Mathematical models.* New York: Oxford University Press.

De Pillis, J. (2002). *777 mathematical conversation starters.* Washington, DC: Mathematical Association of America.

Gardner, M. (1995). *New mathematical diversions.* Washington, DC: Mathematical Association of America.

Honsberger, R. (1978). *Mathematical morsels.* Washington, DC: Mathematics Association of America.

Kahan, S. (1996). *Take a look at a good book: The third collection of additive alphametics for the connoisseur.* Amityville, NY: Baywood.

Kraitchik, M. (1942). *Mathematical recreations.* New York: Dover.

Madachy, J. (1966). *Mathematics on vacation.* New York: Scribner.

Nelsen, R. B. (2000). *Proofs without words 2: More exercises in visual thinking.* Washington, DC: Mathematical Association of America.

Northrop, E. (1944). *Riddles in mathematics.* Princeton, NJ: Van Nostrand.

Ogilvy, C. S. (1956). *Through the mathescope.* New York: Oxford University Press.

Pickover, C. A. (2001). *Wonders of numbers.* New York: Oxford University Press.

Posamentier, A. S. (1988). *Advanced geometric constructions.* White Plains, NY: Seymour.

Posamentier, A. S. (2000a). *Making algebra come alive.* Thousand Oaks, CA: Corwin.

Posamentier, A. S. (2000b). *Making geometry come alive.* Thousand Oaks, CA: Corwin.

Posamentier, A. S. (2000c). *Making pre-algebra come alive.* Thousand Oaks, CA: Corwin.

Posamentier, A. S. (2002). *Advanced Euclidean geometry: Excursions for secondary teachers and students.* Emeryville, CA: Key College Press.

Posamentier, A. S. (2003). *Math wonders to inspire teachers and students.* Alexandria, VA: Association for Supervision and Curriculum Development.

Posamentier, A. S., & Lehmann, I. (2004). π: *A biography of the world's most mysterious number.* Amherst, NY: Prometheus Books.

Schuh, F. (1968). *The master book of mathematical recreations.* New York: Dover.

Stevenson, F. W. (1992). *Exploratory problems in mathematics.* Reston, VA: National Council of Teachers of Mathematics.

Vanderlind, P., Guy, R., & Larson, L. (2002). *The inquisitive problem solver.* Washington, DC: Mathematical Association of America.

Mathematics Clubs

Carnahan, W. H. (Ed.). (1958). *Mathematics clubs in high schools.* Washington, DC: National Council of Teachers of Mathematics.

Devlin, K. (1994). *All the math that's fit to print.* (1994). Washington, DC: Mathematical Association of America.

Gruver, H. L. (1968). *School mathematics contests: A report.* Washington, DC: National Council of Teachers of Mathematics.

Hess, A. L. (1977). *Mathematics projects handbook.* Washington, DC: National Council of Teachers of Mathematics.

Morgan, F., Melnick, E. R., & Nicholson, R. (1997, December). The soap-bubble-geometry contest. *Mathematics Teacher, 90*(9), 746–750.

Mu Alpha Theta. (1970). *Handbook for sponsors*. Norman: University of Oklahoma.

Paulos, J. A. (1995). *A mathematician reads the newspaper*. New York: Basic Books.

Ransom, W. R. (1961). *Thirty projects for mathematical clubs and exhibitions*. Portland, ME: Walch.

Schumer, P. D. (2004). *Mathematical journeys*. Hoboken, NJ: Wiley.

Teppo, A. R., & Hodgson, T. (2001, February). Dinosaurs, dinosaur eggs, and probability. *Mathematics Teacher, 94*(2), 86–92.

Problem Solving

Andreescu, T., & Feng, Z. (2000). *Mathematical olympiads 1998–1999*. Washington, DC: Mathematical Association of America.

Artino, R. A., Gaglione, A. M., & Shell, N. (1982). *The contest problem book 4: Annual high school examinations, 1973–1982*. Washington, DC: Mathematical Association of America.

Berzsenyi, G., & Mauer, S. B. (1997). *The contest problem book 5: American high school mathematics examinations and American invitational mathematics examinations, 1983–1988*. Washington, DC: Mathematical Association of America.

Conference Board of Mathematical Sciences. (1966). *The role of axiomatics and problem solving in mathematics*. Boston: Ginn.

Gardiner, T. (1996). *Mathematical challenge*. Cambridge: Cambridge University Press.

Gardiner, T. (1997). *More mathematical challenges*. Cambridge: Cambridge University Press.

Hayes, J. R. (1989). *The complete problem solver* (2nd ed.). Hillsdale, NJ: Erlbaum.

Holton, D. (1993). *Let's solve some math problems*. Waterloo, ON, Canada: Waterloo Mathematics Foundation, University of Waterloo.

Honsberger, R. (1996). *From Erdös to Kiev, problems of olympiad caliber*. Washington, DC: Mathematical Association of America.

Hudgins, B. B. (1966). *Problem solving in the classroom*. New York: Macmillan.

Krantz, S. G. (1997). *Techniques of problem solving*. Providence, RI: American Mathematical Society.

Krulik, S., & Rudnick, J. A. (1980). *Problem solving: A handbook for teachers*. Boston: Allyn & Bacon.

Polya, G. (1945). *How to solve it*. Princeton, NJ: Princeton University Press.

Polya, G. (1954). *Mathematics and plausible reasoning*. Princeton, NJ: Princeton University Press.

Polya, G. (1962). *Mathematical discovery.* New York: Wiley.

Posamentier, A. S. (1996). *Students! Get ready for the mathematics for SAT I: Problem-solving strategies and practical tests.* Thousand Oaks, CA: Corwin.

Posamentier, A. S., & Krulik, S. (1996). *Teachers! Prepare your students for the mathematics for SAT I: Methods and problem-solving strategies.* Thousand Oaks, CA: Corwin.

Posamentier, A. S., & Krulik, S. (1998). *Problem-solving strategies for efficient and elegant solutions: A resource for the mathematics teacher.* Thousand Oaks, CA: Corwin.

Posamentier, A. S., & Schulz, W. (1996). *The art of problem solving: A resource for the mathematics teacher.* Thousand Oaks, CA: Corwin.

Schneider, L. J. (2000). *The contest problem book 6: American high school mathematics examinations 1989–1994.* Washington, DC: Mathematical Association of America.

Whimbey, A., & Lochhead, J. (1980). *Problem solving and comprehension: A short course in analytical reasoning* (2nd ed.). Philadelphia: Franklin Institute Press.

Wickelgren, W. A. (1974). *How to solve problems.* San Francisco: Freeman.

Zeitz, P. (1999). *The art and craft of problem solving.* New York: Wiley.

Sources for Mathematics Team Problems

Andreescu, T., & Feng, Z. (2000). *Mathematical olympiads: Problems and solutions from around the world, 1998–1999.* Washington, DC: Mathematical Association of America.

Andreescu, T., & Feng, Z. (2001). *USA and international mathematical olympiads 2000.* Washington, DC: Mathematical Association of America.

Andreescu, T., & Feng, Z. (2002a). *Mathematical olympiads: Problems and solutions from around the world 1999–2000.* Washington, DC: Mathematical Association of America.

Andreescu, T., & Feng, Z. (2002b). *USA and international mathematical olympiads 2001.* Washington, DC: Mathematical Association of America.

Andreescu, T., & Feng, Z. (2003). *Mathematical olympiads: Problems and solutions from around the world 2000–2001.* Washington, DC: Mathematical Association of America.

Aref, M. N., & Wernick, W. (1968). *Problems and solutions in Euclidean geometry.* New York: Dover.

Artino, R. A., Gaglione, A. M., & Shell, N. (1982). *The contest problem book 4: Annual high school examinations, 1973–1982.* Washington, DC: Mathematical Association of America.

Barbeau, E., Klamkin, M., & Moser, W. (1975). *Five hundred mathematical challenges.* Washington, DC: Mathematical Association of America.

Barbeau, E., Klamkin, M., & Moser, W. (1978). *1001 problems in high school mathematics.* Montreal, QC, Canada: Canadian Mathematics Congress, 1978.

Barry, D. T., & Lux, J. R. (1984). *The Philips Academy prize examinations in mathematics.* Palo Alto, CA: Seymour.

Berzsenyi, G., & Mauer, S. B. (1997). *The contest problem book 5: American high school mathematics examinations and American invitational mathematics examinations, 1983–1988.* Washington, DC: Mathematical Association of America.

Brousseau, A. (Ed.). (1972). *Mathematics contest problems.* Palo Alto, CA: Creative Publications.

Bryant, S. J., Graham, G. E., & Wiley, K. G. (1965). *Nonroutine problems in algebra, geometry, and trigonometry.* New York: McGraw-Hill.

Butts, T. (1973). *Problem solving in mathematics.* Glenview, IL: Scott, Foresman.

Charosh, M. (Ed.). (1965). *Mathematical challenges.* Washington, DC: National Council of Teachers of Mathematics.

Dowlen, M., Powers, S., & Florence, H. (1987). *College of Charleston mathematics contest book.* Palo Alto, CA: Seymour.

Dunn, A. (Ed.). (1964). *Mathematical bafflers.* New York: McGraw-Hill.

Dunn, A. (Ed.). (1983). *Second book of mathematical bafflers.* New York: Dover.

Edwards, J. D., King, D. J., & O'Halloran, P. J. (1986). *All the best from the Australian mathematics competition.* Melbourne, Australia: Ruskin Press.

Engel, A. (1998). *Problem-solving strategies.* New York: Springer.

Fisher, L., & Kennedy, B. (1984). *Brother Alfred Brousseau problem-solving and mathematics competition: Introductory division.* Palo Alto, CA: Seymour.

Fisher, L., & Medigovich, W. (1984). *Brother Alfred Brousseau problem-solving and mathematics competition.* Palo Alto, CA: Seymour.

Gardiner, A. (1997). *The mathematical olympiad handbook: An introduction to problem solving.* New York: Oxford University Press.

Gillman, R. (Ed.) (2003). *A friendly mathematics competition: 35 years of teamwork in Indiana.* Washington, DC: Mathematical Association of America.

Greitzer, S. L. (1978). *International mathematical olympiads.* Washington, DC: Mathematical Association of America.

Hajós, G., Neukomm, G., & Surányi, J. (1963). *Hungarian problem book: Based on the Eötvös competitions, 1894–1928* (E. Rapaport, Trans.). New York: Random House.

Hajós, G., Neukomm, G., & Surányi, J. (2001). *Hungarian problem book 3: Based on the Eötvös Competition, 1929–1943* (A. Lui, Ed., Trans.). Washington, DC: Mathematical Association of America.

Hill, T. J. (Ed.). (1974). *Mathematical challenges 2: Plus six.* Washington, DC: National Council of Teachers of Mathematics.

Honsberger, R. (1997). *In Polya's footsteps: Miscellaneous problems and essays.* Washington, DC: Mathematical Association of America.

Polya, G., & Kilpatrick, J. (1974). *The Stanford mathematics book.* New York: Teachers College Press.

Posamentier, A. S., & Salkind, C. T. (1996). *Challenging problems in algebra.* New York: Dover.

Posamentier, A. S., & Salkind, C. T. (1996). *Challenging problems in geometry.* New York: Dover.

Salkind, C. T. (Ed.). (1961). *The contest problem book.* New York: Random House.

Salkind, C. T. (Ed.). (1966). *The Mathematical Association of America problem book II.* New York: Random House.

Salkind, C. T., & Earl, J. M. (Eds.). (1973). *The Mathematical Association of America problem book III.* New York: Random House.

Saul, M. E., Kessler, G. W., Krilov, S., & Zimmerman, L. (1986). *The New York City contest problem book.* Palo Alto, CA: Seymour.

Schneider, L. J. (2000). *The contest problem book VI: American high school mathematics examinations 1989–1994.* Washington, DC: Mathematical Association of America.

Shklarsky, D. O., Chentzov, N. N., & Yaglom, I. M. (1962). *The USSR olympiad problem book.* San Francisco: Freeman.

Sitomer, H. (1974). *The new mathlete problem book.* Nassau County, NY: Interscholastic Mathematics League.

Steinhaus, H. (1963). *One hundred problems in elementary mathematics.* New York: Pergamon Press.

Straszewicz, S. (1965). *Mathematical problems and puzzles from the Polish mathematical olympiads* (J. Smslika, Trans.). New York: Pergamon Press.

Trigg, C. W. (1967). *Mathematical quickies.* New York: McGraw-Hill.

Further Suggested Reading

Sources for Problems

Abraham, R. M. (1961). *Easy-to-do entertainments and diversions with coins, cards, string, paper and matches.* New York: Dover.

Ainley, S. (1977). *Mathematical puzzles.* London: Bell.

Alexanderson, G. L., Klosinski, L. F., & Larson, L. C. (1985). *The William Lowell Putnam mathematical competition: Problems and solutions: 1965–1984.* Washington, DC: Mathematical Association of America.

Allen, L. (1991). *Brainsharpeners*. London: Hodder & Stoughton, New English Library.

Andreescu, T., & Feng, Z. (2000). *Mathematical olympiads: Problems and solutions from around the world 1998–1999*. Washington, DC: Mathematical Association of America.

Andreescu, T., & Feng, Z. (2001). *USA and international mathematical olympiads 2000*. Washington, DC: Mathematical Association of America.

Andreescu, T., & Feng, Z. (2002a). *Mathematical olympiads: Problems and solutions from around the world 1999–2000*. Washington, DC: Mathematical Association of America.

Andreescu, T., & Feng, Z. (2002b). *USA and international mathematical olympiads 2001*. Washington, DC: Mathematical Association of America.

Andreescu, T., Feng, Z., & Lee Jr., G. (2003). *Mathematical olympiads: Problems and solutions from around the world 2000–2001*. Washington, DC: Mathematical Association of America.

ApSimon, H. (1984). *Mathematical byways*. New York: Oxford University Press.

ApSimon, H. (1990). *More mathematical byways in ayling, beeling and ceiling*. New York: Oxford University Press.

Aref, M. N., & Wernick, W. (1986). *Problems and solutions in Euclidean geometry*. New York: Dover.

Artino, R. A., Gaglione, A. M., & Shell, N. (1982). *The contest problem book IV: Annual high school examinations, 1973–1982*. Washington, DC: Mathematical Association of America.

Barbeau, E., Klamkin, M, & Moser, W. (Eds.). (1985). *1001 problems in high school mathematics*. Montreal: Canadian Mathematical Congress.

Barbeau, E., Klamkin, M., & Moser, W. (1995). *Five hundred mathematical challenges*. Washington, DC: Mathematical Association of America.

Barr, S. (1965). *A miscellany of puzzles*. New York: Crowell.

Barr, S. (1982). *Mathematical brain benders*. New York: Dover.

Barry, D. T., & Lux, J. R. (1984). *The Philips Academy prize examination in mathematics*. Palo Alto, CA: Seymour.

Bates, N. B., & Smith, S. M. (1980). *101 puzzle problems*. Concord, MA: Bates.

Berloquin, P. (1976a). *100 geometric games*. New York: Scribner's.

Berloquin, P. (1976b). *100 numerical games*. New York: Scribner's.

Berloquin, P. (1977). *100 games of logic*. New York: Scribner's.

Berloquin, P. (1985). *The garden of the sphinx*. New York: Scribner's.

Berzsenyi, G., & Maurer, S. B. (1997). *The contest problem book V.* Washington, DC: Mathematical Association of America.

Birtwistle, C. (1971). *Mathematical puzzles and perplexities*. London: Allen & Unwin.

Brandes, L. G. (1975). *The math wizard* (rev. ed.). Portland, ME: Walch.

Bridgman, G. (1981). *Lake Wobegon math problems* (rev. & enlarged ed.). Minneapolis, MN: Author.

Brousseau, A. (1972). *Saint Mary's College mathematics contest problems.* Palo Alto, CA: Creative.

Bryant, S. J., Graham, G. E., & Wiley, K. G. (1965). *Nonroutine problems in algebra, geometry, and trigonometry.* New York: McGraw-Hill.

Bryant, V., & Postill, R. (1983). *The* Sunday Times *book of brain teasers—Book 2.* Englewood Cliffs, NJ: Prentice-Hall.

Bryant, V., & Raymond, P. (1982). *The* Sunday Times *book of brain teasers.* New York: St. Martin's Press.

Burkill, J. C., & Kundy, H. M. (1961). *Mathematical scholarship problems.* London: Cambridge University Press.

Butts, T. (1973). *Problem solving in mathematics.* Glenview, IL: Scott, Foresman.

Canadian Mathematical Society. *Crux Mathematicorum: The problem solving journal.* Ottawa, ON, Canada: Author. Available at http://journals.cms.math.ca/CRUX/

Central Midwest Regional Educational Laboratory. (1975). *Elements of mathematics problem book.* St. Louis, MO: Author.

Charosh, M. (1965). *Mathematical challenges.* Washington, DC: National Council of Teachers of Mathematics.

Clarke, B. R. (1994). *Puzzles for pleasure.* New York: Cambridge University Press.

Clarke, B. R., Gooch, R, Newing, A., & Singmaster, D. (1993). *The* Daily Telegraph *book of brain twisters, No. 1.* London: Pan.

Conrad, S. R., & Flegler, D. (1994a). *Math contests grades 4, 5, and 6.* Tenafly, NJ: Math League Press.

Conrad, S. R., & Flegler, D. (1994b). *Math contests grades 7 and 8.* Tenafly, NJ: Math League Press.

Conrad, S. R., & Flegler, D. (1995). *Math contests for high school.* Tenafly, NJ: Math League Press.

Dorrie, H. (1965). *100 great problems of elementary mathematics.* New York: Dover.

Dowlen, M., Powers, S., & Florence, H. (1987). *College of Charleston mathematics contest book.* Palo Alto, CA: Seymour.

Dudney, H. E. (1958). *The Canterbury puzzles.* New York: Dover.

Dudney, H. E. (1970). *Amusements in mathematics.* New York: Dover.

Dunn, A. (1964). *Mathematical bafflers.* New York: McGraw-Hill.

Dunn, A. F. (1983). *Second book of mathematical bafflers.* New York: Dover.

Edwards, J. D., King, D. J., & O'Halloran, P. J. (1986). *All the best from the Australian mathematics competition.* Melbourne, Australia: Ruskin Press.

Emmet, E. R. (1976). *Mind tickling brain teasers.* Buchanan, NY: Emerson Books.

Emmet, E. R. (1977a). *A diversity of puzzles.* New York: Barnes & Noble.

Emmet, E. R. (1977b). *Puzzles for pleasure.* Buchanan, NY: Emerson Books.

Emmet, E. R. (1979). *The great detective puzzle book.* New York: Barnes & Noble.

Emmet, E. R. (1980). *The island of imperfection puzzle book.* New York: Barnes & Noble.

Emmet, E. R. (1984). *The Penguin book of brain teasers* (D. Hall & A. Summers, Comp.). New York: Viking.

Emmet, E. R. (1993). *Brain puzzler's delight.* New York: Sterling.

Engel, A. (1998). *Problem solving strategies.* New York: Springer-Verlag.

Filipiak, A. S. (1942). *Mathematical puzzles.* New York: Bell.

Fisher, L., & Kennedy, B. (1984). *Brother Alfred Brousseau problem solving and mathematics competition, introductory division.* Palo Alto, CA: Seymour.

Fisher, L., & Medigovich, W. (1984). *Brother Alfred Brousseau problem solving and mathematics competition, senior division.* Palo Alto, CA: Seymour.

Fleener, F. O. (1990). *Mathematics contests: A guide for involving students and schools.* Reston, VA: National Council of Teachers of Mathematics.

Friedland, A. J. (1970). *Puzzles in math and logic.* New York: Dover.

Frohlichstein, J. (1962). *Mathematical fun, games and puzzles.* New York: Dover.

Fujimura, K. (1978). *The Tokyo puzzles* (M. Gardner, Ed.). New York: Scribner's.

Gardner, M. (1959). *Arrow book of brain teasers.* New York: Scholastic.

Gardner, M. (1961). *The second* Scientific American *book of mathematical puzzles and diversions.* New York: Simon & Schuster.

Gardner, M. (1969). *Perplexing puzzles and tantalizing teasers.* New York: Simon & Schuster.

Gardner, M. (1983). *Martin Gardner's sixth book of mathematical games from* Scientific American. Chicago: University of Chicago Press.

Gardner, M. (1977). *More perplexing puzzles and tantalizing teasers.* New York: Pocket Books, Archway.

Gardner, M. (1978). *Aha! Unsight.* New York: Scientific American & Freeman.

Gardner, M. (1981). *Science fiction puzzle tales.* New York: Potter.

Gardner, M. (1982). *Aha! Gotcha.* New York: Freeman.

Gardner, M. (1983). *Wheels, life and other mathematical amusements.* New York: Freeman.

Gardner, M. (1985). *The magic numbers of Dr. Matrix.* Buffalo, NY: Prometheus.

Gardner, M. (1986a). *Entertaining mathematical puzzles.* New York: Dover.

Gardner, M. (1986b). *Knotted doughnuts and other mathematical entertainments.* New York: Freeman.

Gardner, M. (1986c). *Puzzles from other worlds.* New York: Random House, Vintage.

Gardner, M. (1987). *Riddles of the sphinx.* Washington, DC: Mathematical Association of America, New Mathematical Library.

Gardner, M. (1988a). *Hexaflexagons and other mathematical diversions*. Chicago: University of Chicago Press.

Gardner, M. (1988b). *Time travel and other mathematical bewilderments*. New York: Freeman.

Gardner, M. (1989a). *Mathematical carnival* (rev. ed.). Washington, DC: Mathematical Association of America.

Gardner, M. (1989b). *Penrose tiles to trapdoor ciphers*. New York: Freeman.

Gardner, M (1990). *Mathematical magic show* (rev. ed.). Washington, DC: Mathematical Association of America.

Gardner, M. (1991). *The unexpected hanging and other mathematical diversions* (rev. ed.). Chicago: University of Chicago Press.

Gardner, M. (1992a). *Fractal music, hypercards and more*. New York: Freeman.

Gardner, M. (1992b). *Mathematical circus* (rev. ed.). Washington, DC: Mathematical Association of America.

Gardner, M. (1994). *My best mathematical and logical puzzles*. New York: Dover.

Gardner, M. (1995). *Martin Gardner's new mathematical diversions from* Scientific American. Washington, DC: Mathematical Association of America.

Garvin, A. D. (1975). *Discovery problems for better students*. Portland, ME: Weston Walch.

Gleason, A. M., Greenwood, R. E., & Kelly, L. M. (1980). *The William Lowell Putnam mathematical competitions. Problems and solutions: 1938–1964*. Washington, DC: Mathematical Association of America.

Gould, P. (1992). *Senior challenge '85–'91*. Mathematical Education on Merseyside, University of Liverpool, Liverpool, UK.

Gould, P., & Porteous, I. (1984). *Senior challenge '80–'84*. Mathematical Education on Merseyside, University of Liverpool, Liverpool, UK.

Graham, L. A. (1959). *Ingenious mathematical problems and methods*. New York: Dover.

Graham, L. A. (1968). *The surprise attack in mathematical problems*. New York: Dover.

Greitzer, S. L. (1978). *International mathematical olympiads 1959–1977*. Washington, DC: Mathematical Association of America.

Haber, P. (1957). *Mathematical puzzles and pastimes*. Mount Vernon, NY: Peter Pauper.

Hadley, J., & Singmaster, D. (1992, March). Problems to sharpen the young: An annotated translation of Propositiones alcuini doctoris caroli magni imperatoris ad acuendos juvenes. *Mathematical Gazette, 76*(475), 102–126.

Hahn, L.-S. (2005). *New Mexico mathematics contest problem book*. Albuquerque: University of New Mexico Press.

Halmos, P. R. (1991). *Problems for mathematicians young and old* (Dolciani Mathematical Expositions No. 12). Washington, DC: Mathematical Association of America.

Higgins, A. M. (1971). *Geometry problems*. Portland, ME: Walch.

Hill, T. J. (1974). *Mathematical challenges 2—Plus six*. Washington, DC: National Council of Teachers of Mathematics.

Honsberger, R. (1978). *Mathematical morsels*. Washington, DC: Mathematical Association of America.

Honsberger, R. (1996). *From Erdös to Kiev: Problems of olympiad caliber*. Washington, DC: Mathematical Association of America.

Honsberger, R. (1997). *In Polya's footsteps: Miscellaneous problems and essays*. Washington, DC: Mathematical Association of America.

Holton, D. (1988–1991). *Problem solving series*. 1. *How to*; 2: *Combinatorics 1;* 3. *Graph theory*; 4. *Number theory;* 5. *Geometry 1;* 6. *Proof;* 7. *Geometry 2;* 8. *IMO problems 1;* 9. *Combinatorics 2;* 10. *Geometry 2;* 11. *Number theory 2;* 12. *Inequalities;* 13. *Combinatorics 3;* 14. *IMO problems 2;* 15. *Creating problems*. Leicester, UK: Mathematical Association.

Hunter, J. A. H. (1965). *Fun with figures*. New York: Dover.

Hunter, J. A. H. (1966). *More fun with figures*. New York: Dover.

Hunter, J. A. H. (1972). *Figures for fun* (2nd ed.). London: Dent Aldine.

Hunter, J. A. H. (1976). *Mathematical brain teasers*. New York: Dover.

Hunter, J. A. H. (1977). *Challenging mathematical teasers*. New York: Dover.

Hunter, J. A. H. (1983). *Entertaining mathematical teasers and how to solve them*. New York: Dover.

Kahan, S. (1978). *Have some sums to solve: The compleat alphametics book*. Farmingdale, NY: Baywood.

Kahan, S. (1994). *At last!! Encoded totals second addition: The long awaited sequel to "Have Some Sums to Solve."* Farmingdale, NY: Baywood.

Kahan, S. (1996). *Take a look at a good book: The third collection of additive alphametics for the connoisseur*. Farmingdale, NY: Baywood.

Klamkin, M. S. (1986). *International mathematical olympiads, 1979–1985*. Washington, DC: Mathematical Association of America.

Konhauser, J. D. E., Velleman, D., & Wagon, S. (1996). *Which way did the bicycle go?* Washington, DC: Mathematical Association of America.

Kordemsky, B. A. (1972). *The Moscow puzzles* (M. Gardner, Ed.). New York: Scribner's.

Krechmer, V. A. (1974). *A problem book in algebra* (V. Shiffer, Trans.). Moscow: Mir.

Krulik, S., & Rudnick, J. A. (1980). *Problem solving: A handbook for teachers*. Boston: Allyn & Bacon.

Krulik, S., & Rudnick, J. A. (1996). *The new sourcebook for teaching reasoning and problem solving in junior and senior high schools*. Boston: Allyn & Bacon.

Kuczma, M. E. (2003). *International mathematical olympiads 1986–1999*. Washington, DC: Mathematical Association of America.

Larson, L. C. (1983). *Problem solving through problems*. New York: Springer-Verlag.

Lenchner, G. (1983). *Creative problem solving in school mathematics*. Boston: Houghton Mifflin.

Lenchner, G. (1997). *Math olympiad contest problems for elementary and middle schools*. East Meadow, NY: Glenwood.

Luckács, C., & Tarján, E. (1968). *Mathematical games*. New York: Walker.

Moser, W., & Barbeau, E. (1976). *The Canadian mathematics olympiads 1969, 1975*. Montreal: Canadian Mathematical Congress.

Morris, I. (1969). *The riverside puzzles*. New York: Walker.

Morris, I. (1970). *The lonely monk and other puzzles*. Boston: Little, Brown.

Morris, I. (1972). *Foul play and other puzzles of all kinds*. New York: Random House, Vintage.

Morris, I. (1984). *Super-games*. London: Hutchinson.

Morris, I. (1991a). *Fiendishly difficult math puzzles*. New York: Sterling.

Morris, I. (1991b). *Fiendishly difficult visual perception puzzles*. New York: Sterling.

Moser, W. O. J., & Barbeau, E. J. (1978). *The first 10 Canadian mathematics olympiads (1969–1978)*. Montreal: Canadian Mathematical Society.

Mosteller, F. (1965). *Fifty challenging problems in probability*. New York: Dover.

Mott-Smith, G. (1954). *Mathematical puzzles for beginners and enthusiasts*. New York: Dover.

Newton, D. E. (1972). *One hundred quickies for math classes*. Portland, ME: Walch.

Phillips, H. (1932a). *The playtime omnibus*. London: Faber & Faber.

Phillips, H. (1932b). *The week-end problems book*. London: Nonesuch.

Phillips, H. (1934). *The sphinx problem book*. London: Faber.

Phillips, H. (1936). *Brush up your wits*. London: Dent.

Phillips, H. (1938). *Question time*. New York: Farrar & Rinehart.

Phillips, H. (1945a). *Ask me another*. London: Ptarmigan.

Phillips, H. (1945b). *Hubert Phillips's heptameron*. London: Eyre & Spottiswoode.

Phillips, H. (1958). *Something to think about*. London: Parrish.

Phillips, H. (1947). *Playtime*. London: Ptarmigan.

Phillips, H. (1950). *The Hubert Phillips annual 1951*. London: Hamish Hamilton.

Phillips, H. (1960). *Problems omnibus* (Vol. 1). London: Arco.

Phillips, H. (1961a). *My best puzzles in logic and reasoning*. New York: Dover.

Phillips, H. (1961b). *My best puzzles in mathematics*. New York: Dover.

Phillips, H. (1962). *Problems omnibus* (Vol. 2). London: Arco.

Phillips, H., Shovelton, S. T., & Marshal, G. S. (1961). *Caliban's problem book.* New York: Dover.

Polya, G., & Kilpatrick, J. (1974). *The Stanford mathematics book.* New York: Teachers College Press.

Posamentier, A. S. (1996). *Students! Get ready for the mathematics for SAT I: Problem-solving strategies and practical tests.* Thousand Oaks, CA: Corwin.

Posamentier, A. S. (2002). *Advanced Euclidean geometry: Excursions for secondary teachers and students.* Emeryville, CA: Key College Press.

Posamentier, A. S., & Krulik, S. (1996). *Teachers! Prepare your students for the mathematics for SAT I: Methods and problem-solving strategies.* Thousand Oaks, CA: Corwin.

Posamentier, A. S., & Krulik, S. (1998). *Problem-solving strategies for efficient and elegant solutions: A resource for the mathematics teacher.* Thousand Oaks, CA: Corwin.

Posamentier, A. S., & Salkind, C. T. (1996a). *Challenging problems in algebra* (rev. ed). New York: Dover.

Posamentier, A. S., & Salkind, C. T. (1996b). *Challenging problems in geometry* (rev. ed.). New York: Dover.

Posamentier, A. S., & Schulz, W. (1996). *The art of problem solving: A resource for the mathematics teacher.* Thousand Oaks, CA: Corwin.

Posamentier, A. S., & Wernick, W. (1988). *Advanced geometric constructions.* Palo Alto, CA: Seymour.

Ransom, W. R. (1955). *One hundred mathematical curiosities.* Portland, ME: J. Weston Walch.

Reis, C. M., & Ditor, S. Z. (Eds.). (1988). *The Canadian mathematics olympiads (1979–1985).* Ottawa, ON, Canada: Canadian Mathematical Society.

Ruderman, H. D. (1983). NYSML-ARML *Contests 1973–1982.* Norman, OK: Mu Alpha Theta.

Salkind, C. T. (Ed.). (1961). *The contest problem book.* New York: Random House.

Salkind, C. T. (Ed.). (1966). *The Mathematical Association of America problem book II.* New York: Random House.

Salkind, C. T., & Earl, J. M. (1973). *The Mathematical Association of America problem book III.* New York: Random House.

Saul, M. E., Kessler, G. W., Krilov, S., & Zimmerman, L. (1986). *The New York City contest problem book.* Palo Alto, CA: Seymour.

Schneider, L. J. (2000). *The contest problem book 6: American high school mathematics examinations 1989–1994.* Washington, DC: Mathematical Association of America.

Shklarsky, D. O., Chentzov, N. N., & Yaglom, I. M. (1962). *The USSR olympiad problem book.* San Francisco: Freeman.

Shklarsky, D. O., Chentzov, N. N., & Yaglom, I. M. (1979). *Selected problems and theorems in elementary mathematics* (V. M. Volosov & I. G. Volsova, Trans.). Moscow: Mir.

Shortz, W. (1991). *Will Shortz's best brain busters*. New York: Random House, Times Books.

Shortz, W. (1993). *Brain twisters from the First World Puzzle Championships*. New York: Random House, Times Books.

Sierpinski, W. (1964). *A selection of problems in the theory of numbers*. London: Pergamon/ Macmillan.

Sierpinski, W. (1970). *Two hundred fifty problems in elementary number theory*. New York: American Elsevier.

Sitomer, H. (1974). *The new mathlete problem book*. Nassau County, NY: Interscholastic Mathematics League.

Snape, C., & Scott, H. (1991). *How puzzling*. New York: Cambridge University Press.

Soifer, A. (1987). *Mathematics as problem solving*. Colorado Springs, CO: Center for Excellence in Mathematics Education.

Sole, T. (1988). *The ticket to heaven and other superior puzzles*. London: Penguin.

Steinhaus, H. (1963). *One hundred problems in elementary mathematics*. New York: Pergamon Press.

Straszewicz, S. (1965). *Mathematical problems and puzzles from the Polish mathematical olympiads* (J. Smslika, Trans.). New York: Pergamon Press.

Trigg, C. W. (1967). *Mathematical quickies*. New York: McGraw-Hill.

Ulam, S. M. (1960). *Problems in modern mathematics*. New York: Wiley.

Vakil, R. (1996). *A mathematical mosaic: Patterns and problem solving*. Burlington, ON, Canada: Kelly.

Vout, C., & Gray, G. (1993). *Challenging puzzles*. New York: Cambridge University Press.

Wall, H. S. (1963). *Creative mathematics*. Austin: University of Texas Press.

Wells, D. G. (1979). *Recreations in logic*. New York: Dover.

Williams, W. T, & Savage, G. H. (1940). *The Penguin problems book*. London: Penguin.

Williams, W. T, & Savage, G. H. (1944). *The second Penguin problems book*. London: Penguin.

Williams, W. T, & Savage, G. H. (1946). *The third Penguin problems book*. London: Penguin.

Yaglom, A. M., &. Yaglom, I. M. (1964). *Challenging mathematical problems with elementary solutions* (Vol. 1). San Francisco: Holden-Day.

Yaglom, A. M., &. Yaglom, I. M. (1967). *Challenging mathematical problems with elementary solutions* (Vol. 2). San Francisco: Holden-Day.

Readings on Problem Solving

Ackoff, R. L. (1978). *The art of problem solving*. New York: Wiley.

Adams, J. L. (1974). *Conceptual blockbusting*. San Francisco: Freeman.

Adler, I. (1970). *Mathematics and mental growth.* London: Dobson.

Andre, T. (1986). Problem solving and education. In G. Phye and T. Andre (Eds.), *Cognitive classroom learning: Understanding, thinking, and problem solving* (pp. 169–204). Orlando, FL: Academic Press.

Arnold, W. R. (1971). Students can pose and solve original problems. *The Mathematics Teacher, 64,* 325.

Averbach, B., & Chein, O. (1980). *Mathematics: Problem solving through recreational mathematics.* San Francisco: Freeman.

Bransford, J. D., & Stein, B. S. (1984). *The ideal problem solver.* New York: Freeman.

Brown, S. I., & Walter, M. I. (1983). *The art of problem posing.* Hillsdale, NJ: Erlbaum.

Butts, T. (1985). In praise of trial and error. *Mathematics Teacher, 78,* 167.

Charles, R., & Lester, F. (1982). *Teaching problem solving: What, why, and how.* Palo Alto, CA: Seymour.

Chipman, S., Segal, J., & Glaser, R. (1985). *Thinking and learning skills. Vol. 2: Research and open questions.* Hillsdale, NJ: Erlbaum.

Cofman, J. (1990). *What to solve? Problems and suggestions for young mathematicians.* Oxford: Oxford University Press.

Cofman, J. (1995). *Numbers and shapes revisited: More problems for young mathematicians.* Oxford: Oxford University Press.

Costa, A. (1984, November). Mediating the metacognitive. *Educational Leadership,* 57–62.

Curcio, F. (Ed.). (1987). *Teaching and learning, a problem solving focus.* Reston, VA: National Council of Teachers of Mathematics.

Davis, R., Jockusch, E., & McKnight, C. (1978, Spring). Cognitive processes in learning algebra. *Journal of Children's Mathematical Behavior, 2*(1).

Derry, S. J., & Murphy, D. A. (1986, Spring). Designing systems that train learning ability: From theory to practice. *Review of Educational Research, 56*(1), 1–39.

Emmet, E. R. (1981). *Learning to think.* Verplanck, NY: Emerson Books.

Fisher, R. B. (1981). *Brain games.* London: Fontana.

Fixx, J. F. (1978). *Solve it!* New York: Doubleday.

Frederiksen, N. (1984, Fall). Implications of cognitive theory for instruction on problem solving. *Review of Educational Research, 54*(3), 363–407.

Gardner, M. (1978). *Aha! Insight.* New York: Scientific American & Freeman.

Gardner, M. (1982). *Aha! Gotcha.* San Francisco: Freeman.

Gifted students. (1983). *Mathematics Teacher, 76.*

Gordon, W. J. J. (1961). *Synectics—The development of creative capacity.* New York: Harper & Row.

Hadamard, J. (1954). *The psychology of invention in the mathematical field.* New York: Dover.

Heiman, M., Narode, R., Slomianko, J., & Lochhead, J. (1987). *Thinking skills: Mathematics, teaching.* Washington, DC: National Education Association.

Honsberger, R. (1970). *Ingenuity in mathematics.* Washington, DC: Mathematical Association of America, New Mathematical Library.

Honsberger, R. (1973). *Mathematical gems* (Vol. 1, Dolciani Mathematical Expositions No. 1). Washington, DC: Mathematical Association of America.

Honsberger, R. (1976). *Mathematical gems* (Vol. 2, Dolciani Mathematical Expositions No. 2). Washington, DC: Mathematical Association of America.

Honsberger, R. (1978). *Mathematical morsels* (Dolciani Mathematical Expositions No. 3). Washington, DC: Mathematical Association of America.

Honsberger, R. (1979). *Mathematical plums* (Dolciani Mathematical Expositions No. 4). Washington, DC: Mathematical Association of America.

Honsberger, R. (1985). *Mathematical gems 3* (Dolciani Mathematical Expositions No. 9). Washington, DC: Mathematical Association of America.

Honsberger, R. (1991). *More mathematical morsels* (Dolciani Mathematical Expositions No. 10). Washington, DC: Mathematical Association of America.

Hough, J. S. (Ed.). (1984). *Problem solving* (Newsletter, Vols. 1–5). Philadelphia: Franklin Institute Press.

Hughes, B. (1975). *Thinking through problems.* Palo Alto, CA: Creative.

Jensen, R. J. (1987). Stuck? Don't give up! Subgoal-generation strategies in problem solving. *The Mathematics Teacher, 80,* 614.

Karmos, J., & Karmos, A. (1987). Strategies for active involvement in problem solving. In M. Heiman & J. Slomianko (Eds.), *Thinking skills instruction: Concepts and techniques* (pp. 99–110). Washington, DC: National Education Association.

Kluwe, R. (1987). Executive decisions and regulation of problem solving behavior. In F. Weinert & R. Kluwe (Eds.), *Metacognition, motivation and understanding.* Hillsdale, NJ: Erlbaum.

Krantz, S. G. (1997). *Techniques of problems solving.* Providence, RI: American Mathematical Society.

Krulik, S. (Ed.). (1980). *Problem solving in school mathematics, 1980 yearbook.* Reston, VA: National Council of Teachers of Mathematics.

Krulik, S., & Rudnick, J. (1987). *Problem solving: A handbook for teachers* (2nd ed.). Boston: Allyn & Bacon.

Krulik, S., & Rudnick, J. (1989). *Problem solving: A handbook for senior high school teachers.* Boston: Allyn & Bacon.

Krulik, S., & Rudnick, J. (1993). *Reasoning and problem solving: A handbook for elementary school teachers.* Boston: Allyn & Bacon.

Krulik, S., & Rudnick, J. (1995). *The new sourcebook for teaching reasoning and problem solving in elementary schools.* Boston: Allyn & Bacon.

Krulik, S., & Rudnick, J. (1996). *The new sourcebook for teaching reasoning and problem solving in secondary schools.* Boston: Allyn & Bacon.

Mason, J. (1984). *Learning and doing mathematics.* Milton Keynes, England: Open University Press.

Mason, J. (with Burton, L., & Stacey, K.) (1985). *Thinking mathematically.* Reading, MA: Addison-Wesley.

Mayer, R. (1986). Mathematics. In R. Dillon & R. Sternberg (Eds.), *Cognition and instruction.* Orlando, FL: Academic Press.

McKim, R. H. (1980). *Thinking visually: A strategy manual for problem solving.* Palo Alto, CA: Seymour.

Moses, S. (1974). *The art of problem-solving.* London: Transworld.

Mottershead, L. (1978). *Sources of mathematical discovery.* Oxford, UK: Blackwell.

Mottershead, L. (1985). *Investigations in mathematics.* Oxford, UK: Blackwell.

Nickerson, R. (1981, October). Thoughts on teaching thinking. *Educational Leadership,* 21–24.

Nickerson, R., Perkins, D., & Smith, E. (1985). *The teaching of thinking.* Hillsdale, NJ: Erlbaum.

Noller, R. B., Heintz, R. E., & Blaeuer, D. A. (1978). *Creative problem solving in mathematics.* Buffalo, NY: D. O. K..

Polya, G. (1945). *How to solve it.* Princeton, NJ: Princeton University Press.

Polya, G. (1954a). *Introduction and analogy in mathematics.* Princeton, NJ: Princeton University Press.

Polya, G. (1954b). *Patterns of plausible inference.* Princeton, NJ: Princeton University Press.

Polya, G. (1981). *Mathematical discovery* (Vols. 1–2, combined ed. with foreword by P. Hilton, bibliography extended by G. Alexanderson, & index extended by J. Pedersen). New York: Wiley. (Original works published 1962, 1965)

Posamentier, A. S. (1996). *Teachers! Prepare your students for the mathematics for SAT I: Methods and problem-solving strategies.* Thousand Oaks, CA: Corwin.

Posamentier, A. S., & Krulik, S. (1998). *Problem solving strategies for efficient and elegant solutions: A resource for the mathematics teacher.* Thousand Oaks, CA: Corwin.

Posamentier, A. S., & Schulz, W. (1996). *The art of problem solving: A resource for the mathematics teacher.* Thousand Oaks, CA: Corwin.

Reeves, C. A. (1987). *Problem solving techniques helpful in mathematics and science.* Reston, VA: National Council of Teachers of Mathematics.

Schoenfeld, A. H. (1983). *Problem solving in the mathematics curriculum.* Washington, DC: Mathematical Association of America.

Schoenfeld, A. H. (1985). *Mathematical problem solving.* Orlando, FL: Academic Press.

Segal, J., Chipman, S., & Glaser, R. (Eds.). (1985). *Thinking and learning skills, Vol. 1: Relating instruction to research.* Hillsdale, NJ: Erlbaum.

Silver, E. A. (Ed.). (1985). *Teaching and learning mathematical problem solving.* Hillsdale, NJ: Erlbaum.

Simon, M. A. (1986, April). The teacher's role in increasing student understanding of mathematics. *Educational Leadership, 43*(7), 40–43.

Skemp, R. R. (1971). *The psychology of learning mathematics.* Baltimore, MD: Penguin Books.

Smullyan, R. (1978). *What is the name of this book?* Englewood Cliffs, NJ: Prentice-Hall.

Soifer, A. (1987). *Mathematics as problem solving.* Colorado Springs, CO: Center for Excellence in Mathematics Education.

Troutman, A., & Lichtenberg, B. P. (1974, November). Problem solving in the general mathematics classroom. *Mathematics Teacher, 67*(7), 590–597.

Walter, M. I., & Brown, S. I. (1977, January). Problem posing and problem solving. *Mathematics Teacher, 70*(1), 4–13.

Whirl, R. J. (1973, October). Problem solving—solution or technique? *Mathematics Teacher, 66*(6), 551–553.

Winckelgren, W. A. (1974). *How to solve problems.* San Francisco: Freeman.

INDEX

The letter *f* following a page number denotes a figure.

ABOUT THE AUTHORS

Alfred S. Posamentier is Professor of Mathematics Education and Dean of the School of Education of the City College of the City University of New York. He is the author and coauthor of more than 40 mathematics books for teachers, secondary and elementary school students, and the general readership. Dr. Posamentier is also a frequent commentator in newspapers on topics relating to education, and he works with mathematics teachers and supervisors, nationally and internationally, to help them maximize their effectiveness.

He completed his Bachelor of Arts degree in mathematics at Hunter College of the City University of New York and began his career as a teacher of mathematics at Theodore Roosevelt High School in the Bronx (New York). He joined the faculty of the City College after receiving his master's degree there and immediately began to develop inservice courses for secondary school mathematics teachers; these courses included such special areas as recreational mathematics and problem solving in mathematics. He received his Ph.D. in mathematics education from Fordham University (New York) and has since extended his reputation in mathematics education to Europe, where he has been visiting professor at universities in England, Germany, Poland, and Austria. He was Fulbright Professor at the University of Vienna (1990).

Dr. Posamentier's many honors include Honorary Fellow at the South Bank University in London, England (1989); Grand Medal of Honor from the Federal Republic of Austria (1994); University Professor of Austria (1999); Honorary Fellow of the Vienna Institute of Technology (2003); and the Austrian Cross of Honor for Arts and Science First Class (2004). In recognition of his outstanding teaching, the City College Alumni Association named him Educator of the Year in

1994, and the New York City Council named May 1, 1994, in his honor. In 2005, he was inducted into the Hunter College Alumni Hall of Fame, and, in 2006, he was awarded the Townsend Harris medal from the City College Alumni Association, its highest honor.

Dr. Posamentier was a member of the New York State Education Commissioner's Blue Ribbon Panel on the Math-A Regents Exams and the Commissioner's Mathematics Standards Committee, which redefined the standards for New York State. He also serves on the New York City schools' Chancellor's Math Advisory Panel.

Now in his 37th year on the faculty of the City College, Dr. Posamentier remains a leading commentator on educational issues and continues his long-time passion of seeking ways to make mathematics interesting to teachers, students, and the general public. His most recent books include *Math Wonders to Inspire Teachers and Students* (2003); for the general readership, π: *A Biography of the World's Most Mysterious Number* (2004) and *The Fabulous Fibonacci Numbers* (2007).

Daniel Jaye is Director of Academy Programs at the Bergen County (NJ) Academy, a high school for gifted students, and was formerly Chair of Mathematics at Stuyvesant High School in New York City. He lectures frequently and enjoys presenting interesting techniques in problem solving as well as problems that provide enrichment for the mathematics classroom. He is also interested in comparing math standards throughout the nation and the world.

Mr. Jaye graduated from the City College of New York and began his career teaching at Seward Park High School in New York City before accepting an invitation to teach at the prestigious Stuyvesant High School, where he distinguished himself as a teacher of algebra through advanced placement calculus.

After receiving his Master's Degree in mathematics from the City College of New York, Mr. Jaye took an interest in guiding student research projects in mathematics at Stuyvesant High School, where he served as the math research coordinator and coordinated the submission of thousands of student-generated research papers to local and national competitions, including the Westinghouse and Intel Science Talent Search competitions. In 2001, he was awarded the Mathematical Association of America's Edyth Sliffe Award for Excellence in Teaching. His other honors include Education Update's Outstanding Teacher of the Year award (2004) and Phi Delta Kappa's Leadership in Education award (2004). In 2006 he was awarded Educator of the Year by the City College of New York Alumni Association.

In 2004, Mr. Jaye was selected for the New York State Math Standards Committee, for which he served on a team that authored the new state standards in mathematics. Also in 2004, he was elected president of the Association of Mathematics Assistant Principals of Supervision. He was selected in 2005 to serve on New York State's Curriculum Committee on Mathematics, and he currently serves on the Chancellor's Math Advisory Panel.

Stephen Krulik is Professor Emeritus of Mathematics Education at Temple University in Philadelphia, Pennsylvania, where he has taught courses in methods of teaching mathematics at all levels. His special areas of expertise include the history of mathematics, the teaching of problem solving, and methods of teaching mathematics. He has been at Temple for 37 years. In 2001, Dr. Krulik received the Lindbach Award as an outstanding college professor and in 2003 he was honored by Temple University with the Great Teacher Award.

Dr. Krulik received his Bachelor of Arts degree in Mathematics from Brooklyn College of the City University of New York and his Master of Arts and Doctor of Education degrees from Teachers College, Columbia University, New York. Before coming to Temple, Dr. Krulik taught mathematics in the New York City public schools for 15 years.

Nationally, Dr. Krulik has served as a member of the committee responsible for preparing the Professional Standards for Teaching Mathematics. He edited the National Council of Teachers of Mathematics 1980 yearbook, *Problem Solving in School Mathematics,* and is the author or coauthor of more than 30 textbooks on the teaching of mathematics and the teaching of problem solving, as well as several nationally known textbook series for students in elementary, middle, and high schools. He has served as a consultant to school districts throughout the United States and Canada and has presented internationally in Vienna, Budapest, Quebec City, Adelaide, and San Juan. One of his major interests is preparing teachers to succeed in helping every student learn mathematics.

Related ASCD Resources: Mathematics

At the time of publication, the following ASCD resources were available (ASCD stock numbers appear in parentheses). For up-to-date information about ASCD resources, go to www.ascd.org.

Audios

Improving Mathematics Instruction Through Coaching by Glenda Copeland (CD: #505298)

Linking Classroom Practice to Student Learning in Mathematics by Kathleen Morris and Jo Ellen Roseman (audiotape: #204095; CD: #504129)

Reading Strategies for the Math Classroom by Rachel Billmeyer (audiotape: #205063; CD: #505087)

Books

Concept-Rich Mathematics Instruction: Building a Strong Foundation for Reasoning and Problem Solving by Meir Ben Hur (#106008)

Literacy Strategies for Improving Mathematics Instruction by Joan M. Kenney et al. (#105137)

The Mathematics Program Improvement Review: A Comprehensive Evaluation Process for K–12 Schools by Ron Pelfrey (#105126)

Math Wonders to Inspire Teachers and Students by Alfred S. Posamentier (#103010)

Priorities in Practice: The Essentials of Mathematics 7–12: Effective Curriculum, Instruction, and Assessment by Kathy Checkley (#106129)

Videos and Mixed Media

The Brain and Mathematics (2 tapes and 136-page facilitator's guide, #400237)

The Lesson Collection: Math Strategies, Tapes 17–24 (8 tapes, #401044)

TechPaths for Math 1.02 (CD-ROM with 104-page user's manual, #598238; Spanish version, #598240)

For more information: send e-mail to member@ascd.org; call 1-800-933-2723 or 703-578-9600, press 2; send a fax to 703-575-5400; or write to Information Services, ASCD, 1703 N. Beauregard St., Alexandria, VA 22311-1714 USA.